WEBSITE SOUND

Jim Cline
Patrick Seaman

New Riders Publishing, Indianapolis, Indiana

Website Sound

By Jim Cline and Patrick Seaman

Published by:
New Riders Publishing
201 West 103rd Street
Indianapolis, IN 46290 USA

Printed in the United States of America 1 2 3 4 5 6 7 8 9 0

Library of Congress Cataloging-in-Publication Data

```
***CIP data available upon request***
```

Warning and Disclaimer

PUBLISHER	Don Fowley
PUBLISHING MANAGER	David Dwyer
MARKETING MANAGER	Mary Foote
MANAGING EDITOR	Carla Hall

PRODUCT DEVELOPMENT SPECIALIST
Alicia Buckley

ACQUISITIONS EDITOR
Steve Weiss

SENIOR EDITOR
Sarah Kearns

DEVELOPMENT EDITORS
Laura Frey
Tim Huddleston

PROJECT EDITOR
Karen Walsh

COPY EDITORS
Keith Cline
Barb Potter
Molly Warnes

TECHNICAL EDITOR
Richard Yaker

ACQUISITIONS COORDINATOR
Stacy Beheler

ADMINISTRATIVE COORDINATOR
Karen Opal

COVER ILLUSTRATION
Jay Corpus

COVER PRODUCTION
Aren Howell

BOOK DESIGNER
Anne Jones

PRODUCTION MANAGER
Kelly Dobbs

PRODUCTION TEAM SUPERVISORS
Gina Rexrode
Joe Millay

GRAPHICS IMAGE SPECIALISTS
Debi Bolhuis
Tammy Graham
Oliver Jackson

ILLUSTRATORS
Laura Robbins
Bryan Towse

PRODUCTION TEAM
Cynthia Fields
Diana Groth
William Huys Jr.
Christopher Morris
Daniela Raderstorf

INDEXER
Sharon Hilgenberg

About the Authors

Jim Cline (harmaty@onramp.net) is an engineering manager and writer based in the Dallas, TX area. He has a BSEE from Virginia Polytechnic Institute and State University and an MSEE from the University of Kentucky. During his career, he has designed integrated circuits, worked as a consultant on numerous military programs, and led product development and concept exploration efforts. He holds five U.S. patents and is a member of the Institute of Electrical and Electronic Engineers (IEEE). His interest in sound and computers dates back to 1974, when he built his first voice recognition machine while still in high school. The audio version of Jim's science fiction novel, *A Small Percentage*, has the distinction of being the first serialized audio novel on the Internet.

Patrick Seaman (pseaman@audionet.com) is Director of Technology at AudioNet (www.audionet.com), the largest broadcast network on the Internet. He also owns a small multimedia publishing company, Timberwolf Press (www.twolfpress.com), that copublished the first serialized audio novel on the Internet and publishes the software version of the annual trade book *Writer's Guide to Book Editors, Publishers, and Literary Agents* by Jeff Herman. Patrick also writes fiction. His technothriller, *Seed of Fear*, is due to go to press in December, 1996. Patrick lives near Dallas, TX with his wife, two children, and local area network.

Trademark Acknowledgments

All terms mentioned in this book that are known to be trademarks or service marks have been appropriately capitalized. New Riders Publishing cannot attest to the accuracy of this information. Use of a term in this book should not be regarded as affecting the validity of any trademark or service mark.

Dedications

Jim Cline: To the memory of my parents.

Patrick Seaman: To Dawn, the love of my life, for her faith and support, and to my beloved sons, Patrick and Blake.

Acknowledgments

Jim Cline: Many thanks to the folks at AudioNet, especially Patrick Seaman, for encouraging my audio efforts. I am also grateful to the staff and management at Guitar Center (Dallas) and the Brook Mays Pro Shop (Dallas) for their advice and technical assistance. I also wish to thank the companies which have provided pictures and other materials for this book.

Patrick Seaman: I would like to thank my good friend and coauthor, Jim Cline, without whose help I could never have finished this project. Jim is the best engineer I know, and a fine writer with whom it is my privilege to work.

Todd Wagner and Mark Cuban, at AudioNet, are true visionaries whom I thank for the opportunity to participate in and help shape the birth of a new industry. Thank you, Mark and Todd, for believing in and choosing me to help you start and build our labor of love, AudioNet.

Steve Weiss, Laura Frey, Stacey Beheler, Karen Walsh, Barb Potter, and Tim Huddleston at New Riders are the best in the business and a pleasure to work with. Thanks to all of you for your hard work and attention to detail in getting this project out the door! I would especially like to thank Steve Weiss for his encouragement and vision.

Contents at a Glance

Table of Contents

INTRODUCTION

One goal of any website planner is to create and continually improve an effective and vibrant site. By adding sound to your website, you can turn a visually stimulating site into a compelling one that is rich with various aspects of multimedia. Whether your site's focus is business, technology, education, medicine, law, entertainment, or public service, you can use audio to enhance other content or as the site's primary emphasis. At the very least, audio differentiates you from the rest of the Internet hordes—for a while.

Web designers are finding many exciting uses for audio on their sites. The folowing list provides a few examples:

◆ Record companies and independent recording artists are offering samples of the latest cuts from their compact discs. "Indy" (independent) bands are using the web to promote and demonstrate their music, in hopes of joining the ranks of signed bands.

◆ Companies are beginning to add sound capabilities to Intranets (internal networks) so they can broadcast product, sales, human resources, and other internal company news. This capability is especially handy in companies with widely dispersed offices, where employees in remote locations cannot benefit from hearing company direction and strategic plans from the top brass.

◆ Musicians are using the Net to broadcast concerts all over the world. Entire concert series are now regularly made available over the Net. In addition to a live audio feed, these broadcasts often include webcam (still image video capture) presentations, chat boxes, and lively graphics to add an energetic appearance to the website.

◆ Radio and television stations are extending their reach beyond local markets to the rest of the world. Stations are adding websites at a ferocious rate, and many are taking bold steps into the Internet broadcasting medium. As the Internet audience grows, radio stations will begin to create a Net-only version of their programming—complete with web-side audio advertising. This use of Internet technology promises to create a new revenue stream for these broadcasters.

◆ Just like commercial broadcast stations, syndicated and independently produced radio programs can extend their reach on the web. If you are producing such a program, you can broadcast it on the web and invite radio station programming directors to hear your stuff. It's a lower-cost alternative to expensive satellite uplinks.

◆ By broadcasting annual or shareholder meetings on the Net, companies can increase stockholder participation and awareness. Remote participants can use chat or e-mail to submit questions that can be answered live during the meeting and broadcast back over the Net. Organizations that want to restrict and control access to the broadcast can do so by establishing any of the following:

- Online subscription forms that redirect registrants to a dynamically generated or secret listener page.

- UserID and password protected web pages.

- User accounts or Internet address inclusion/exclusion lists supported by their Internet broadcast software of choice.

- Sales-oriented websites can create a department store atmosphere by adding automatic streamed audio with, say, music and advertisements. These load when a browser loads the site and immediately inform the listener about the organization.

- "Underground" radio stations (those broadcasting without an FCC license) are moving north of the border and proliferating on the web. You can create your own Internet-only radio station without an FCC license and experiment with new broadcasting formats and concepts. This is a great way to try out new ideas without dealing with stiff, FCC radio licensing fees and equipment costs associated with a traditional radio station.

Technology and Content: The Driving Forces Behind Web Sound

The web sound equation has two sides: technology and content. Which of the two is the driving force? Like software and hardware vendors, both lay claim to the driver's seat, saying that one would not exist without the other. In many ways, they are both right, although the scales are leaning toward the content side.

Technology

If your site is going to use non-streaming—or downloadable—formats such as WAV or AU, the technology players are largely relegated to those making editing tools. All major web servers and browsers, such as Netscape Navigator and Microsoft Internet Explorer products, support these formats.

Use of these formats requires that the site's visitor first download the entire file; then a "helper" program spawns to play the file. This process is often disappointingly slow. The relatively large size of these files—and the resulting lengthy download times—limit the use of these formats to such low-volume applications as archiving.

On the other hand, streaming technologies, including RealAudio, Shockwave, VDO, and StreamWorks, were designed for transmission over the Net. RealAudio currently holds the lion's share of the market—especially on live broadcasts. The fight for market dominance is really only just now warming up. If history is a guide, the software companies will attempt to leapfrog each other technologically in an attempt to gain market share. Keep in mind, though, that it isn't always the best technology that wins.

Browser Support

The major browser software publishers are quickly adding helper applications, called *players*, for streaming formats. For example, as of this writing, Internet Explorer includes a built-in RealAudio player and support for QuickTime, WAV, MIDI, AU, and AIFF. Netscape Navigator includes support for AIFF, AU, MIDI, WAV, and QuickTime.

If the browser doesn't include a specific helper (player), or your visitors want to obtain the latest version, they must visit the player's web- or FTP site and download what is often a multimegabyte file, then install it on their local computer.

After the player is installed, the client can visit the appropriate website and click on the Play or Listen button. This usually invokes a special URL that sends a request to the media server to begin streaming to the client's TCP/IP address, where the player briefly buffers and sorts the packets before playing the stream through the computer's sound card.

The Rush to Standards

Attempts are being made to standardize multimedia streaming. These attempts include Microsoft's ActiveMovie Streaming Format (ASF) initiative, which works with multiple network transport protocols such as TCP/IP, UDP, RTP, IPX/SPX and ATM. It promises to eliminate or reduce the need for separate helper applications and also support many of the major multimedia formats.

The truth is that companies in every segment of the Internet multimedia explosion have a stake in the standards and formats that ultimately dominate the market. Chip makers and network router/switch manufacturers optimize their architectures on certain assumptions, then bet their manufacturing capital on the outcome. Similarly, Internet backbone providers—such as Sprint, MCI, or UUNET—invest huge sums in their infrastructure. If their service or product supports the winning standards better than their competition, they'll have an edge.

Content

No matter what technology you use, whether you stream or download, whether you are live or recorded, you are ultimately in a ratings war—and your site's content is your ammunition. Just ask the TV networks whether they would rather have the newest, most exotic technology or a guaranteed number one, prime-time show. They might try to say "Both," but it all boils down to how good your content is.

The race to acquire content rights—and to push the boundaries of the medium—is being run at a fevered pace. In some ways, it is reminiscent of the early days of television or radio, when there was a great deal of exploration, few rules, and no maps.

Whether you are putting up sales information on your company's products or broadcasting a live entertainment program, you are competing for the attention of the Net audience. The better your content, the more often people will come back, the more often people will make bookmarks to your site, the more "favorite links" will point to your site, and the more search engines will include references to your site and drive traffic to you.

To whet your appetite, the following sections offer some websites that currently take advantage of audio technology, using the formats mentioned earlier.

RealAudio Sites

The following list of sites is by no means comprehensive, but is intended to provide a starting point for your exploration of web audio-related sites. Wherever appropriate, additional sites are listed throughout the rest of the book.

- ◆ **AudioNet** (`http://www.audionet.com`)   AudioNet is the largest audio site on the Internet and calls itself a "Broadcast Network" to differentiate itself from other Net sites. AudioNet's rapidly growing programming list includes play-by-play from more than 100 colleges and professional sports teams, more than 130 live radio stations, and more than 10,000 hours of archived programming—including specialty programming, audio novels, the largest archive of full-length music and comedy CDs on the Net, as well as numerous live concerts, conventions, seminars, product launches, political convention coverage, motion picture launches, and more.

- ◆ **c|net radio** (`http://www.cnet.com/Content/Radio/`)   This is the audio-broadcast side of c|net's integrated television/online service network. It is oriented toward computers, multimedia, online services, and other technology-related topics.

- ◆ **RealAudio** (`http://www.realaudio.com/`)   RealAudio's website showcases the RealAudio technology and also provides a home for a few content providers such as ABC and NPR. To help popularize the multitude of sites that use the technology, this site now features `www.timecast.com` to provide a searchable guide to the bulk of available programming.

Shockwave Sites

- ◆ **Virgin Records** (`http://www.virginrecords.com/show/mhzfront.html`) **and Capitol Records** (`http://www.hollywoodandvine.com/` **and** `http://www.macromedia.com/shockwave/epicenter/shockedsites/capitol/index.html`)   Both of these are good examples of established companies exploring their options on the Net. The Virgin Records site includes both Shockwave (`http://www.macromedia.com`) and RealAudio (`http://www.realaudio.com`) content. The Capitol Records sites represent efforts with Xing (`http://www.streamworks.com`) and Shockwave, respectively. Both of these sites use streaming audio to showcase and promote their artists.

VDONet Site

- ◆ **CBS News "Up To The Minute"** (`http://uttm.com`)   This site uses VDOLive (`http://www.vdo.net`) to deliver a slideshow of news snippets.

Streamworks Site

◆ **AudioBookClub** (`http://www.audiobookclub.com`)   Audio books are making their way to the web at sites such as this one, where subscribers can enjoy the online version of a book club that uses Xing Streamworks (`http://www.streamworks.com`).

Where Is All This Going?

In web audio technology—just as in other types of desktop computing technologies—it is a safe bet we are in for the usual software feature wars, leapfrogging, buyouts, takeovers, and various manifestations of the most sincere form of flattery.

Which technology will win? Never forget the old VHS-versus-Betamax battles; it isn't always the best technology that wins and, of course, today's best technology is obsolete tomorrow. RealAudio has a good market lead today, but only time will tell if that lead will last.

As technology, bandwidth, and the Net evolve, look to the content-oriented companies for the biggest growth. All the television and cable networks, such as NBC, ABC, CBS, FOX, UPN, CNN, and even cable operators such as TCI are testing the Internet waters. Content aggregators such as AudioNet have aggressively signed up Internet broadcast rights for a vast array of programming. The winners will be those entities that deliver the most compelling content to the broadest Internet audience over the most comprehensive and reliable Net distribution system. If your site is to be counted among the winners, you must focus your efforts not just on using the hottest technologies, but on providing the most compelling content you possibly can.

Who Is This Book For?

This book is aimed at experimenters, webmasters, site planners, architects, and those charged with maximizing the impact of their organization's web presence.

General familiarity with the Internet, computer hardware and software, and basic HTML concepts are helpful but not required to benefit from reading this book.

This book's emphasis is on practical descriptions and how-to examples, balanced with enough strategic advice and theory to help you decide which options are best for your site and how to effectively implement them.

New Riders Publishing

The staff of New Riders Publishing is committed to bringing you the very best in computer reference material. Each New Riders book is the result of months of work by authors and staff who research and refine the information contained within its covers.

As part of this commitment to you, the reader, New Riders invites your input. Please let us know if you enjoy this book, if you have trouble with the information and examples presented, or if you have a suggestion for the next edition.

Please note, however, that New Riders cannot serve as a technical resource for any of the software, hardware, or other audio- or Internet-related technologies described in this book. If you have questions about a specific product, please refer to the product's documentation, Help system, or vendor for assistance.

If you have a question or comment about any New Riders book, there are several ways to contact New Riders Publishing. We will respond to as many readers as we can. Your name, address, or phone number will never become part of a mailing list or be used for any purpose other than to help us continue to bring you the best books possible. You can write us at the following address:

New Riders Publishing
Attn: Publisher
201 West 103rd Street
Indianapolis, IN 46290

If you prefer, you can fax New Riders at (317) 817-7448.

You also can send electronic mail to New Riders at the following Internet address:

    ddwyer@newriders.mcp.com

New Riders Publishing is an imprint of Macmillan Computer Publishing USA. To obtain a catalog or information, or to purchase any Macmillan Computer Publishing book, call (800) 428-5331.

Thank you for choosing *Website Sound*!

CHAPTER 1

PREPARING TO IMPLEMENT WEBSITE SOUND

This chapter is intended as a shortcut to help you decide which direction and options to choose in your quest to add sound to your website. As you answer the questions posed throughout this chapter, you'll find out which of the later chapters are most relevant to your needs.

Before you begin, consider the kind of content with which you will be working. Will you create it yourself or under contract? Perhaps the content will be under license from a third party. If the content is licensed, what is the financial and contractual impact on your organization? Is your license exclusive, or will your competitors also have the ability to carry the material?

The choices you make in content drive the decisions about which technology you'll choose and the types of employees and skills needed to put the site together and support it. Without the right talent to get the job done, your project is likely to fail. Understanding the skills that are needed helps ensure that you'll get the best people.

Deciding whether you plan to start out with a small or large site drives many decisions. Choosing to build a large site automatically eliminates inadequate technological choices. If you plan to start as a small website, but quickly grow to be a large site, you are wise to choose technology and resources that can grow with you, rather than invest in throw-away technology that won't be able to fulfill the needs of a larger site.

The sections that follow explore these issues, provide tips and examples to help you avoid technological dead ends, and improve your chances for success.

Choosing Your Site's Audio Content

What kind of content—or *programming*—will you be broadcasting from your website? The answer to this question helps you make many decisions as you plan your audio strategy. After you answer this question, most of the other legal, licensing, and technical questions that lie ahead are ALSO more easily answered. The following sections help you examine some of these questions.

Original Versus Borrowed Content: Who Holds the Rights?

Intellectual property rights, copyrights, and licenses are complex issues that cannot be legally ignored and that are gaining increasingly more visibility on the Internet. Gone are the days when enterprising individuals could cavalierly post copyrighted material because the record labels or other copyright holders didn't know what the Internet was. Today, savvy legal departments regularly scour the web looking for rights violators.

> The authors and publisher of this book take no position on this issue.

How serious are these copyright issues? In 1995, a series of now-famous law enforcement raids were carried out against individuals and Internet companies accused of infringing Church of Scientology copyrights. Disks, backups, and computer equipment were seized, and a tortuous trail of lawsuits and legal actions began. The issue was the Internet newsgroup posting (`alt.religion.scientology`) of material written by church founder L. Ron Hubbard. The posters of the material, active critics of the church, felt that their actions were ones of exercising their right to free speech by expressing and supporting their arguments. Reportedly, the church claimed that the materials were church secrets and should not be released to the uninitiated. Ultimately, the claims and counter-claims had to do with the issue of denying the church money from the potential sale of these materials. At last report, many of the charges had been dropped; however, some of those involved have settled out of court, and some legal actions were still ongoing.

Volumes have been written about the moral, ethical, and legal implications of this series of events and the way in which cyberspace intrudes upon reality. For Internet broadcasters, the lessons to be learned emphasize the negative consequences of copyright disputes and the need to make absolutely certain that you've done your legal homework. Failure to do so can swiftly lead to unpleasant consequences.

> None of the comments in this book should be construed as legal advice. If you have any doubts about the legal status of materials that you plan to make available on the Internet, you should first seek the advice of a Net-aware attorney who understands (or better still, specializes in) intellectual property law. Don't post any material—whether it's text, graphics, audio, or video—unless you're sure you have the right or permission to do so.

Now that the disclaimers are out of the way, you should examine your "original" content. How do you know if it is okay to broadcast? Take a common-sense approach to this rule of thumb: Can you get away with the content on television or radio? Suppose that you are a musician, and you record a CD that has several tracks that sound amazingly like those from a Rolling Stone's album. Unless you have secured the necessary legal/licensing rights and permissions, you may be receiving one of those nasty legal letters that everyone dreads.

This rule of thumb also applies if you are creating, for example, business presentations that use copyrighted music in clips or soundtracks.

The bottom line is this: If you are unsure of the legal status of your material, either obtain legal advice or be advised that you are living dangerously.

If you are the rights-holder of the content, make sure that you protect these rights by incorporating copyright notices on your web pages and in the delivery of the audio content. For example, the RealAudio player displays copyright information, as shown in figure 1.1.

FIGURE 1.1

Example showing copyright information on the RealAudio Player.

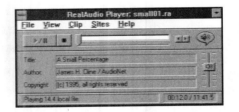

In figure 1.1, co-author James Cline's audio novel is being broadcast by AudioNet (`http://www.AudioNet.com`). As you can see in figure 1.2, in addition to the player, the author and copyright information is also credited on the web page itself.

The HTML code shown in figure 1.2 is as follows:

```
Copyright &#169; James H. Cline
<p>
All writer's works, text, descriptions, etc. ,
are copyrighted to the author, unless otherwise noted.
<hr>
```

```
Copyright &#169; 1995,1996 <a href="http://
www.audionet.com">AudioNet</a>, Inc. All Rights Reserved
</BODY>
</HTML>
```

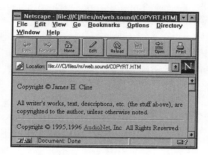

FIGURE 1.2

Sample web page copyright credits.

How Volatile Is Your Content?

For the first year of operations, how often do you expect your audio content to change? The second year? Just as important is how much the volume or quantity of audio content will grow.

How Many Hours of Programming Will You Have at StartUp?

Suppose that you are starting out with 100 hours of programming on cassette. Each hour of tape requires a minimum of one hour to encode. *Encoding* is the process of taking the digital audio source and converting it to the format used on the Internet, such as with Xing Streamworks, Macromedia Shockwave, or RealAudio.

Prior to the encoding step, some audio editing is usually needed to delete unwanted sections or audio artifacts (glitches, chirps, beeps, and so on). How much time do you need to plan for editing? In many cases, little or none, especially if you are working with material that has already been professionally edited and prepared. If the material you receive is a raw, unedited recording, a substantial amount of audio editing may be required to remove unwanted sounds, such as coughs, cue calling, and extraneous speakers or sounds like cars, bells, and aircraft. Depending on how much work your audio source needs, the amount of time needed to edit it may range from a few minutes to several hours, per hour of raw source.

Note

Multitrack recordings in which each audio source is recorded on a separate track might require many hours of editing, per hour of source content. In very complex cases, such as with professionally recorded 48 track music, it might take days or weeks to complete one three minute song. On the other end of the spectrum, a two-track 15 minute recording of a dramatic reading might take two to three hours. Please see Chapter 11 for further discussion on this topic. See Chapters 9, "Sound Basics and Audio Theory" and 11, "Digital Audio Recording and Editing," for more information on sound basics and editing.

Suppose, in your case, that 30 minutes are needed to edit each hour of tape. If you further assume that each hour of tape requires 5 minutes for changing tapes and recueing the tape deck and software, your 100 hours of programming would require

150 hours of editing
+100 hours of encoding
+ ((5 minutes/hour)*100 hours=500 minutes=8.3 hours)
258.3 hours preparation

258.3 hours translates to a little over 32 8-hour work days to prepare your 100 hours. If you plan to have 100 new hours of tape per month, you'll obviously need more than one audio editor.

The number of hours required to prepare your content drives the type and quantity of audio and computer equipment, sound editors, and audio technicians needed to do the job—even if all these jobs are held by you. What if you take 5 to 8 hours or more to edit every hour of tape? You can easily be looking at 1,000 hours of work for 100 hours of programming. Obviously, you need to budget enough time to get the content ready.

Part of your planning process is to determine how much hard disk space is needed to store your content. The RealAudio 28.8 format uses 1.8 KB per second, so 100 hours (360,000 seconds) of content requires about 648,000 KB, or 632 MB of hard disk space, depending on the cluster size and other specifics of the individual hard drive. If you plan to keep all of your content from previous months available to your listeners, you need to plan for adequate hard disk space to maintain your archives. For example, if the 100 hours grows to 110, 120, or more, per month, you may need 10 to 12 GB per year of hard disk space.

How Fast and How Much Will Content Increase?

As you go through the startup content production process, you'll get a better idea of how many hours and how much equipment it takes to produce a given amount of finished product. In the real world, you have to make these plans before you have the benefit of the experience.

If your site is limited in scope and unlikely to grow significantly beyond your initial design, you may not need to worry about planning for production and bandwidth capacity. An example of this might be businesses that plan to use their Internet presence to advertise their traditional products using existing audio advertising material. These types of sites are often static, with any changes replacing, rather than adding to, website audio content. In these cases, there may be little or no growth in the number of hours (or minutes) of audio programming.

If you plan to add new content on a regular basis, you need to plan for the following: adequate content editing and encoding time, HTML programming to keep the site up to date, server support, and more bandwidth.

For example, will the addition of new content require the creation of new graphics? If so, your HTML staff needs to have sufficient artistic talent to produce acceptable designs within the time allotted. Trying to force creativity to follow a schedule can be quite a challenge— don't underestimate this task.

What about bandwidth? If you project your listener growth to be, for example, 35% per month, the computation for how much bandwidth you'll need is simple arithmetic. Many organizations lack the funding to purchase today the bandwidth they'll need a year from now. Indeed, it is probably a poor economic decision to do so.

So how much should you buy, and when? Clearly, no solution works for every situation. A rule of thumb is to look at the lead time required for each expected transition. How long would it take to have each larger circuit type installed and activated? If the lead time for a T-1 in your area or city is 60 days, you'll need to order the T-1 long before you expect to actually need it. The following table illustrates a typical bandwidth growth plan.

	Circuit Type Needed	Circuit Installation Lead Time	Circuit Order/ Request Date
Startup	ISDN	2 weeks	Day 1
3 Months	T-1	30 days	Month 2
6 Months	3 T1s	30 days	Month 5
9 Months	10 MB	30 days	Month 8
12 Months	T-3	60 days	Month 10

Note See Chapter 13, "Bandwidth and Cost Considerations," for a detailed discussion of bandwidth and cost considerations.

Is the Content Live, Recorded, or Both?

Preparation of prerecorded content is often a straightforward editing and encoding process. Planning for the necessary time and resources is usually easy—with a little experience.

If some portion of your content is to be live, the complexity of your production increases because you are now in the realm of professional audio engineers, broadcast studios, and live remotes. Live events exemplify Murphy's Law: Everything that can go wrong will go wrong at the worst possible time. Dealing with these inevitable problems requires the experience and planning to avoid them and the professionalism and resources to work around them.

If you plan to produce live events, you should consult a local television or radio station engineer and learn the ropes about having backup equipment, power, connectivity, transportation, personnel, and backups for your backups. This applies to both the sending and receiving end of your broadcasts. Broadcast feeds should be structured with automatic failover equipment and methods. Drill and practice procedures for dealing with problems such as equipment and line failures. What will you do if your line goes dead? Where is your spare telephone hybrid? Spare microphone(s)?

When things go wrong during a live event, there is no time to fix or repair equipment, or diagnose network or line problems. You must have backup solutions in place and ready for failover both at the live event venue and also back at your broadcast center. Live events are very unforgiving. When they are over, that's it. If you missed it, it's gone. Dress rehearsals and constant testing are musts. If possible, try to start out with smaller, less critical events, to help your organization get a handle on the learning curve.

Critical live events should be configured with backup, or multiple Internet broadcast bandwidth options. If your MCI line goes down, for example, your staff should be trained to move the traffic to that backup UUNET line you had installed.

"Okay," you say, "so doing live programming can be difficult. Is anyone else doing it?" The answer is yes, and at two levels. Most of the programs being broadcast are *single-product* efforts, in which a company produces an Internet talk show, for example, and concentrates on producing one show or a very small number of highly targeted shows. An excellent example is PC Week Radio (`http://www.pcweek.com`).

Multiple Product Efforts—that is, Internet broadcasters that specialize in delivering a wide variety of programming—are rare. The best example is AudioNet (`www.audionet.com`), the "Wal-Mart of Internet audio." AudioNet has thousands of hours of recorded programming and a vast selection of live sports, radio stations, concerts, and other offerings.

You will probably find yourself somewhere in the middle of this spectrum; therefore, you must plan accordingly. You need to anticipate the number of HTML programmers, audio engineers, audio technicians, and network engineers that you will need. You also should plan for the network hardware and software and, once again, the amount of network bandwidth that you'll need to get started.

Do You Need to Convert the Content to a Different Format?

Dealing with a different format is another "gotcha." If you receive the content in a different format from the one you plan to use, you need to convert the content to the correct format. You also need to be certain that no quality is lost during the conversion process, and, of course, you must plan for the extra time required to convert and edit the content.

All content production elements require an investment in that most expensive of commodities: time. If you think the process through and budget your time and resources wisely, however, you'll be way ahead of most of your competition.

What Are Your Content's Quality Assurance Demands?

The issue of quality assurance may seem obvious, but you don't have to surf the Net long to find out how often it is ignored. After your content is produced and HTML is edited, make sure that you schedule someone to be responsible for reviewing and testing the pages and content. Be certain that the reviewer is a good editor because it takes only one syntax error to disable the audio or some other feature of your site and pages.

A frequent mistake of programmers occurs when they test the page during development and then make one last change before turning on the page. Because they fail to retest the page after the change, they frequently create an error.

The consequences of small mistakes can be profound. In June 1996, NETCOM's 400,000 subscribers were offline for 13 hours due to a routing table programming error. Routing tables guide networks in ways to distribute traffic. During routine maintenance, a NETCOM programmer introduced a small flaw that propagated to other routers in Netcom's network. Each time the flaw was corrected on one router, it was reintroduced by another router in the system. The solution was a complete shutdown of the system and a lot of unhappy customers.

After the pages and audio are up, retest. Minor editing changes that can accidentally disable the audio are often made to HTML pages. Also, depending on how your shop is run, audio can be moved from one server to another and sometimes the links get broken.

The bottom line: Test, test, and retest!

Planning Your Technical Approach

After you have decided what your website's content will be and have an idea of the kind of resources you'll need to acquire or develop it, it is time to plan your technical approach. Will your website be large or small? Will you use a streaming or nonstreaming broadcast format? Starting out small, with a low volume or experimental site, may be a great fit for your project and budget. If you are planning a large, high volume website, you need to make additional considerations during the planning stages.

The type of content you choose to broadcast has less to do with the size of your site than with the kind of hardware, software, and staffing you'll need. Conversely, the relative size of your site is more of a function of your business model and the quantity of material you plan to broadcast.

The sections that follow explore the implications of starting out with small or large sites, music and speech-only content, as well as bandwidth and other related issues.

Starting Out Small

As with many endeavors, starting out small can have many advantages, especially in the reduced costs associated with personnel and equipment. Starting out small also enables you to focus the scope of your project and narrowly define the parameters of success. Another major benefit is the shortened amount of time it takes to bring an operational site online.

The following two sections present different methods for implementing a small site, starting with nonstreaming, downloadable files. The downloadable category includes .WAV and similar formats. The second method uses a small streaming-audio license.

The Implications of Format on Sound Quality

Carefully evaluate how much fidelity, dynamic range your broadcast is going to require. In general, music found on an FM radio station is high fidelity, whereas music found on an AM radio station is low fidelity.

You can probably use a sub-14.4 Kbps format for low-fidelity material. The bandwidth requirements for these formats range from 6 Kbps to 10 Kbps. The best quality sounds like AM radio on a good day, which is often pretty good.

What kinds of audio material are low fidelity? Examples include sporting events, audio novels, talk shows, most sales presentations, seminars, conventions, and speeches.

Low-fidelity broadcasts have a couple advantages over high-fidelity broadcasts:

◆ **Cost:** The smaller the bandwidth requirements, the less bandwidth you use. Bandwidth is almost always limited in quantity and availability, and for most organizations it represents a significant monthly expense.

◆ **The number of listeners:** In general, the lower the bandwidth requirements of your broadcast, the more simultaneous listeners you are able to fit into your available bandwidth.

High-fidelity music usually requires streaming formats that consume more bandwidth, increase your operating costs, and often require twice the bandwidth to reach the same number of listeners as nonmusical quality formats.

What about a talk show format? Even talk shows don't sound any better on the faster formats. If the content does not use the greater dynamic range afforded the faster formats, you are simply wasting bandwidth.

For further discussion on audio dynamic range, see Chapter 11.

Static, Nonstreaming, Downloadable Files

All streaming audio formats require some form of audio server. The number of possible concurrent streams is a function of the number of stream licenses you have purchased, the horsepower of the server, and the amount of available bandwidth. Although this section deals with nonstreaming formats, it's important to mention streaming formats here to point out the advantages of using nonstreaming formats on small audio websites.

Nonstreaming formats do not require the purchase of audio server software because the download method is usually a simple FTP (file transfer protocol) process initiated by an URL pointing directly at the sound file. If you have a direct, permanent connection to the Internet and you own your own server, there is usually nothing you'll need to do to your servers because most are preconfigured to handle simple sound file downloads.

If you don't have the luxury of permanent bandwidth and server hardware/software, you need to arrange to have your website hosted by an Internet Service Provider. In this case, you need to make sure that you have made arrangements to allow for the number of megabytes of downloads you are expecting. Be cautious because many ISPs don't really have the hardware and software they need to accurately bill on the basis of megabytes per time period. Unless you are in a rural area, many different ISPs are usually available from which to choose; make sure that you have done a good job of comparison shopping for hosting your website.

For more information on bandwidth considerations, look at Chapter 13.

Using nonstreaming formats is probably the easiest and quickest way to add audio to any website. Virtually any multimedia PC or MAC has built-in hardware and software with which you can create WAV files. With a cassette or CD player and the right cabling, you can input an audio source into your computer and create a WAV file. The WAV file can then be linked on the website for direct download by your listeners.

Being able to create a WAV file is the good news. The bad news is that although WAV files and many other static formats create good-quality sound, they do so at the expense of hard disk space. One minute of full stereo CD-quality sound consumes about 10.5 MB of disk space.

The download time for WAV files is another drawback. Even if you compress your WAV (or other format) file with a compression utility, your one-minute file is still several megabytes and results in download times that can be measured in hours. Even at today's 28.8 Kbps speeds, download time is further increased because many 28.8 Kbps connections have an actual data throughput that is significantly lower than 28.8 Kbps. This situation is due to oversold bandwidth at the ISP or the ISP's bandwidth provider (upstream), bad phone lines, general Internet congestion, or many other possibilities.

Nonetheless, with good sound editing, judicious reductions in audio fidelity, and application of available compression techniques, the file size and download-time problems can be reduced. WAV files and other, similar formats, can add an exciting dimension to your website.

Note See Chapters 8, "MIDI," and 2, "Static (Downloadable) File Formats," for more detailed information on nonstreaming file formats.

Small Streaming Licenses

An alternative to working with nonstreaming technology is to purchase a streaming server license with 5–25 streams. This is a good way to start small and build up your audio website. The following list contains some cost examples, but notice that these costs are for software only; hardware must be purchased separately.

◆ **Progressive Networks** (http://www.realaudio.com/).   At the time of this writing, RealAudio is offering a 5-stream server license for $495, plus $100 for upgrades and support. A 20-user license is $1,895, plus $600 for upgrades and support. If you plan to broadcast 14.4 Kbps streams, the 5-stream license can be supported on a single ISDN B channel or on the older, switched-56 format line. This is because the RealAudio 14.4-class stream actually requires about 10 Kbps of bandwidth. The 28.8-class streams require about 20 Kbps per stream; thus your 5-stream license can be supported on a dual B channel 128 Kbps ISDN line.

◆ **Shockwave** (http://www.macromedia.com).   Shockwave is a hybrid web audio product that depends on the HTML web server, rather than a dedicated audio server, to deliver the streaming audio file. Instead of selling server and stream licenses, Macromedia sells a package of multi-media authoring tools ($995 at the time of this writing). The idea is to use Shockwave as a full multimedia (video and audio) toolkit for developers to create synchronized video/audio "movies." At the time of this writing, Macromedia has not listed any advanced audio server features—such as monitoring tools, replication across multiple servers, and so on—that are a focus of Streamworks and RealAudio.

◆ **VDONet** (http://www.vdo.net/).   The VDOLive Video Server (although it is a video server, it helps illustrate the pricing for small servers) lists at

$1,199 for a 5-stream license, plus $360 for annual support. The 10-stream license lists at $1,995/$599, and a 25-stream license lists at $3,995/$1,199.

◆ **Xing Technology** (`http://www.streamworks.com/`). Xing Streamworks is currently licensed on the basis of bandwidth. The full package, which runs on a 128 Kbps ISDN line, currently costs $1,395.

As with the nonstreaming formats, starting out with a small license can provide a training ground, and even a proving ground, for your project or website. An additional benefit to your listeners is the lowered bandwidth requirements, which reduce your equipment and recurring telecom/bandwidth expenses.

High-Volume and Commercial Sites

If you've started out small and grown your business to the point that you are contemplating jumping into the high-volume category, your experience will be invaluable. By now you should have a good idea about the resources you'll need to expand your audio editing and HTML support. Be warned that the increase in other costs, such as high-capacity bandwidth and the support personnel to manage it, is not linear; it is, in fact, a rather steep curve upward.

If you are jumping straight into this new type of broadcast industry, you should buy the best Net talent you can find. That is, you will need experienced network engineers who understand and can negotiate Internet peering arrangements, design your Internet routing table architecture, and understand the interrelationships between the telcos, first and second tier Internet connectivity providers, and organizations such as your own.

Large Streaming Licenses

Most vendors don't list pricing for more than one hundred streams. If you project pricing based on published stream rates of around $100 per stream, one thousand streams should cost about $100,000 less than whatever volume discount you can negotiate.

Bandwidth Implications of High Traffic Volume

After you have the money for the streams, you need the bandwidth on which to play them. Suppose that you are going to use a low-bandwidth format, such as RealAudio's 14.4 stream, which requires about 10 Kbps. Your 1,000 streams translates into $1,000 \times 10$ Kbps = 10,000 Kbps, or 10 Mbps (a T-1 is 1.54 Mbps). This amount leaves no room for other traffic, such as from your web server, file transfers, or e-mail.

When shopping for bandwidth, be warned that many bandwidth providers are selling their core capacity many times over and are trying to ensure that the total average use of their customers does not overload their capacity. One of the problems is that you may not be getting what you think you have paid for. Your T-1 or 10 Mbps line may only have a real-world capacity of some fraction of that amount because you are sharing the downstream pipe with other customers.

After you are satisfied with the terms of your bandwidth agreement, your network building project requires a significant capital outlay for the bandwidth itself, routers, switches, hubs, computers, and other equipment and software, not to mention qualified staffing.

Content Licensing Expense

The larger your operation and the more content you license or acquire, the greater the expense to obtain that content will be. As the Internet broadcast market matures, demandable costs rise, and available programming grows in acquisition complexity. It is not going to get any easier or cheaper to obtain content.

Intense competition exists for Internet broadcasting rights for available content. Be careful that the content you plan to obtain isn't already taken before you get there. What this situation means for your project or website is that it might be easier for you to develop your content internally than to plan your site around third-party content you have not yet acquired.

Outsourcing

Outsourcing website audio enables you to concentrate on the acquisition and production of content rather than the expensive proposition of building your own high-speed Internet audio distribution network. Outsourcing is also the quickest way to deliver your audio content to the Net.

The following list contains a few questions that you should ask the outsourcing organization:

◆ How much Internet broadcasting experience does the company have? It may be a great ISP, but does it really know anything about Internet broadcasting?

◆ How many streams is the company licensed to broadcast, and what other programming is currently using part of those streams?

◆ How many unique listeners does the company have for its existing content? What is the growth rate, and can the company document the rate?

◆ How much overall bandwidth does the company have available? Does it have enough to handle the number of expected listeners without swamping its network?

◆ How many Internet distribution points does the company have with which to deliver your content with the fewest number of router hops? Does the company have a single "pipe" to the Net, or does it have multiple, independent routes to increase the robustness and reliability of the distribution network?

◆ What kind of network redundancy does the company have in case of Net problems upstream from it? Does the company have the capability to reroute its (your) traffic around Internet congestion areas?

◆ What kind of staff does the company have available during the hours you plan to have your programming? Staffing is important if you plan to do live events during time slots that are outside of normal business hours. Does the company offer telephone technical support for your broadcasts during the hours that are important to you? Many ISPs only offer support via e-mail.

◆ Does the company guarantee a minimum number of available streams for your content? Does it cap your listeners for any given time period, such as *x* many streams per hour?

◆ Is the company's overall site/service popular enough to give you a feel for whether it will help draw listeners to your content? How does the company propose to promote your content and drive new listeners to it?

◆ Does the company have an ASCAP/BMI license to cover any music or music clips you may include on your site? The company should also be able to advise you as to what is and is not permitted under current intellectual property and other law.

Implementation Tips

Implementing website sound is essentially a two step process. The first step is to decide what kind of content you plan to broadcast. In many cases this is easy, especially for existing businesses and organizations wanting to bring their message to the Net. For pioneering Net broadcasters, the decision can be much harder, and should involve a lot of research to see what is already out there. The choices you make drive the kind of personnel, equipment, broadcasting software, and bandwidth you'll need.

The second step begins with deciding how big your effort will be. The choice further defines what resources you need to implement the site. Small sites can be quickly and inexpensively established. Large sites require careful planning in every area to avoid cost and technical pitfalls. Everything from your employees to your equipment, bandwidth, and software costs are significantly higher for large sites.

After you've made the decisions about the kind of content you want and how big a splash you plan to make, you need to find the right people to make it all happen. Then you must take steps to ensure that your content is a success. Following are some tips.

◆ **Finding the right people.**   Artists, HTML, and other programers are easy to find. Qualified Unix systems administrators are hard to find, and true Internet connectivity experts are *very, very* hard to find. The principles of supply and demand are in full effect in this arena, pushing the salary requirements of Unix administrators and Internet connectivity experts to lofty levels. How do you find them? Try hanging around the relevant newsgroups, such as support forums for the type of software you plan to use. Don't be intrusive, but watch the posts for a while and see if anyone stands out, then send that person a discrete, personal e-mail. Be careful that your message does not look like a form letter—the recipient may think he is getting spammed.

◆ **How to make your content a success.**   Ever notice how many television shows are canceled each year? Clearly, a lot of time and money were spent on their production, yet they didn't make it. Popularity is fickle, and success has no guaranteed formula. The following list provides a few things you can do to try to maximize your chances of success.

  ◆ If possible, try to use material that has won in other media forms.

  ◆ If your budget permits, don't pin your hopes on a single program; try running other simultaneous programs. This can build an audience for your site. If you can't try out other material simultaneously, have a backup plan. What do you do if your content flops? You should plan in advance what the parameters are for success or failure. If the content is spiraling downward, don't let it take you with it. Plan ahead for when to cut your losses, and always be on the look-out for new material.

  ◆ Advertise. The number of websites on the Net is staggering. The chances of a significant number of listeners stumbling upon your site and spreading the word is remote. You need to promote your site and content as widely as possible. Here are some tips:

    ◆ Scour the web for sites that are willing to add a link to yours, and don't forget to reciprocate.

    ◆ Go to all the search engines and manually update them with information on your site as often as they will allow.

    ◆ Trade banner ads with other sites.

◆ Start an e-mail newsletter and send updated copies with the latest programming information to everyone who registers in your website guest book.

◆ Start getting press for your site by calling local news papers and magazines. Ask them to mention your program in the entertainment or arts section.

◆ As articles are written about your efforts, add them to your press kit, and keep sending press kits to newspaper editors and other media outlets. Don't worry about including articles from small newspapers or magazines—any press is good press.

◆ Many talk radio stations carry locally produced Internet-related talk shows. Send press kits to all of these shows and try to get them to interview you, or at least mention your website on the air.

CHAPTER 2

STATIC (DOWNLOADABLE) FILE FORMATS

This chapter examines various static audio file formats such as WAVE, AIFF, and AU. For the purposes of this book, static means that the file must first be completely downloaded before it can be played. This is opposed to streaming format audio files (see Chapter 3, "Streaming Technologies"), which are designed to be played as they are downloaded.

No special server software is needed with static format files, which is a major advantage in terms of cost and simplicity. Static format files can be posted and downloaded like any other binary file, whereas streaming format files require special server software to *push* them to the client.

The simplicity of the static formats makes them very popular on the Internet. They are widely used for posting sound clips and other short audio pieces. A major limitation of these files is that they are usually large compared to the streaming format files. Download time becomes a problem for the larger files.

A wide variety of static formats are currently in use. Some, such as WAVE or AIFF, are widely accepted; others are unique to a specific sound tool or other software application.

A large part of this chapter is dedicated to the structure of static file formats. Although few readers need all the details contained in this chapter, a basic understanding of this material helps in the selection of a format for your website application. The formats discussed include the following:

◆ WAVE (.WAV)

◆ AIFF

◆ AIFF-C (AIFC)

◆ AU (Sun audio, NeXT audio, MU-law, u-law)

◆ MPEG

◆ SND (SND Resource)

◆ VOC

A Shortcut to Format Selection

If you are in a hurry and do not want to read all the details about formats, you should know that the two most popular, general-purpose static audio formats on the Internet are WAVE (.WAV) and AIFF (.AIF). WAVE, the more common of the two, is the Windows audio standard. AIFF is the Macintosh audio standard. AIFF also is used on other machines such as the Silicon Graphics workstations. The PC/Mac distinction is somewhat blurred because most sound players on either machine read either format equally well.

If your goal is just to place a few short (that is, a minute or so in length) sound clips on your website, go with WAVE or AIFF or both. Post your audio files with the lowest sampling rate and shortest word length you can stand. Files with higher sampling rates and longer word length sound better, but they take up more disk space and take much longer to download.

If you want to post instrumental music, you may want to consider MIDI. Although not an audio format, MIDI is efficient and widely used to distribute music on the Internet. It is discussed in detail in Chapter 8, "MIDI."

If your Internet audio application is neither short nor instrumental, you probably need a streaming audio format. See Chapter 3 for details.

Digitized Audio

To store audio in a computer file or transmit it across the Internet, it must first be converted to digital form. This *raw audio* is then encoded using a standard format that can be efficiently stored in a file, retrieved at some later time, decoded, and played. Use of a standard format ensures it will be readable by all users of your website.

Figure 2.1 shows this process in schematic form. Various blocks in this system, such as the analog-to-digital converter and the anti-aliasing filters, are discussed in Chapter 9, "Sound Basics and Audio Theory."

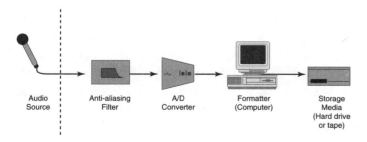

Audio Source — Anti-aliasing Filter — A/D Converter — Formatter (Computer) — Storage Media (Hard drive or tape)

FIGURE 2.1

Converting audio to digital form involves removing high frequencies (anti-aliasing), converting to a raw digital code, formatting the audio data into a usable form, and storing the data until needed.

At first look, encoding appears to be nothing more than the simple packing of a large number of digitized audio samples into a file. Rarely is it that simple though, because formats are designed to minimize the size of the file or optimize the quality of the audio. Encoding is often the most complicated part of the process. Selecting the right (or wrong) encoding format can have a dramatic effect on audio file properties, such as those in the following list:

◆ Size of the audio file

◆ Degradation of the audio due to format-related noise

◆ Tonal quality (frequency range) of the stored audio

◆ Range of possible loudness levels (dynamic range)

◆ Number of audio channels supported

◆ Special features such as three-dimensional sound

The oldest and simplest formats involve storing the digitized audio stream as is, directly into the file. These raw audio formats are almost always proprietary and are rarely used on the Internet. Their main deficiency is that nothing inside them defines how the audio should be played. Playback rate, word length (the number of bits in each sample), and other critical parameters are not defined in the format. You must know exactly what all these parameters are before you can use the data; nothing in the file provides this information.

More advanced formats, including all those commonly used on the Internet, are *self-describing*. They add a header that identifies format parameters such as sampling rate and word length. Many format parameters exist. That is, an audio file can be put together in many ways. The following list shows these parameters. They are discussed in the sections immediately following the list. The way these parameters affect basic format properties is also discussed in these sections, along with example formats.

◆ Header format and content

◆ Number of audio tracks

◆ Sampling rate

◆ Word length

◆ Compression method (if any)

◆ Number system

◆ Addressing method (big endian versus little endian)

◆ Frame length

◆ Parity bits and error-correcting codes

Header Format and Content

Header information at the front of the file almost always contains a field to identify the sampling rate and the word length (in bits). This is essential in formats that enable different sampling rates or bit lengths. WAVE, AIFF, and AU are examples of such formats. Without this information, the data stored in the file cannot be decoded easily, turning it into a useless block of random numbers.

Number of Audio Tracks

The simpler formats support only mono (a single audio track) or stereo (two tracks). An example is the .AU format used on many Unix machines. More sophisticated formats, such as those used with sound-editing software programs, can support many tracks. WAVE can support an arbitrary number of tracks, although players or other applications supporting more than two tracks are rare. AIFF can support one to six channels.

Sampling Rates

Digital audio is a long series of samples derived from analog audio. The number of samples taken per second is called the *sampling rate*. Sampling rate is a key factor in audio quality; it defines the highest frequencies that can be stored and reproduced—the higher the sampling rate, the higher the maximum frequency. Theoretically, the highest frequency is half the sampling rate. In practice, the highest frequency is usually 10–20 percent lower than the theoretical value due to practical circuit design considerations.

The format used on audio CDs, for example, follows the Red Book Standard, which uses a 44.1 KHz sampling rate. Two samples, one each for the left and right channel, are read off the CD at a 44.1 KHz rate. The maximum frequency that can be practically reproduced is 20 KHz, which meets the upper end of the human auditory range of 20 Hz–20 KHz.

Increasing the sampling rate beyond 44.1 KHz has rapidly diminishing returns. In fact, the improvement is insignificant, except for a few special applications. For this reason, sampling rates higher than 48 KHz are rare, even if the digital audio format can support it.

Note

> The audio from an AM radio tops out at about 8 KHz. An FM radio can reproduce audio frequencies up to 15 KHz. Most of the energy content of human voice resides in frequencies of 1 KHz or less, although a small but significant content extends past 5 KHz. As mentioned earlier, the minimum sampling rate to fully support each of these maximum audio frequencies is twice the maximum frequency plus a small margin. Reproducing FM-radio quality sound requires an absolute minimum sampling rate of 15 KHz×2, or 30 KHz. In practice a 32 KHz rate would be adequate, but just barely.

The possible number of sampling rates is large, but only a few are *standard* sampling rates. Consider the 44.1 KHz rate used for CD-quality audio, for example. Why 44.1 KHz? Wouldn't 44.05 KHz or 43.923277 KHz or any other sampling rate near 44.1 KHz work just as well? The answer is yes. Although nothing is magical about 44.1 KHz, it serves as a standard for equipment manufacturers and software designers. Without such standards, an electronic Tower of Babel would result, with every sound file sampled at a different rate. Standard sampling rates and other audio format features often come about by the actions of standards committees and equipment manufacturers.

Common standard sampling rates include

8 KHz	Commonly used with WAVE, AIFF
8.013 KHz	Supported by some u-law formats including .AU
11.025 KHz	Called *1/4 CD* rate. Common with WAVE
11.127 KHz	AIFF

16 KHz	Supported by MPEG-2
22.05 KHz	Supported by MPEG-2, .AU
24 KHz	Supported by MPEG-2
32 KHz	Supported by some Digital Audio Tape (DAT) formats, MPEG-1, and MPEG-2
44.1 KHz	Supported by DAT formats, MPEG-1, MPEG-2, Red Book (audio CD), .AU, and AIFF
48 KHz	DAT formats, MPEG-1, MPEG-2

Some formats support arbitrary sampling rates. WAVE and AIFF can do this, although only a few rates are shown for them in the list.

Even though a format supports arbitrary sampling rates, this provides no guarantee that an audio player or other audio tool can handle an audio file formatted in this manner. For this reason, a good practice is to test a new audio file on several different audio players before posting it on a website. This testing helps ensure that all visitors to your website can access the audio and that it plays correctly.

Sampling rate is a major driver of audio file size. The higher the sampling rate, the larger the file and the more time needed to download it. Suppose that you want to post a one-minute-long sound clip on your website. Furthermore, suppose it is in mono and uses 8-bit samples (see the next section, "Word Length"). If a 44.1 KHz sampling rate is used, this file requires 44,100 bytes for every second of audio. That works out to over 2.6 MB (60×44,100) for the one-minute-long audio clip! Most users of your website won't bother with such a massive download unless they know the file contains something very special.

By dropping the sampling rate to 8 KHz, the file size reduces to 60×8,000 or 480 KB—less than one fifth the size. This is still a large file, but it is much more manageable. More users will take the effort to download it. It won't have the frequency range of the 44.1 KHz-sampled file, of course. Fortunately, this extra frequency range is often unnecessary, especially for nonmusical clips.

Word Length

An audio sample is nothing more than a binary number containing a certain number of bits. The more bits, the higher the quality of the audio, but also the more disk space (or Internet bandwidth) required to store or transmit the bits.

Almost all formats, including WAVE and AIFF, support both 8- and 16-bit word lengths. The 8-bit word length version is inherently noisy because digital audio is an approximation to real-world analog audio. Short word lengths do not enable as accurate an approximation as the longer word lengths. Engineers call this *quantization error*, and it is equivalent to noise.

8-bit audio is tinny, sounding something like what you hear on a telephone. As more bits are added, the quality improves. 12-bit audio sounds much better, but some *fuzz* can still be heard on careful listening. 16-bit audio is excellent, at least if the sampling rate is high enough (see the previous section, "Sampling Rates"). 16-bit audio is used on audio CDs and other high-quality formats.

Despite the potential quality of the 16-bit audio, use 8-bit audio on your website whenever possible. 8-bit audio requires only half as much disk space. This conserves Internet bandwidth and keeps download time for your sound clips as short as possible.

Some formats support arbitrary word length. WAVE supports multiple formats, some of which can support arbitrary word lengths. AIFF can also support arbitrary word lengths.

Please note, however, that most audio formats supporting arbitrary word lengths still use whole bytes to store samples. An AIFF or WAVE file using 14-bit samples, for example, stores those 14 bits as two full bytes (16 bits). Two bits are therefore wasted.

Compression

Some audio file formats support compression to save file space. Compression can make a major difference in file size, which in turn saves time as users download a file from your website. As a result, longer-playing sound files can be supported comfortably. It is not uncommon to have *compression ratios* of 3:1 or higher. (The compressed data requires only 1/3 the space of the original data.)

The downside to compression is that it requires more complex software to handle the compression and decompression necessary to store and later retrieve the audio data. This is generally not a significant issue compared to the savings that can be gained with compression.

An audio-specific compression algorithm is generally much faster and much more efficient (for audio) than a generic data compression algorithm such as those used in ZIP or STUFFIT. Speed and efficiency are achieved by a knowledge of the properties of audio and also through the use of lossy compression algorithms. *Lossy* means that these algorithms tolerate a small amount of audio quality degradation to obtain higher compression ratios.

Ratios of 3:1 or higher are usually achieved through lossy compression. Even higher compression ratios can be achieved if more degradation can be tolerated.

AIFF does not support compression, but AIFF/C (also known as AIFC) does. Commonly used AIFF/C compression ratios are 3:1 and 6:1. MPEG uses a lossy compression algorithm to achieve high compression with little loss of quality. As a result, MPEG audio files are often smaller than equivalent files that use other formats.

Number Systems

> This and the next three sections delve into some of the more esoteric details of the way in which data is actually stored in an audio file. If your interests are more practical than technical, you may want to skip these topics and go instead to the section entitled "Memory Requirements of Audio Files."

Several number systems are used to represent audio in binary form. The two most common are 1's (ones) complement and 2's (twos) complement. In 1's complement, a negative number is represented by inverting the positive number. In an 8-bit 1's complement system, for example, 17 is represented as 00010001, and –17 is represented as 11101110.

A 2's complement system is identical, except that negative numbers are represented by inverting the positive, and then adding 1. Using the prior example, 17 is represented in an 8-bit 2's complement system as 00010001. This is identical to the 1's complement form. –17, however, is represented as 11101111. The following table shows other examples.

TABLE 2.1

8-BIT BINARY NUMBER SYSTEMS			
Number	1's Complement	2's Complement	Unsigned
0	0 0 0 0 0 0 0 0	0 0 0 0 0 0 0 0	0 0 0 0 0 0 0 0
1	0 0 0 0 0 0 0 1	0 0 0 0 0 0 0 1	0 0 0 0 0 0 0 1
2	0 0 0 0 0 0 1 0	0 0 0 0 0 0 1 0	0 0 0 0 0 0 1 0
4	0 0 0 0 0 1 0 0	0 0 0 0 0 1 0 0	0 0 0 0 0 1 0 0
127	0 1 1 1 1 1 1 1	0 1 1 1 1 1 1 1	0 1 1 1 1 1 1 1
128	1 0 0 0 0 0 0 0	n/a	1 0 0 0 0 0 0 0
129	n/a	n/a	1 0 0 0 0 0 0 1
255	n/a	n/a	1 1 1 1 1 1 1 1
–1	1 1 1 1 1 1 1 0	1 1 1 1 1 1 1 1	n/a
–2	1 1 1 1 1 1 0 1	1 1 1 1 1 1 1 0	n/a

Number	1's Complement	2's Complement	Unsigned
-4	1 1 1 1 1 0 1 1	1 1 1 1 1 1 0 0	n/a
-127	1 0 0 0 0 0 0 0	1 0 0 0 0 0 0 1	n/a
-128	n/a	1 0 0 0 0 0 0 0	n/a

Data can also be represented as signed or unsigned. The 2's and 1's complement systems are signed because they support negative and positive numbers. The unsigned number system represents only positive numbers.

No system is superior to any other; they are merely different. The advantages of one over the other for audio are insignificant. The existence of these three systems seems confusing, and indeed it can be. Using the wrong number system when playing a sound file produces strange-sounding results. Fortunately, this is a problem for the designers of audio software, not the users.

All three of these numbering systems are *linear*, meaning the difference between each step is a fixed amount. A truly different system uses *logarithmic* encoding.

Logarithmic encoding involves storing the logarithm of the audio samples rather than the actual values. Mu-law PCM (Pulse Code Modulation), widely used in digital telephone lines and as a basis for several file formats including AU and several WAVE modes, converts a 12-bit linear range to only 8 bits by using logarithmic encoding. This encoding increases dynamic range at the expense of adding noise.

Addressing Methods

The data in an audio format file is stored in either *big endian* or *little endian* order. A 16-bit word, for example, consists of two 8-bit bytes. This two-byte pair can be stored with the most significant byte first (big endian), or with the least significant byte first (little endian). For an audio format, no real advantage accrues from either method; some computer systems, however, can address one method easier than another. Intel x86 processors, for example, use a little endian addressing scheme. As no surprise, WAVE uses a little endian addressing scheme.

Motorola 680xx processors, as used in all Macs until the introduction of the Power Macintosh, use big endian addressing, as does the AIFF format. Power PC CPU chips, as used in Power Macs, can address either method.

> **Note** Just because a processor does not support an addressing method does not mean it cannot read an audio file. It merely means that the coding is a little more complicated.

Unless you are writing your own audio player or other application, the addressing method used by your software is transparent to you.

Frames

Frames are blocks of audio data. Some formats do not use frames, and audio is considered one long string of samples. Others, particularly those designed for multiple audio tracks or for synchronization with other media (video), do use frames. AIFF, for example, uses frames for multichannel data. One frame contains a single sample from each channel.

Error Detection and Correction

Some audio formats contain parity bits or extra bytes for error correction. Audio CDs, for example, use a Reed-Soloman encoding algorithm that provides efficient, robust error recovery in the event of partial data loss.

Memory Requirements of Audio Files

Whatever the encoding technique, any static audio format requires ample space to store a small amount of audio. CD-quality audio at 16 bits (2 bytes) per sample and 44,100 samples per second requires 88,100 bytes of storage for every second of audio.

That's for mono. If the audio is in stereo (as all audio CDs are), the memory requirements are doubled to 176,400 bytes/sec. That's 10.584 *megabytes* per minute! That's okay on a CD, but it's a killer over the Internet.

Calculating the Size of an Audio File

The following formula can be used to calculate the number of bytes required to store a digital audio file:

Bytes = (TM)×(SR)×(WL/8)×(CH) / (CR)

in which

Bytes = the length of the audio file in bytes
TM = the total playing time of the audio in seconds
SR = the sampling rate in samples per second
WL = the word length in bits, rounded up to the nearest multiple of 8
CH = the number of audio channels
CR = the compression ratio

For example, a WAVE file storing 1 minute (60 seconds) of uncompressed CD-quality audio (SR=44,100; WL=16; CH=2; CR=1) has the following memory requirements:

Bytes = (60)×(44,100)×(16/8)×(2) / 1 = 10,584,000 bytes

You can reduce the size of an audio file by using any of the following methods:

◆ Reduce the sampling rate

◆ Reduce the word length

◆ Reduce the number of channels

◆ Increase the compression ratio

◆ Reduce the play time of the sample

Suppose, for example, that you want to post a one-minute-long sound clip on your website. In original form, it is CD-quality stereo, which requires 176,400 bytes for each second (a total of approximately 10.5 MB for the entire one-minute clip). A user connected to the Internet by a 28.8 Kbaud modem needs (optimistically) just over an hour to download this file. Obviously, you won't have many takers of this offering.

Fortunately, this huge file can be reduced in size. Going from stereo to mono reduces the file size by half. Going to 8-bit word length cuts it in half again.

Reducing the sampling rate to 22.05 KHz cuts it in half again. Using a format such as AIFF/C that supports a 3:1 compression ratio further reduces the size by a factor of three. Plugging all these factors yields a total file size of 441 KB for the entire one-minute clip, a savings of almost 96 percent. Instead of taking over an hour, the file can now be downloaded in less than three minutes (at least on a good day).

Admittedly, these space-saving measures degrade the quality of the audio. This raises the question of how much degradation can be tolerated. The answer depends on which type of audio it is. Sampling human voice at an 8 KHz sample rate, using 8-bit samples, produces a telephone-quality result. It's not particularly pretty, but it is reasonably intelligible, and it requires only 8 KB per second of uncompressed audio. That's an 11:1 improvement over monophonic, CD-quality audio. Although not of the best quality, it is usually quite acceptable for simple speech, sound effects, and noncritical music.

Better quality music reproduction can be achieved at a 22 KHz sampling rate, while staying with an 8-bit word length. Compression ratios of 3:1 generally have minimal impact on sound quality.

These basic guidelines are only intended as a starting point. Determining what is adequate sound quality is a matter of personal taste, experience, and intended application. Be prepared to experiment. Some types of audio can take more degradation than others. Also, try not to be overly critical. It does no good to have the best audio files on the Internet if those files are too big for the average web surfer to download.

If you insist on maximum audio fidelity, you may want to post both high-quality and minimum-sized versions of your sound clips. If properly labeled, this pairing gives the users of your website the option of sampling your offerings without investing inordinate amounts of time.

Creative Compensation Techniques

Some simple, creative techniques can sometimes be used to compensate for the loss of quality, and yet still get the message across. Suppose you are the manager, engineer, and webmaster for a new rock band. Your band just released its first album on CD, and you have to set up a website to advertise it. The album contains 45 minutes of CD-quality audio, roughly 500 MB of data. Obviously, posting all 500 MB is impractical.

Fortunately, posting the entire album is neither necessary nor a good idea. Your purpose is to entice people to buy the album, not give it away. After consulting with the band, you decide to post only the two best songs, about seven minutes of audio. At full quality, this is still about 73 MB of data, and too much to post.

The solution to this problem is to reduce the audio quality of that seven minutes of audio. Converting to 22 KHz, 8-bit mono format reduces the data to only 9.2 MB. That's still too big, but at least it's starting to get into the best range. Further reduction can be achieved by using a compressed format. Suppose MPEG with a 3:1 compression is used. That gets the files down to a little over 3 MB, a very manageable size.

Entertain Your Visitors

Use a diversion to keep website visitors' attention away from how long it takes to download an audio file. Invite your visitors to start the download, then enjoy the splendid graphics, an online article, or other feature of your website while they wait.

This trick works best when no more than a few minutes of download time are needed.

But what about the lost quality? Your two best songs, crafted with infinite attention to detail, now sound like they are coming over a telephone. The solution is to add a few brief clips at full CD quality. This adds another megabyte or two. You clearly label everything on the site and add a few sentences that explain that bandwidth considerations limit your ability to post everything at full CD quality. The two main tracks enable surfers to hear what your music sounds like, and the short clips assure them that the CD is professionally done. Your message is delivered using only 4–5 MB of audio data.

This example shows that significant savings in audio file size are achieved by reducing the amount of material, scaling back on quality, and using compression. Clever presentation on the website reduces the negative impact of these reductions.

But what happens if after all the cutbacks and gimmicks, there is still too much audio to comfortably download? One example of this is a nightly 30-minute news program. Even with all the tricks, it would take about 6–8 MB of audio data to store one program. That takes over 40 minutes to download at 28.8 Kbaud—longer than the length of the program.

The problem gets worse if you must post something even longer: an hour-long *radio* play or the complete works of Mozart. Unfortunately, such cases exceed the practical capabilities of static audio formats, at least with current Internet bandwidths.

For these longer works, an entirely different class of formats must be used. MIDI (see Chapter 8) is often used for long instrumental works. It is extremely compact, because it stores what amounts to musical notes rather than audio. For general audio work, including voice and music, a streaming audio format (see Chapter 3) is more appropriate. Streaming audio formats offer aggressive compression and are played directly from a digital data stream instead of being downloaded.

A Brief Survey of Digitized Audio Formats

Commonly-used digitized audio formats include the following:

◆ **WAVE (.WAV):**   The Waveform Audio File Format is the Windows-native audio format. It is the most common audio format on the Internet. IBM and Microsoft developed it as part of the RIFF (Resource Information File Format) specification for various files used with Windows. The default format is Microsoft Pulse Code Modulation (PCM), which uses logarithmic encoding. Other PCM formats are supported as alternatives. WAVE supports arbitrary sampling rates and numbers of channels. Arbitrary word lengths up to 16 bits are supported, although 8 and 16 bits are most common. WAVE also supports playlists that enable sound segments to be played in an order different from how they are stored. See the "Further Reading" section at the end of this chapter for the location of a WAVE specification.

◆ **AIFF:**   The Audio Interchange File Format is widely used on the Internet, especially in Macintosh and cross-platform applications. Apple Computer developed it for the Macintosh, but it has spread to many other platforms. AIFF supports mono, stereo, 3-channel, quadraphonic, and four- and six-channel Surround Sound. AIFF also supports MIDI. Arbitrary word lengths from 1 to 32 bits, and arbitrary sample rates are also supported. Linear encoding is used. See the "Further Reading " section at the end of this chapter for the location of the AIFF specification.

◆ **AIFF-C or AIFC:**   This format is an extension of AIFF that supports compression.

◆ **AU (Sun audio, NeXT audio, MU-law, u-law):**   The Unix sound format, .AU is common on the Internet. It is, however, less common than WAVE or AIFF. It supports mono or stereo, 8- to 32-bit samples, and a u-law format. Sampling rates include 44.1, 22.050 and 8.013 KHz.

◆ **MPEG:**   Created by the Motion Picture Experts Group, this multimedia format is usually associated with video, but it also supports sound. MPEG-1 was designed for movie-quality audio; MPEG-2 was designed for TV-quality audio. Different *layers* are defined to achieve different levels of compression. 4:1 compression can be achieved with only a slight loss of sound quality. Much higher levels are also possible, with increasing losses of quality. MPEG files can be somewhat smaller than many other equivalent audio files because of this high compression ratio.

◆ **QuickTime:**   This is another multimedia format that supports sound. It is common on the Internet and is supported by Windows, Mac, SGI, and other machines. It supports an arbitrary number of channels, 8- to 16-bit word length, and variable sampling rates up to 65.535 KHz. A 4:1 compression option is available in newer versions of this format. QuickTime files also support MIDI (see Chapter 8).

◆ **SND (SND Resource):**   This is a specialized, Mac-specific format used by the Macintosh OS and a few applications such as Hypercard. This format is rarely seen on the Internet. For general audio work on a Mac, the AIFF format is preferred.

◆ **VOC:**   This is a proprietary format created by Creative Labs for use with its SoundBlaster audio cards.

Sampled Audio Formats

Some types of sounds, instrumental music in particular, are highly redundant and repetitious. Consider a guitar, for example. It produces only so many chords and notes in any given song, even though each may be repeated many times.

Instead of digitizing and storing the entire song, only samples of each unique sound need to be stored. A format employing this technique must also contain a play list, describing how to play the samples in the proper order, at what volume, and for how long. Pitch information is also usually included.

A player program designed to read such a format can reconstruct the original song. Quality is dependent on the quality of the stored samples. Because the samples are relatively short, they do not require a lot of storage space. The play list is small compared to the space required for direct storage. Sampled audio formats may be one or even two orders of magnitude smaller than a direct storage format of equivalent quality.

Sampled audio formats have disadvantages, however. They are used almost exclusively for instrumental music and do not work for human voice or other semi-random sounds. Quality of the reconstructed result also depends highly on the quality of the samples. Incorrect selection of the samples results in a distorted reconstruction. In cases where many samples exist, the files can become fairly large—although nowhere near as large as an equivalent direct-storage format file.

The most common sampled audio format is MOD. It is used for music, although nonmusical samples can also be stored. Originally developed for the Amiga computer, MOD eventually spread to other computers.

MOD contains a set of samples and a playlist that defines the order, pitch, and distortion on four channels. MOD's main limitation is its limitation to 8-bit resolution and a sampling rate of 32 KHz. High-quality sound is thus impossible.

Once relatively popular, MOD is now declining rapidly. It receives little commercial support, has the aforementioned quality limitations, and has been largely replaced on the Internet by MIDI (see Chapter 8). MIDI is even more compact than MOD because it does not contain audio. MIDI also does not suffer from the quality limits inherent to MOD, and it is widely supported.

Unless you are operating a website specializing in Amiga or already have a large collection of MOD files, MOD is not a good choice for new works.

Summary

Static audio file formats are a reasonable Internet audio solution for works of a minute or so in length. Their main limitation is their large size. By using compression, reduced quality, and longer files several minutes in length, you can place audio on websites without incurring excessive download times.

Static formats can be used to store any sound, are very flexible, and require no *push* from special server software. Audio tools of all types support these formats, at least the more common ones, such as AIFF and WAVE. Due to their simplicity and the availability of tools, static file formats are a good first choice for webmasters beginning to use audio.

Static audio formats are less useful for long audio works. For bandwidth reasons, their main Internet use is for short sound clips. In the future, when Internet bandwidths increase significantly, this will be less of a problem. Until then, streaming audio file formats (Chapter 3) or MIDI (Chapter 8) are usually a better solution for longer works.

Further Reading

Specifications for AIFF and WAVE can be found on the Internet:

"Audio Interchange File Format (AIFF): A Standard for Sampled Sound Files," version 1.3., Apple Computer.
At the time this chapter was written, an online version could be downloaded from `ftp.cwin.nl/pub/audio/AudioIFF1.3.hqz` by using FTP. If this file has been removed, a web search using the keywords *AIFF specification* should find an online copy.

"Multimedia Programming Interface and Data Specification," v 1.0.
This document, created by IBM and Microsoft, defines RIFF, of which WAVE is a part. A web search on *RIFFMCI.RTF* or *RIFF WAVE* should lead to an online copy.

C H A P T E R 3

STREAMING TECHNOLOGIES

Streaming audio (playing audio from a continuous stream of audio data packets) and video—if your client has enough bandwidth—brings a sense of immediacy to your website pages. If your webmaster has done a good job of keeping your graphics small and your page load time fast, streaming audio offers a natural extension to your well-designed site. Of course, it is no panacea for those lumbering, webartist-gone-wild site surfers who have suffered through loading on their browsers.

This chapter covers important issues that impact streaming technology:

◆ Streaming software

◆ Using plug-ins versus players on website design

◆ Copyright issues

◆ Competition, Internet brownouts, and the relative merits of live and recorded (on-demand) programming

Streaming Software

Streaming software consists of three main components: the encoder, the server, and the client. An encoder converts audio from its source format into the streaming format. The source can either be a pre-existing audio file, such as a .WAV file, or audio currently being processed by the computer's sound card. The server makes the resulting stream, or streamable file, available to the client. The client is the helper-player, plug-in, or browser built-in player used by your listeners to hear your broadcast.

The capability to process live audio, input it through the sound card, convert it immediately into the streaming format, and then make it immediately available to your listeners constitutes a live encoder/server. Examples of a live solution include Xing Streamworks (http://www.streamworks.com) and RealAudio (http://www.realaudio.com). Of course, these formats can also be used to create static, prerecorded, playable-on-demand streamable files.

By contrast, some streaming software requires that a pre-existing .WAV file or other audio source be completely processed, creating a streamable file (after the entire audio source is encoded). An example of this approach is Macromedia's (http://www.macromedia.com) Shockwave, which appears to be aimed at those who want to create highly integrated audio/video presentations, referred to as *movies*.

These nonlive multimedia objects are available on-demand to your clients. In some cases, you may want to take a recording of an event that you carried live and make it immediately available afterward as an archive. Archives may be as simple as taking the audio file created during your live broadcast and relabeling the now static file as an archive rather than a live show on your web page. In other cases, you or your customer might want to take the recording and synchronize it with graphics or still images to create a more dynamic, on-demand presentation.

If you choose to work with a format that does not have live broadcast capability, you should consider whether you want to have the option to do live audio at some point in the future. Perhaps, by then, your software vendor of choice will include a live capability. If not, you may be faced with considerable time and expense to convert to a system that supports live encoding. This can be disruptive for your listeners if you want to maintain a consistent streaming audio format on your site.

Either way, with good equipment, wiring, and quality audio sources (see Chapters 9, "Sound Basics and Audio Theory" and 11, "Digital Audio Recording and Editing"), you can produce and broadcast first class programming of which everyone in your organization can be proud.

Plug-Ins Versus Players

Your listeners are able to hear your programming, whether your web pages use a plug-in, helper-player, or browser built-in player. In fact, many of the players have a corresponding plug-in, and some even offer Software Development Kits (SDK) for you to design your own interface. An important design consideration arises when choosing which of these options is right for a particular web page. If you use a plug-in, the audio stream is severed as soon the listener leaves the page. If you use a separate player, the listener can go to other web pages at your site or leave your site entirely while continuing to listen to the audio stream.

Your choice of designs, plug-in, or player is driven by the nature of your content and the objectives of your site. If you create a multimedia presentation with streaming audio and possibly other content such as a slide show or video still-image capture, for example, a plug-in may be the most appropriate design because it integrates the player controls more seamlessly into the page.

If you are broadcasting a college football game, live radio station, or hot music CD, you probably don't want to lose listeners if they leave your web page(s), which would call for a player-based design. Indeed, if you market commercial spots in your audio stream, it becomes a selling point for your advertisers that the client will still hear the ads while surfing the web.

Copyright Issues

Streaming audio packets might arrive out of sequence at a listener's computer. This is due to the nature of delivery over the Internet. Individual packets may travel different routes to reach the final destination. After the packets arrive at the client computer, they are buffered in memory and reassembled for playback. Depending on the circumstances, the buffer is usually only for a few seconds-worth of data.

Depending on which streaming software you choose, a side benefit of this design is that the sound the listener hears is not stored or written to disk. Because the audio stream is *listen and forget*, the only way for the listener to hear it again is to stop the stream and then reinitiate it. If it is a live broadcast, it cannot be retrieved after it's gone. This could actually work to your advantage in some copyright situations.

Unless the broadcaster configures the encoder(s) to allow it, the RealAudio player does not enable the user to make a digital copy of the audio stream. In contrast, the Shockwave player has no such restriction.

Of course, the listener could connect a tape recorder to his computer's sound jack and make an analog recording of the audio stream; this would, however, induce a certain amount of signal loss and frequency dispersion in the physical connection. Also, to conserve bandwidth and reach more listeners, streaming audio is usually transmitted at a lower fidelity level. Combine this with Internet congestion packet loss and the final recording is not of digital quality.

Which Technology Is Your Competition Using?

Which streaming technology should you use? Each has different strengths and weaknesses; also, as with most software or hardware vendors, expect frequent feature leapfrogging and fierce market share battles. To find out which path is best for your website, start out by researching your competition. Are there other sites similar to what you are trying to do? How successful are they, and which technology do they use?

The web is replete with proof of the truism that imitation is the sincerest form of flattery. The savvy webmaster is constantly scouring the web looking for new techniques and approaches that can be incorporated into his own website. No one wants to be in a position of not having an answer to the question, "Why aren't *we* doing this?"

Doing your web homework also affords you the opportunity to learn from the mistakes of others. If you notice that a much publicized web event does not go well, find out whether it was the fault of the organization that tried to produce it, the technology, or a general web glitch. Studying the mistakes and misfortunes of others should help you make better informed decisions about your own plans and strategies.

Some of the Major Net Broadcasters

Just like the old west gold towns, Net broadcasting websites are springing up everywhere. Some sites switch technology allegiances as fast as they hear of a better stream to pan (pun intended) or their free evaluation license runs out, whichever comes first. Some entertainment and mass media companies openly play one technology against another, hoping to see which can outperform the other.

By the time you read this book, some of these sites might no longer exist or might have switched to a different technology. If you cannot find the specific page listed in the URL, try working your way down the URL to a lower level. If `http://www.mongomedia.com/try/this/out/index.html` doesn't work, for example, try going to the home page `http://www.mongomedia.com` and see if it lists any links similar to what you are looking for.

The examples given in this section are intended to provide a sampling of what is out there. Throughout this book, these and other sites are described within the context of the technology they employ. For the latest list of hot sites, be certain to visit the website dedicated to this book: `http://www.websitesound.com`.

◆ Virgin Records (`http://www.virginrecords.com/ show/mhzfront.html`) and Capitol Records (`http://www.hollywoodandvine.com/` and `http://www.macromedia.com/shockwave/epicenter/shockedsites/capitol/index.html`) are good examples of established companies exploring their options on the Net. The Virgin Records site includes both Shockwave (`http://www.macromedia.com`) and RealAudio (`http://www.realaudio.com`) content. The Capitol Records sites represent efforts with Xing (`http://www.streamworks.com`) and Shockwave, respectively. Both of these sites use streaming audio to showcase and promote their artists.

◆ c|net, the popular television and website, has a radio page at `http://www.news.com/Radio/`. This site features a daily news report focusing on the computer and Net industries that use RealAudio (`http://www.realaudio.com`).

◆ CBS News "Up To The Minute" (`http://uttm.com`) uses VDOLive (`http://www.vdo.net`) to deliver a slideshow of news snippets.

◆ Another example of television dabbling in website sound can be found at the "Dr. Quinn, Medicine Woman" website (`http://www.aspenlinx.com/DrQuinn/`). This site uses IWAVE downloadable files.

Audio Book Club

◆ AudioBooks are making their way to the web at sites such as the Audio Book Club (http://www.audiobookclub.com), where subscribers can enjoy the online version of a book club that uses Xing Streamworks (http://www.streamworks.com).

What if you are not an entertainment or other media company? Any organization, whether it is government, commercial, or otherwise, can use website sound to deliver information and updates to customers and employees.

HERBALIFE.

◆ Herbalife (http://www.herbalife.com/page8a.html), for example, the folks with the bumper stickers (as you know), have found that website sound, using Xing Streamworks (http://www.streamworks.com), can be a great way to distribute daily sales pep talks to a widely distributed sales force.

AudioNet

◆ AudioNet (http://www.AudioNet.com) broadcasts a vast selection of live and recorded sports, full-length music CDs, concerts, entertainment, news, books, seminars, annual meetings, product launches, politics, and more than 130 radio stations. With strategic partners such as Host Communications (one of the largest sports event marketing firms in the U.S.) and Motorola, AudioNet is quickly defining itself as a new breed of broadcast network, similar in some ways to a cable network, but without many of the limits of the traditional entities.

Internet Brownouts and Packet Loss

Much has been said in the trade and traditional press about Internet *brown-outs* and other congestion problems; doomsayers regularly predict the collapse of the Net under its own weight. Conversely, others admonish to take the *don't worry, be happy* approach. The growth or collapse of the web can be likened to the life of a star, with its opposing forces of gravity and outward pressure. If the outward pressure weakens and succumbs to the force of gravity, the star collapses. Similarly, as long as the growth of the Net infrastructure outstrips the collective inertia of its own existence, the Net will stay ahead of the spectre of Net calamity. At least, that's the hope of those who earn a living on the web!

If the web does collapse, there will be less to worry about. As long as that calamity is avioded, web broadcasters will only need to deal with packet loss and routing failures due to the inherent design of the Net. Packet loss, which degrades the audio quality of your streaming broadcasts, often results from local or regional ISPs who have oversold their bandwidth.

Bandwidth

If bandwidth is oversold, the listener's 28.8 or 33.6 connection may have dramatically lower actual throughput than the listener is aware of. If the listener's throughput is only 19.2, 14.4, or even 9.6, the 20 Kbps stream to which she is trying to listen sounds choppy or has other problems, including complete failure. One of the joys of Internet broadcasting is that the listener usually assumes that the problem is the broadcaster's fault rather than some problem on the Net or with her ISP.

Even if your listener's ISP is not overbooked, analog dial-up modem perfor-mance is also dictated by the quality of the telephone lines between the client and her ISP. Even with 33.6 Kbps direct-dial connections to identical modems on an uncongested private network, for example, the actual connec-tion rate observed by the authors is often only 24 Kbps or slightly higher.

Rockwell Semiconductor Systems, which manufactures modem chip sets (among other things), is reportedly working on a 56 Kbps analog modem chip set. Rockwell and others are expected to release these higher-speed chip sets to modem manufacturers in 1997. Similarly, popular modem manufacturer US Robotics has announced a 56 Kbps modem of their own with an expected January 1997 release.

With the kinds of telephone line performance seen today on 28.8 and 33.6 modems, it remains to be seen whether these higher-speed modems will be capable of achieving actual throughputs high enough to justify their cost and help them compete against ISDN or ADSL products. For further discussion of bandwidth issues, please skip to Chapter 13, "Bandwidth and Cost Considerations."

Broadcast Conditions

Router configuration problems, such as Netcom's and AOL's mid-1996 multi-hour and day-long outages, can leave entire segments of your listening audience unreachable. Another regular Net hazard is caused by actions in the physical world, such as the backhoe that slices through fiber pairs.

One of the best illustrations of how dynamic the Net is can be found at Matrix Information and Directory Services' website (`http://www.mids.org`). MIDS publishes legal and technical analysis of web topics, including a subscription-based Internet weather map in MPEG format. The MPEG file overlays a map with animated Internet weather symbols. Multiple concentric circles depict the relative amount of Internet traffic across the country in terms of millisecond delay (see fig. 3.1).

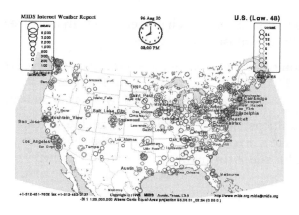

FIGURE 3.1

MIDS Internet Weather Report.

The MIDS services are an excellent resource for website planners who want to better understand the broadcast conditions on the web. They are also a great way to help illustrate these concepts to your sales and marketing staff. Static images as well as time-lapsed MPEG video files are available from MIDS on a subscription basis.

For more discussion of web traffic and bandwidth issues, please refer to Chapter 13, "Bandwidth and Cost Considerations," and Chapter 14, "Future of Audio on the Web."

Streaming Technology Pros and Cons

Streaming technology currently dominates website sound. .WAV and other downloadable formats are usually too large for use on a significant scale because of their lengthy download times. Some of the strengths of streaming audio include the following:

◆ Play begins soon after the stream begins, reducing end-user frustration over access speeds and download times.

◆ Versions exist for both small and large sites.

◆ A large installed-base of client (end-user) software exists.

◆ The technology has gone through several version changes and is usually stable and reliable.

Streaming is not the best solution for all situations. Some of the weaknesses include the following:

◆ The software cost is usually much higher than with non-streaming alternatives like downloadable .WAV files.

◆ Streaming requires a dedicated audio server or web server that has been pre-configured to support streaming audio. This can be a problem for sites that are hosted on servers provided by other organizations or ISPs.

◆ If and when multicasting becomes widely available, unicast technologies will begin to take a marketshare back seat. Make sure that your streaming software vendor supports multicasting for future growth.

C H A P T E R

4

REALAUDIO

At the time of this writing, RealAudio (Progressive Networks,

Inc.: `http://www.realaudio.com`*) has the largest installed*

base of players and a solid set of server and broadcast

distribution tools. The encoding and streaming formats are

proprietary, and are therefore listed separately in this book

from others, such as MPEG.

RealAudio software is available in both Intranet and Internet flavors, and it has been optimized to deliver content on low to medium bandwidth connections ranging from 14.4 to 28.8 to ISDN. Clients can listen to streamed RealAudio files (.RA) or to complete .RA files located on local hard disk space. Listeners cannot, however, download a copy of the original digital .RA file unless that option is enabled on the live encoder.

Until recently, comparisons of RealAudio and its main competitor, Xing (pronounced *zing*) Technology Corporation's (`http://www.Xingech.com` or `http://www.streamworks.com`) Streamworks server, have focused on two main areas: sound quality and integrated video streaming. With the release of Beta RealAudio 3.0 in September 1996, Progressive Networks has largely closed the sound quality gap; the addition of video streaming, however, remains an unfulfilled area that requires some catching up.

On the other hand, video streaming is still a much smaller market than audio. For the vast majority of Internet clients who have a dial-up 28.8 or 14.4 connection, the video streaming experience is of poor quality, with just a handful of frames per second and a tiny picture that fills only a small portion of a computer screen.

The prospects for video will gradually improve, but not without vast improvements in frame compression, increases in client bandwidth capacity, and increases in client CPU horsepower. And don't wait for the mythical cable modems to cure all that. It will be years—if ever—before cable modems are a significant player (see Chapter 13, "Bandwidth and Cost Considerations").

Although RealAudio does not yet support streaming video, it does support synchronized multimedia presentations. If you are broadcasting a conference, you might display *webcam* type still images on the same page where the audio link is, providing a live, and yet separate presentation. Afterward, you can use the RealAudio TimeLine Editor software to take those images and combine them with the now static .RA file; this results in your archived version having the same look and feel as the original.

Browser Support

For the end user, browsers are the primary interface to the Net. Third-party applications such as RealAudio are supported either by being bundled with the browser or by requiring the end user to download and install the player or plug-in. A RealAudio player is bundled with Microsoft's Internet Explorer and has long been rumored to *soon* be included with Netscape Navigator. The RealAudio plug-in is supported in recent editions of the following web browsers:

- Microsoft Internet Explorer
- Netscape Navigator
- NCSA Mosaic
- NetCruiser
- MacWEB
- AIR Mosaic (Internet in a Box)
- Cello WWW Browser
- EINet WinWeb
- Internet MCI Navigator
- Spyglass Mosaic and Enhanced Mosaic
- Quarterdeck Mosaic
- NetManage WebSurfer
- America Online (Windows)

Hardware Requirements

Hardware requirements for the RealAudio encoder vary, depending on whether you are planning on encoding only prerecorded files, or if you plan on using live encoding.

For encoding prerecorded files, you need a minimum of a 486/66 DX PC with 8 MB RAM and 1 MB free disk space for the RealAudio software and another 1 KB per second for 14.4 files. You also need a 16-bit sound card capable of recording an 8 KHz signal.

> **Note**
>
> If you plan to use Windows NT, make certain that you have the appropriate NT driver for your sound card. It may be difficult to find drivers for, and configure, some OEM sound cards. Mainstream sound cards, such as the SoundBlaster line from Creative Labs, are more likely to be supported than the cheap OEM cards some manufacturers bundle with their PCs.

For live encoding, you need a minimum of a 75 MHz Pentium PC with 8 MB RAM (16 MB is highly recommended) and 1 MB free disk space for the RealAudio software, and another 1.8 KB per second for 28.8 files. You also need a 16-bit sound card capable of recording an 8 KHz signal.

The Macintosh version of the RealAudio encoder requires a minimum of an Apple System 7.1 (or later) or a 68030 Macintosh with FPU (floating point processor). RealAudio highly recommends the latest PowerMac or Quadra 700 for better performance and results, especially for live encoding.

Supported Prerecorded Digital File Formats

RealAudio supports numerous prerecorded digital file formats that are available in both stereo and mono output. A stereo file can be used to create either a stereo or mono output file. A mono file lacks stereo data; thus, you cannot make a stereo file out of a mono source. Not all types of prerecorded formats are supported on all platforms. The .AIFF format, for example, is supported only on the Mac. Table 4.1 details which formats are supported on each platform.

TABLE 4.1

REALAUDIO ENCODER INPUT TYPES		
Format	**Hardware/OS**	**Sampling**
.AIFF	Mac	8- or 16-bit mono or stereo
.AU	Windows, Unix, Mac	8-bit mono or stereo or 16-bit linear mono or stereo
.PCM	Windows, Unix	8- or 16-bit mono or stereo

Format	Hardware/OS	Sampling
.SD2	Mac	8- or 16-bit mono or stereo
.SND	Windows, Mac	8- or 16-bit mono or stereo
.WAV	Windows, Unix	8- or 16-bit mono or stereo
Live feed	Windows Live, Mac Live, Unix Live	8- or 16-bit mono or stereo

If you are experiencing problems converting a file, make certain that it has not been previously compressed. Sampling options include 8 KHz, 11.025 KHz, 16 KHz, 22.05 KHz, and 44.1 KHz.

Encoding Algorithms and Bandwidth Requirements

With the release of RealAudio 3.0, the number of available encoding algorithms has grown from two to ten, including stereo formats and broadcast-quality ISDN formats (see Table 4.2). Single stream bandwidth requirements now range from 10 Kbps to 100 Kbps.

The RealAudio encoding and playback technology has always leaned more toward the robust approach rather than the perfect-sounding approach. Although some streaming players pause or stop when packet loss gets high enough to cause audio artifacts, the RealAudio player keeps trying, even when the stream degrades to unlistenable garbage. Although this may be considered admirable tenacity, it has resulted in a general perception of poorer quality audio.

The new PlayerPlus Perfect Play option adds several seconds of buffering to enable tardy packets to catch up, lending to its name *Perfect Play*. This additional robustness, combined with the multitude of new high-quality encoding algorithms, has significantly raised the stakes in Internet broadcasting.

TABLE 4.2

REALAUDIO 3.0 ENCODING ALGORITHMS

RealAudio 3.0	Frequency	Bandwidth	Description Encoding Response Algorithms
14.4	4.0 KHz	10 Kbps	Original 14.4 CODEC. Speech, AM Radio
28.8	4.0 KHz	20 Kbps	Original 28.8 CODEC. Mono, FM Mono
28.8 Instrumental	5.5 KHz	20 Kbps	Instrumental, classical, and other music needing wider dynamic range
28.8 Pop	4.7 KHz	20 Kbps	Musical selections including snare drums, cymbals, and vocals
28.8 Voice	4.0 KHz	20 Kbps	Optimized for speech over dial-up 28.8 modems
28.8 Stereo	4.0 KHz	25 Kbps	General stereo content
ISDN Mono	11 KHz	50 Kbps	General mono content over single channel ISDN
ISDN Stereo	8 KHz	50 Kbps	General stereo content over single channel ISDN
Dual ISDN Mono	20 KHz	100 Kbps	CD-quality mono, dual-channel ISDN
Dual ISDN Stereo	16 KHz	100 Kbps	Broadcast quality, dual-channel ISDN

Now that you have an idea about how much bandwidth each of your listeners needs to receive your broadcast(s), how much bandwidth do you need for all your listeners? If you plan to provide more than one of the available options, such as 14.4 and 28.8, the total bandwidth required is a function of how many of each is in use. To simplify things, Table 4.3 illustrates the total number of listeners you can have, assuming that you use only one of the available options. This should give you an idea of the kind of bandwidth you need to reach the desired number of listeners.

TABLE 4.3

BANDWIDTH REQUIREMENTS FOR REALAUDIO

Actual Throughput to the Internet, Excluding All Other Traffic	Simultaneous 14.4 Sounds like AM Radio 10 Kbps	Simultaneous 28.8 Mono Each, FM Mono 20 Kbps	Simultaneous 28.8 Stereo 25 Kbps	Simultaneous ISDN Mono/Stereo 50 Kbps	Simultaneous DUAL ISDN Mono/Stereo 100 Kbps
Modem: 28.8 Kbps	2	1	1	0	0
Cable Modem: 28.8 Kbps (outbound rate) (Note: This format may never make it to real-life.)	2 (Best possible range; no test data available. Actual performance may be lower.)	1 (Best possible range; no test data available. Actual performance may be lower.)	1 (Best possible range; no test data available. Actual performance may be lower.)	0	0
RF Cable Modem: 28.8 Kbps (outbound rate)	2 (Best possible range; no test data available. Actual performance may be lower.)	1 (Best possible range; no test data available. Actual performance may be lower.)	1 (Best possible range; no test data available. Actual performance may be lower.)	0	0
Switched 56/Frame Relay: 56 Kbps	5	3	3	1	0
ADSL: 64 Kbps to 640 Kbps (outbound rate) (Note: This format is new and not widely available.)	6 to 60 (Best possible range; no test data available. Actual performance may be lower.)	3 to 32 (Best possible range; no test data available. Actual performance may be lower.)	2 to 25 (Best possible range; no test data available. Actual performance may be lower.)	1 to 12 (Best possible range; no test data available. Actual performance may be lower.)	0 to 6 (Best possible range; no test data available. Actual performance may be lower.)
ISDN: 128 Kbps (2 "B" channels)	12	8	5	2	1
T-1: 1.54 Mbps	150	90	61	30	15
10BaseT / Ethernet: 10 MB (Overhead often lowers performance by 30%)	560 (Estimate based on LAN collision assumptions and format overhead)	350 (Estimate based on LAN collision assumptions and format overhead)	280 (Estimate based on LAN collision assumptions and format overhead)	140 (Estimate based on LAN collision assumptions and format overhead)	70 (Estimate based on LAN collision assumptions and format overhead)
T-3/DS3: 45 Mbps	4,500	2,700	2,160	1,080	540
100BaseT (100Mbps)	6,000	3,600	2,880	1,440	720
100BaseT/FDDI LAN (100 Mbps)	10,000	6,000	4,800	2,400	1,200

See Chapter 11 for details on inbound/outbound rates and ADSL.

Note that the last two bandwidth options (at 100 Mbps) are usually LAN/ WAN configurations because the maximum (single) connection to the Net for most organizations is 45 Mbps (T3/DS3). Multiple T3/DS3s can be combined to increase the total bandwidth. Large carriers such as MCI are building more and more 155 Mbps+ backbone segments.

With web server traffic, e-mail, ftp, and so on, your throughput is likely to be significantly less than the figures listed in the preceding table, so treat the numbers in Table 4.3 as the absolute best performance possible. Remember also to subtract bandwidth you use for other traffic.

The RealAudio Encoder

The RealAudio encoder currently has several encoding algorithm options (refer to Table 4.2). Bandwidth requirements for these algorithms are 10, 20, 25, 50, and 100 Kbps. RealAudio 3.0 includes an option to provide a stereo stream for clients with 28.8 connections (requires 25 Kbps actual bandwidth).

Figure 4.1 shows a typical RealAudio encoder session. In this example, the author selected a favorite CD.

The authors would like to take this opportunity to again remind web broadcasters that all appropriate permissions and licenses must be obtained before you make broadcasts of copyrighted material available on the Net (and, no, we did not broadcast this CD!).

In figure 4.1, notice the inclusion of Windows NT built-in recording control; the Microphone and Line-in check boxes are not checked. This is to prevent any crossover hiss from these inputs bleeding into the recording. Depending on your system, this problem can occur even if nothing is plugged into the microphone port on your sound card.

The 14.4 option essentially drops off the highs and lows from the signal, with the result sounding like a strong AM radio station. This format is excellent for many types of broadcasts, including, of course, AM radio stations. It is also excellent for speeches, conventions, sporting events, and any other audio source that does not have a wide dynamic range, such as most music. If you are only using music as background material, this format may do quite nicely.

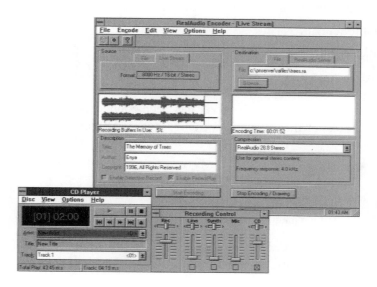

FIGURE 4.1

RealAudio Encoder example.

The various 28.8 formats take a less draconian approach to compressing the sound and result in audio quality ranging from FM Mono to FM Stereo, depending on the encoding algorithm chosen. If you increase bandwidth consumption into the ISDN range, you can achieve an even clearer result, up to full Broadcast Quality.

Web Server Support

The RealAudio server supports any web server that enables you to customize MIME types, such as the following servers that RealAudio has tested:

◆ Apache 1.1.1

◆ CERN HTTPD (v3.0)

◆ Emwac HTTPS 0.96

◆ HTTPD4Mac

◆ Mac HTTPD

◆ Microsoft IIS

◆ NCSA HTTPD (v1.3 or v1.4)

◆ Netscape Netsite and Enterprise Servers

◆ O'Reilly Website NT

◆ Spinner 1.0b12–10.b15

◆ Webstar and Webstar PS

To find out whether your web server has been configured for RealAudio, check the MIME table for the following entries (server MIME table formats vary):

MIME Type	Extension/Suffix
audio/x-pn-realaudio	.ra and .ram
audio/x-pn-realaudio-plugin	.rpm

Progressive Networks maintains an updated list of compatible web servers at `http://www.RealAudio.com/help`.

The RealAudio Server

The RealAudio Server (PNServer—Progressive Networks Server) is available for many platforms. This book's examples use the Intel/Windows NT version of the server. A quick check of the RealAudio (`http://www.RealAudio.com`) website yielded the list of currently supported server environments found in Table 4.4.

TABLE 4.4

REALAUDIO-SUPPORTED OPERATING SYSTEMS AND HARDWARE PLATFORMS

Hardware Platform	Operating System
Apple Macintosh; Motorola 68000 based systems and the PowerPC	Mac Open Transport MacTCP
DEC Alpha	DEC Alpha UNIX 3.2 DEC Alpha Windows NT 3.51+

Hardware Platform	Operating System
Hewlett Packard PA/RISC	HP/UX 10.x
Intel Pentium or 66 MHz 80486	BSDI 2.0 or later FreeBSD 2.x Linux 1.2+ Linux 1.2+ ELF Windows NT 3.51+
IBM PowerPC	AIX 4.0+
Sun SPARC	Solaris 2.x SunOS 4.1x
Silicon Graphics Indy	SGI/IRIX 5.3 or later

If some Internet streaming audio packages use only a web server, why is a separate server important? If website sound is to be a small component in your web presence, a separate server may not be very important to you. If you are planning a medium- to large-scale audio site, however, a separate audio server and its related tools provide better scalability, control, and logging features.

Which Platform Is Best for You?

AudioNet (http://www.AudioNet.com), RealAudio's largest customer—and by virtue of its shear volume of content, the largest audio broadcaster on the Net—uses Intel-based, Windows NT platforms exclusively. If your existing operation is predominantly Unix-based, you should probably stick with that which you are comfortable. All the platforms work, but it is a myth that you must have a Unix, Mac, Sun, or SGI network to be an Internet multimedia contender.

Running PNServer

PNServer can be run from the command prompt or, more commonly, as an NT service (see fig. 4.2).

FIGURE 4.2

*RealAudio
Server Service in
Windows NT.*

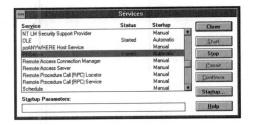

Configuration of the server is controlled via the SERVER.CFG file.

```
CustomerName XXXXXXXXXX
LicenseKey XXXXXXXXXXXXXXXXXXXXXXXXXXXXXXXXXXXXXXXXXXXXXXXXXXXXXXXXXXX
BasePath C:\PNSERVER\RAFILES
LogPath C:\PNSERVER\LOGS\PNACCESS.LOG
ErrorLogPath C:\PNSERVER\LOGS\PNERROR.LOG
PnaPort 7070
AudioConnections 100
EncoderPassword mypassword
MailMessageUser mymail
MailMessageSMTPHost mailhost.mysite.com
MailMessageLimit 2
MailMessageLevel INFO
MailUsageCC auto-feedback@prognet.com
MailUsageThreshold 90
MailUsagePeriod 24
```

The RealAudio License Key defines how many simultaneous connections
your server can have based on the number of stream licenses you have
purchased. The sample RealAudio Configuration file listed previously limits
simultaneous connections under the AudioConnections tag to 100. You may
want to set the number lower than the total number you have purchased; if
you have more than one server/license, and your servers are located at
different sites with different bandwidths, you can lower the number for a
particular server to be consistent with the amount of available bandwidth at
that location. As with any software installation, be aware that license rules

change from time to time. Check your license agreement or with the software vendor if you have any questions about your configuration or rollout plans.

Numerous other configuration parameters are not included by default in the SERVER.CFG file. These include monitor passwords, cluster server information, and other advanced features.

Scalability, Splitters, and Clustering

If a server is combined with splitters and server clusters, the audio stream can be arranged among many servers on different Internet Service Providers (ISPs). This architecture enables you to distribute the audio closer to your listeners, provide more aggregate bandwidth, and ultimately reduce the number of hops between your server(s) and your clients. A clustered server can distribute both live and recorded streams.

Individual PNServers can be grouped in server clusters under the control of a main or control server. New client requests are routed to the next available subserver in the cluster by the control server. If any server in the cluster runs out of available streams, the client is automatically sent the next free subserver, helping to reduce the possibility of having the client's request refused due to lack of bandwidth or stream licenses from any particular server.

To enable clustering, the following entries should be added to the SERVER.CFG file on the master or control server:

```
ClusterPassword <clusterpassword>
```

For example

```
ClusterPassword mypassword
```

Similarly, each subserver must have a section added to its SERVER.CFG file:

```
ClusterHost          <clusterhost>
ClusterPort          <clusterport>
ClusterPassword      <Control Server password>
```

For example

```
ClusterHost        George
ClusterPort        7070
ClusterPassword    mypassword
```

Control

With a separate audio server such as PNServer, you can control how much bandwidth is used on each server by setting the maximum number of simultaneous users. By the time this book goes to print, you should also be able to control bandwidth by including a max-bandwidth parameter in the SERVER.CFG file. You can also achieve the same result by carefully setting the max-users parameter.

> The RealAudio server examples used in this book are from the Windows NT version of the software. As detailed in Table 4.4, many other versions are available. Please refer to the RealAudio server documentation provided by Progressive Networks for details on your specific operating system.

Using the RealAudio Hosting Service, you can configure your PNServer(s) with group or individual accounts, guaranteeing minimum and maximum stream limits. This feature proves especially useful for special events in which you want to ensure that certain parts of your audience are guaranteed a seat in your virtual audience.

These kinds of features give you the flexibility to respond to changing Internet conditions and broadcast requirements. They make your broadcasts more reachable to your listeners and thus more salable to your management or advertisers.

Monitoring

Real-time PNServer monitoring software is included with the server. As shown in figure 4.3, the monitor shows the listeners currently connected. It also shows the listeners' DNS information (if available); a graph detailing all connections over the last couple of minutes; and a list of the files currently being played and how many clients are listening to them. This powerful real-time software provides detailed information on your servers regardless of their location. You can open multiple sessions to track all your servers and their current traffic loads.

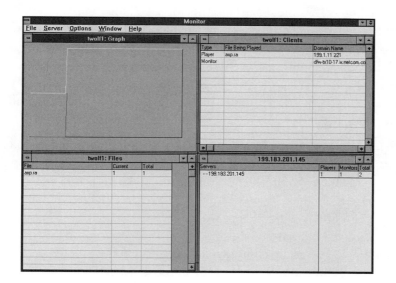

FIGURE 4.3

RealAudio Monitor: real-time listener statistics.

This kind of information can alert you to problems. If the number of listeners on a server suddenly drops to zero, a problem with the server or with a live feed may exist. Similarly, if the number of listeners keeps climbing to a point that will exhaust your available bandwidth, you have enough warning to do something about it, such as change the web page URL to point to a server that has more room.

Logging

The PNServer log file uses the familiar web server record format of one time/date-stamped line per transaction. The log file records the number of listeners who have connected to your server, their DNS names (if you have turned this feature on—it consumes CPU cycles and can be a drain on high-volume servers), and, of course, which file was listened to. Audio server errors are also logged, helping you pinpoint where problems are being experienced by your listeners. The following is an example of a PNServer log file record.

```
199.1.11.221 - - [08/Sep/1996:22:26:51 -0500] "GET asp.ra PNA/8" 200
255600 [MacTCP_7.5.3_2.0.2_play_PN01_EN_PPC]
```

In this example (a single record, but wrapped around to fit on this page), coauthor James H. Cline dialed into his local ISP and connected via the Internet to coauthor Patrick Seaman's evaluation PNServer. He then played a sample from James' audio novel, *A Small Percentage*. This record makes available James' IP address, the date/time stamp, the file name, the exact protocol requested (PNA/8), the transfer code (200 is the standard web server success code), the number of bytes transferred (255600), and also the fact that he uses a Mac in the Client Player version variable.

These log files are rich hunting grounds for content planners. By loading the logs into your favorite spreadsheet, you can quickly analyze program popularity, listener habits, and volumes and make informed decisions about future content choices. If you examine the DNS host names of your listeners, you can get a pretty good idea of which networks they are using. With this information, you can often determine listeners' geographic locations. This information can be an invaluable marketing tool to help convince regional advertisers of the value of putting ads on your website.

Firewalls and RealAudio

A *firewall* is a security package that protects internal networks from the outside world, competitors, hackers, and so on. RealAudio servers are customarily installed outside of firewalls to protect the rest of a network, unless the server is intended for use only on your Intranet.

In many cases, users inside a firewall try to access RealAudio servers outside their firewall on the Internet. Many firewalls can be configured to enable RealAudio traffic, and many specifically support RealAudio streams.

In many cases, no firewall reconfiguration is required if the user selects the TCP option on the RealAudio Player (View, Preferences, Network). Otherwise, the firewall software should be configured to enable traffic on TPC port 7070 and UDP ports 6970 through 7170 (for the UDP ports, incoming traffic only). The client uses the TCP port to negotiate with the external RealAudio server, and the incoming audio stream transmits the range of UDP ports.

A breakdown of firewalls that support RealAudio is included in Table 4.5, along with the software manufacturer's URL.

TABLE 4.5

RealAudio-Supported Firewalls		
Firewall Version	**Source/Company**	**URL**
ANS Interlock	ANS CO+RE Systems	http://www.ans.net/
Borderware	Border Network Technologies	http://www.border.com/
Cypress Labyrinth	Cypress Consulting	http://www.cycon.com:8080/ firewall/firewall.html
Firewall-1	Checkpoint Software Technologies, LTD.	http:// www.checkpoint.com/
Firewall/Plus	Network-1	http://www.network-1.com/
Gauntlet	Trusted Information Systems	http://www.tis.com/ docs/products/gauntlet/ index.html
GFX System	Global Technology Associates	http://www.gta.com/
IBM Secured Network Gateway	IBM	http://www.ibm.com.au/ ProdServ/network/ firewall.html
Interceptor	Technologic	http://www.tlogic.com/
Iway one	BateTech Software	http://www.batetech.com/ IWay-One/
Linux IP Masquerading	Linux	http://www.indyramp.com/masq/
NetSeer	enterWorks	http://www.enterworks.com./ netseer/netseertop.html
Private Internet Exchange	Cisco	http://www.cisco.com/ univercd/data/doc/cintrnet/ prod_cat/pcpix.htm
SecureConnect	Morning Star Technologies (acquired by Ascend)	http://www.ascend.com/ products/firewall/index.html
WinGate	Qbix Software	http://nz.com/webnz/ creative-cgi/special/ qbik/qbik.htm

For the latest information on firewalls and RealAudio, check out the FAQs at `http://www.realaudio.com/help/faq/`.

Network Protocols

The PNServer uses either UDP or TCP/IP packets to deliver audio streams to the listeners, depending on how the listener has configured his RealAudio Player (see fig. 4.4). The option of TCP or UDP enables RealAudio to bypass some of the shortcomings of using only TCP streams, such as TCP retransmission problems and the inefficiencies of TCP header segments. Next generation Net standards, such as RSVP and future multicast solutions, are based on UDP.

FIGURE 4.4

RealAudio Player configuration: TCP/IP or UDP packet selection.

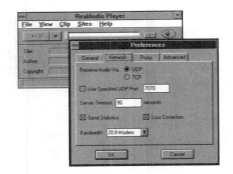

Player

The RealAudio Player and its non-free cousin, Player Plus, are the front-line client-access options. Progressive Networks also includes a browser plug-in; some browsers, such as Microsoft Internet Explorer, have the free version built in. If these options are too limiting, the RealAudio SDK is available (see the next section, "RealAudio SDK and Custom Interfaces"), which can be used to create highly customized interfaces to your website (real)audio.

The RealAudio Player Plus supports Windows 3.1, Windows 95, Windows NT, and Mac PowerPC. The standard RealAudio Player is available for Windows, Macintosh, and Unix platforms. RealAudio is not currently supported on Prodigy or the AOL Mac dial-up accounts.

The standard RealAudio Player has options for configuring CPU utilization, TCP versus UDP protocol use, UDP port, bandwidth choice, proxy server settings, and even options to force your sound card to play only 8-bit sound or to convert the output to 11 KHz (see fig. 4.5). In addition, it will display a statistics dialog box showing lost packets and so on. This information can be used to diagnose connection problems and to enhance the quality control efforts of any Net broadcaster.

FIGURE 4.5

The RealAudio Player, its preferences settings, and its connection statistics.

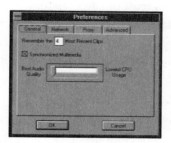

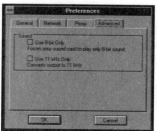

RealAudio SDK and Custom Interfaces

Using the RealAudio Software Development Kit, programmers can customize the look and feel of the way in which users access their website. The SDK supports Java and Macromedia's Shockwave, giving you a great deal of freedom in mixing components.

RealAudio also supports Microsoft's ActiveX and Netscape plug-in tools, making website customization even easier.

Why create a custom interface if you can use traditional HTML web programming? The RealAudio Player already has plug-in support, enabling you to place VCR-like controls on a standard HTML web page. Furthermore, the external player can be configured to display only with the controls, dropping the title information and status bar. The answer can be found in examples such as `http://www.thedj.com`, in which a snazzy, colorful, customized radio/ jukebox appears rather than the now staid-looking HTML pages so familiar to everyone (see figs. 4.6 and 4.7). Similarly, if you are putting together a company Intranet with audio, building a highly customized interface is a natural for many organizations with special interests and needs.

In this example, `http://www.thedj.com` has provided both HTML-based (as shown in fig. 4.6) and plug-in-based (as shown in fig. 4.7) interfaces. The plug-in version was created using a Software Development Kit (SDK) to create customized software that the end user must download and install on his computer. This has the advantage of presenting a highly tailored interface for the user and the disadvantage of putting web publishers in the software publishing and support business. The next section discusses this further.

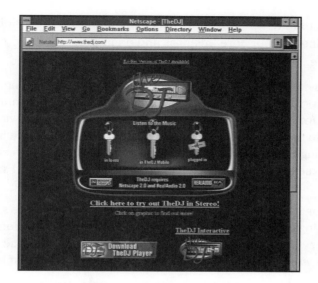

FIGURE 4.6

HTML custom interface example (www.thedj.com).

FIGURE 4.7

SDK custom example: www.thedj.com.

Custom Interface Pros and Cons

A custom interface for your website can provide a unique ambiance and can enhance the visual representation of your content. Some things to keep in mind include the following:

◆ If the scope of your content remains narrow enough, regular aesthetic updates may provide everything necessary to keep the interface from growing stale.

◆ If you have a tightly defined content focus, a custom interface may be just the ticket to draw attention to and differentiate your site from others.

On the other hand, keeping up with a custom interface might divert you from focusing on your core business and on improving the actual content. For example

◆ HTML is easy. The client software, the web browser, is manufactured and supported by other companies, so your web page cannot really be blamed for crashing someone's computer. This is not so with a plug-in. After you develop and distribute a custom plug-in, you are in the software publishing business. This means that you are dealing with software life-cycle issues such as maintenance, support, upgrades, and so on—all this in addition to your web publishing efforts.

◆ If a major bug exists in your plug-in, it could ruin your site's reputation with a single flaming spam by a disgruntled user. In addition, it may be necessary to divert resources from other projects to fix the bug. As Murphy would have it, this is likely to happen at the worst possible time.

If you accept as an axiom that no bugless significantly complex software exists (most who have been in the business very long do), you must plan ahead for how to deal with bugs if they arise. Who will fix it, and how will you test the fixes, notify your listeners, and distribute the updated software? Keep in mind also that users don't like to download plug-ins very often due to the often lengthy download time.

◆ Many of the newest Internet users lack the knowledge and confidence to download and install software. For them, if it is not bundled with the browser, they are unlikely to use it. For those users who decide to try, your instructions and installation program must be *very* well tested. Put another way, could you explain to your grandparent(s) how to do it?

◆ If your content base changes significantly, it may quickly outgrow a hardcoded plug-in suddenly struggling to effectively represent your content.

◆ If your site is evolving and you do not feel confident about what it will look like in a few months, you may be well advised to stick to a less sexy, but more flexible HTML-centric website.

Editing Prerecorded Audio Files

If you are working with prerecorded material rather than a live broadcast, you are facing the same type of audio editing issues as any other Internet broadcaster and much of the audio broadcasting world in general. The same rules that would apply to preparing audio clips for other software, such as Xing Streamworks, apply to RealAudio.

Any audio source you are converting to RealAudio format should be of the best possible quality. Please refer to Chapter 11, "Digital Audio Recording and Editing," for more information on how to make your prerecorded audio files sound their best on RealAudio.

How to Create Content

The basic steps to create audio content are shown in figure 4.8. Step one is where the audio originates. This can be via microphones, cassette tapes, and so on. You might record a speech, song, or other type of content using a microphone. If, for example, you are a reporter, you might have an interview recorded on tape, or the content might have been sent to you by an artist or other content provider.

The second step is to route your content through a mixer, and then in step three, route it through a compressor or limitor, depending on your needs. In step four, the audio is input into your computer, where, if it is not live, it can be preprocessed and edited using various digital editing techniques. After editing, or if it is a live broadcast, the RealAudio Encoder is used to create a playable-on-demand streaming audio file, or a live streaming audio file.

In step five, the file or live stream is delivered to an audio server for distribution to your listeners. In some cases, this is the same machine as the encoder in step four. In other cases, you may have many encoders sending files or streams to a central, high-capacity server. Finally, in step six, the stream is delivered to your Intranet or Internet listeners.

FIGURE 4.8

*The basic steps
involved in creating
audio content.*

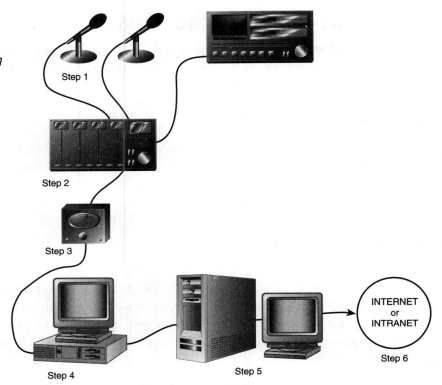

How to Integrate RealAudio
into Your Website

After configuring your web server to support the RealAudio MIME type
(see the earlier section, "Web Server Support"), you are ready to begin. The
following code contains abbreviated HTML from coauthor James H. Cline's
audio novel web page.

```
<HTML><HEAD>
<TITLE>AudioNet: A Small Percentage, by James H. Cline</TITLE></head>
<body bgcolor=#ffffff text=#000000 link=#ff0000 vlink=#ff0000
➥alink=#ffff00>
<center><img src="asphead.gif"></center>
<hr>
```

```
<a href="http://www.twolfpress.com" border=""><img src="twolf.jpg"
➥align=left></a>
<b>AudioNet and <a href="http://www.twolfpress.com/
➥jcline1.htm">Timberwolf Press</a>
present the first serialized Audio-Novel on the Internet:<br><p></b>
<b>"A Small Percentage,"</b> <i>by James H. Cline</i> -- An action-
➥filled tale of alien
invasion. At the dawn of the twenty-first century, Earth
becomes the prize in a deadly battle between warring
➥extraterrestrials. Technology and intrigue blend to
form a graphic study of politics, morality and the brutality of
➥total war. <br><p>
<a href="harmaty.jpg">Click here for a sneak preview of the cover art
➥for the soon to be released hardback edition of "A Small
➥Percentage"</a>
<p>
<center><a href="smallall.ram"><b>Listen to all the current episodes
➥back to back</b></a></center><p>
<a href="small01.ram"><b>Episode 1</b></a> - A sinister alien force
➥secretly threatens Earth in the early twenty-first century.<br>
<a href="small02.ram"><b>Episode 2</b></a> - A U.S. Navy fighter is
➥shot down by an elusive aircraft with remarkable capabilities.<br>
<a href="small03.ram"><b>Episode 3</b></a> - Air Force jets
➥investigate strange happenings in the skies over a small Texas
➥town.<br>
<a href="small04b.ram"><b>Episode 4</b></a> - A secret alien assault
➥begins.<br>
  .
  .
  .
```

Figure 4.9 demonstrates that you can have more than one clip included in a RealAudio Metafile. In this case, the broadcaster of this audio novel, AudioNet (`http://www.AudioNet.com`), includes a lead-in audio clip that includes a sub-thirty-second thank you and advertisement (thanks.ra). The actual audio novel episode is invoked after the first clip finishes (small01.ra). The Metafiles, or *RAM* files, are usually located in the same directory as the corresponding HTML files on your web server(s).

```
pnm://199.179.200.62/thanks.ra
pnm://199.179.200.51/small01.ra
```

FIGURE 4.9

*Example web page
with RealAudio
Metafile link.*

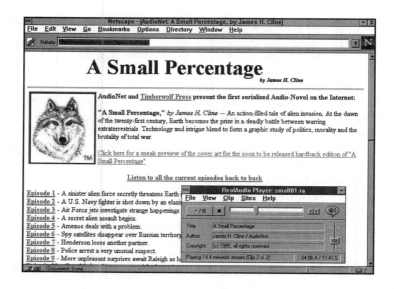

Why use a Metafile instead of simply putting the URLs in the original HTML? If you attempt the latter, your web server tries to send the RealAudio data, but because RealAudio requires a separate audio server, the web server is unable to stream RealAudio. Your web server returns the contents of the Metafile to the client browser, which passes the URLs on to the RealAudio Player (or plug-in, if the extension is .rpm rather than .ram). The player then sends a request to the RealAudio server for the specified .ra file(s).

You may have noticed that the URL contains the locator type PNM as opposed to HTTP or FTP. PNM is a proprietary RealAudio type that stands for Progressive Networks Metafile.

RealAudio Metafile Options

RealAudio Metafiles can be further enhanced by using optional parameters that can control starting, stopping, and RealAudio Player title, author, and copyright information. If you add parameters to a Metafile, you must start with a "?" character and delimit each parameter with an "&" character:

```
pnm://[my.pnserver.ip.address]/[myfile.ra] ?[Parameter 1]&[Parameter 2]
```

For example

```
pnm://199.179.200.51/small01.ra ? start="12"&end="10:15"
```

starts playing the .ra file at the twelve second point, and then stops ten minutes, fifteen seconds from the very beginning of the clip. The format of the time stamps is as follows:

```
"dd:hh:mm:ss.ss"
```

in which ss.ss refers to seconds:tenths_of_seconds. As obvious from the previous example, rather than specifying 00:00:00:12.00 to represent twelve seconds, you can simply say 12.

In the previous audio novel example, separate .ra files were created for each episode. What if, instead, there was a single, large .ra file? Clearly, you could use the previously described start and end parameters to control the section of the .ra file being played. If left at that, the title and other information displayed on the RealAudio Player would be the same regardless of the segment being played. The following code is an example of how the Metafile could be configured to change the title information for each new segment.

```
pnm://199.179.200.51/small01.ra ? start="12" & end="10:15" &
➡title="Episode 1" & author="James
H. Cline" & copyright="Timberwolf Press"
```

Web Page Design Considerations

This chapter has discussed the mechanics of .RAM files, HTML, SDKs, plug-ins, and so on. A larger concern is the amount of thought that goes into how to make website sound a fully integrated and indispensable part of your web presence. Part of this design philosophy is to make the implementation of audio consistent from one page to the next. Always provide a link to a help page for users who have just discovered you and do not understand what they need to do to listen. Another consideration is to lay out your page with a design that includes the audio content from the beginning. Afterthoughts always look like afterthoughts.

Don't hide your audio content! An amazing number of sites bury the audio links on their web pages. The situation is very much like the early days of the desktop publishing craze, when graphic-arts-challenged individuals flamboyantly expressed their lack of creativity in ungainly newsletters with a cacophony of mismatched fonts and clip art. Our best advice is to put feedback mail-tos on all your pages, keep surfing until your fingers ache, and learn the good and the bad from those who have gone before you.

RealAudio Pros and Cons

The RealAudio solution can be expensive to implement compared to non-server-based delivery systems such as Macromedia Shockwave. Shockwave, however, does not have the infrastructure for audio distribution on a significant scale.

Prior to the release of 3.0, RealAudio lagged behind archrival Xing Streamworks in audio quality. That gap is now effectively closed. Xing still has the advantage of integrated MPEG video, although a lack of a significant audience with adequate bandwidth to take advantage of video on the Net nonetheless remains.

RealAudio's player installed base, tool set, and scalability are second to none—today. Whether Progressive Networks can sustain its market share and tool set lead remains to be seen.

C H A P T E R

5

OTHER STREAMING AUDIO FORMATS

Although RealAudio remains the dominant streaming audio presence on the web, its competitors offer many compelling alternatives. The advantages brought to the table by these large and small rivals include important features such as image, video, and MPEG support, as well as sophisticated multimedia development tools, and in some cases, much lower startup costs.

Microsoft reportedly spent $300 million to $400 million in 1996 on its online service (MSN), Internet news and Cable TV operation (MSNBC), and other Internet services. This figure does not include its Internet software development costs, which are spread across many different areas of the company as part of an across-the-board effort to integrate Internet functionality into their entire prodcuct line. Clearly, Microsoft is serious about not only competing in the Internet arena, but dominating it as they do the software market.

Whether Microsoft or any other rival manages to dethrone RealAudio's hold on web audio remains to be seen, although there can be little doubt that Progressive Networks faces stiff competition. This chapter introduces the competition and provides details to help website planners compare and decide which technology best fits their needs.

The complete list of MPEG format standards can be found in Appendix A, "Glossary of Internet Terms."

Xing Streamworks

The feature of handling both audio and video in one format distinguishes MPEG from other codecs and makes a compelling case for RealAudio's archrival, Xing (pronounced *zing*) Technology Corporation's (`http://www.Xingech.com` or `http://www.streamworks.com`) Streamworks server. Even if you are only encoding audio today, who is to say that you won't want or need to combine that audio with video in the future. Because this is built into the Stream-works server technology today, you have the comfort of knowing that it will be there for you tomorrow.

Streamworks also has the distinction of being the first relatively low-cost commercial application of its class. It was designed for LANs, WANs, and Internet distribution of MPEG audio, video, or audio/video streams.

Xing Streamworks delivers digital audio and video in a variety of bit rates and stream types and in mono or stereo. Both MPEG-1 audio (32 to 192 Kbps) and MPEG-2 audio (8 Kbps to 80 Kbps) standards are supported for Layer II audio. MPEG video is supported under the MPEG-1 standard.

Bandwidth and Source File Requirements

Xing Streamworks has numerous audio encoding algorithm stream size options in both MPEG-1 and MPEG-2 formats. Table 5.1 lists a variety of bandwidth options from 28.8 all the way up to a 100BaseT/FDDI (Intranet/ LAN) configuration. By cross referencing bandwidth capacities with stream size, this table provides a quick guide to the amount of bandwidth you need to provide for the number of simultaneous listeners you want to reach.

Mono Low Bit Rate (LBR) streams are available in 8, 9, 10, 11, 12, 13, 14, 15, or 16 Kbps. Mono and joint stereo MPEG-2 audio streams are available in 8, 16, 24, 32, 40, 48, 56, 64, or 80 Kbps per channel. Similarly, MPEG-1 audio streams are available in 32, 48, 56, 64, 80, 96, 112, 128, 160, or 192 Kbps per channel.

All these bandwidth stream sizes help Streamworks deliver a scalable platform from which clients can receive on-demand re-encoded streams tailored to their actual network capacities. This is a powerful feature. If streams are provided with higher bandwidth usage than the content warrants, however, precious bandwidth can be quickly consumed without payback and at the expense of the total number of streams available for other listeners. With careful management and attention to the realistic fidelity requirements of your content, you can strike a balance between stream size and bandwidth used.

Streamworks accepts input from the static file formats .AVI and .WAV at 11, 22, and 44 KHz, mono or stereo. As with any audio codec, always strive for the highest quality source file possible, regardless of the target stream size and encoding algorithm.

TABLE 5.1

ESTIMATED MAXIMUM NUMBER OF SIMULTANEOUS STREAMWORKS STREAMS BY SIZE AND BANDWIDTH

Stream	Stream Size, Kbps	28.8 Modem	28.8 Cable Modem	28.8 RF Cable Modem	56 Switched/ Frame Relay	64 ADSL	640 ADSL	128 ISDN	1.54 Mbps T-1	7 MB 10BaseT (Less Overhead)	45 MB T-3/D S3	100BaseT/ FDDI
MPEG-2, LBR	8	3	3	3	7	8	80	16	192	875	5,625	12,500
LBR	9	3	3	3	6	7	71	14	171	777	5,000	11,111
LBR	10	2	2	2	5	6	64	12	154	700	4,500	10,000
LBR	11	2	2	2	5	5	58	11	140	636	4,090	9,090
LBR	12	2	2	2	4	5	53	10	128	583	3,750	8,333
LBR	13	2	2	2	4	4	49	9	118	538	3,461	7,692
LBR	14	2	2	2	4	4	45	9	110	500	3,214	7,142
LBR	15	1	1	1	3	4	42	8	102	466	3,000	6,666
MPEG-2	16	1	1	1	3	4	40	8	96	437	2,812	6,250
MPEG-2	24	1	1	1	2	2	26	5	64	291	1,875	4,166
MPEG-1,2	32	0	0	0	1	2	20	4	48	218	1,406	3,125
MPEG-2	40	0	0	0	1	1	16	3	38	175	1,125	2,500
MPEG-1,2	48	0	0	0	1	1	13	2	32	145	937	2,083
MPEG-1,2	56	0	0	0	1	1	11	2	27	125	803	1,785
MPEG-1,2	64	0	0	0	0	1	10	2	24	109	703	1,562
MPEG-1,2	80	0	0	0	0	0	8	1	19	87	562	1,250
MPEG-1	96	0	0	0	0	0	6	1	16	72	468	1,041
MPEG-1	112	0	0	0	0	0	5	1	13	62	401	892
MPEG-1	128	0	0	0	0	0	5	1	12	54	351	781
MPEG-1	160	0	0	0	0	0	4	0	9	43	281	625
MPEG-1	192	0	0	0	0	0	3	0	8	36	234	520

> With web server traffic, e-mail, ftp, and so on, your real-life throughput is likely to be significantly less than the figures listed in Table 5.1, so treat those numbers as the absolute best performance possible and remember to subtract bandwidth you use for other traffic. See Chapter 13, "Bandwidth and Cost Considerations," for more details.

Servers

Servers are available for Windows NT, SGI IRIX, Solaris for Sparc, and Linux; they are sold on the basis of bandwidth used, as described in Table 5.2.

TABLE 5.2

STREAMWORKS COST BY BANDWIDTH

Bandwidth to Internet or LAN/WAN	Streamwork Server	PlusPack	Propagation Server
ISDN 128 Kbps	$795	$200	$400
Fractional T1 512 Kbps	$1,495	$400	$750
T1 1.54 Mbps	$3,500	$875	$1,750
10BaseT 10 Mbps	$4,950	$1,250	$2,500
T3/DS3 45 Mbps	$9,950	$2,500	$4,950
Unlimited	$14,950	$3,750	$7,500

Note: All prices are for comparison purposes and were accurate at the time of this writing.

The StreamWorks Server streams audio, video, or audio/video over the Net or your LAN/WAN. As noted in the preceding table, the cost is based on bandwidth, and hardware is sold separately. Streams are distributed via TCP/IP unicast transmission.

The PlusPack adds LiveFile and Propagation features. LiveFile enables you to simulate a live feed from prerecorded files.

The Propagation Server increases the bandwidth available for listeners to receive live streams, expanding the potential audience by propagating streams across multiple servers. The Propagation Server requires separate hardware and network bandwidth from the StreamWorks Server.

The StreamWorks Transmitter is needed to produce live audio, video, or audio/video events. It requires dedicated hardware and software to encode MPEG and to transmit to your LAN/WAN or Internet clients. The Transmitter is priced separately from Xing's other products, at $2,500 for audio only, and $6,500 for audio/video.

Players

The StreamWorks Player delivers live and on-demand MPEG audio and video streams. The player works as a helper application for Microsoft Internet Explorer and Netscape Navigator. A built-in intelligent decoder scales data rates, maximizing the quality of the listening experience on Mac, Windows 3.1, Windows 95, Windows NT, and X-Windows platforms. The StreamWorks player is shown in figure 5.1.

FIGURE 5.1

Xing Streamworks Player.

Player Hardware/OS Requirements

Xing has released players (`http://www.xingtech.com/sw_now.html`) for a variety of platforms, including the Windows/Intel combination, Macintosh, and X-Windows environments, as described in the following list:

Windows 3.1, Windows 95, Windows NT:

◆ Minimum: 80386, 4 MB RAM (note that Windows 95 and Windows NT will not run well (if at all) on this hardware).

◆ Recommended: Pentium, 8 MB RAM, Accelerated VGA card with DCI driver, 16-bit audio card

Macintosh:

◆ Minimum: 68040, Sound Manager 3.0+

◆ Recommended: Power Mac, 8 MB, System 7.5+

X-Windows Supported Platforms:

◆ SGI IRIX

◆ Solaris for Sparc

◆ Linux

How to Create Content

Several tools are available from Xing for creating audio/video files, including the following:

◆ **The StreamWorks Capture Program (Unix):** Receives a live stream from a StreamWorks Transmitter and stores it as a file.

◆ **XingMPEG Encoder (Windows):** Converts .AVI digital video into MPEG video files.

◆ **Third-Party Software:** Can be used to create MPEG files, provided the audio files are standard MPEG-1 or MPEG-2 files. Video files must meet the constrained parameter MPEG-1 video compression standard, and stream files must contain constrained parameter MPEG-1 video and MPEG-1 audio data.

How to Integrate StreamWorks into Your Website

Like other environments, Xing uses the Metafile approach to link client users to streaming content. End users click on an HTML hyperlink that points to the Xing Metafile, or .XDM file. This action causes the Metafile to be down-loaded to the client web browser. If the player is correctly installed, the browser launches the StreamWorks Player, which then reads the URL embedded in the Metafile and attempts to access the stream.

The HTML hyperlink, for example, resembles the following:

```
<a HREF="http://your.server.address/yoursound.xdm">Click here to
➥listen.</a>
```

The .XDM file is a simple text file that contains an URL redirection, like this one to a live source:

```
STREAM = XDMA://your.server.address:portnumber/yoursound.ply
```

or this one to a prerecorded file:

```
STREAM = XDMA://your.server.address:portnumber/yoursound.mpa
```

Xing StreamWorks Pros and Cons

Xing has provided a compelling environment for the creation and delivery of high-quality audio/video streams over the Internet or an Intranet. Some of Xing's strengths include the following:

◆ Xing Streamworks' sound quality is on par with any of its rivals, and, some may argue, still has a technological edge.

◆ By sticking to the MPEG standard, Xing has positioned itself as a standard, especially with regard to its interoperability with third-party MPEG software. This flexibility makes it attractive for cross-platform development.

◆ By providing the capability to convert and stream industry standard .AVI files, Xing has positioned itself as a powerful audio/video Internet broadcasting platform.

Xing does, however, face some weaknesses:

◆ Xing has the advantage of built-in support for video streaming in the MPEG format; however without substantial improvements in Internet backbone and end-user bandwidth capacities, not enough clients exist with fast enough connections to make video a significant factor.

◆ Xing Streamworks is good technology, but it lags significantly in marketshare.

If you are trying to decide between Xing and a competitor, take a hard look at the relative costs for the software, hardware, and network bandwidth resources. You should also look at the browsers and environments supported on both the client and server side. Will they meet the needs of your listeners?

.TSP (TrueSpeech)

TrueSpeech is a set of audio compression algorithms optimized for speech, rather than music. This approach makes possible rates as low as 3.7 Kbps and as high as 8.5 Kbps, keeping this format well under the 14.4 Kbps modem watermark. The TrueSpeech algorithm produces a file that is a variant of the .WAV format.

Available for licensing by the DSP Group, Inc. (http://www.dspg.com/), the TrueSpeech technology arguably received its biggest boost after Microsoft selected it for multimedia applications on PCs (that is, Windows 95) and other devices. TrueSpeech algorithms have also been licensed by ATMEL, AT&T, Cirrus Logic, Creative Labs, Intel, Jetstream, NEC, NetSpeak, Phylon, Physio Control, Prodigy, Siemens, Sierra Semiconductor, Southwest Research, Telescape, TRW, U.S. Robotics, VDOnet, and Visible Interactive.

As with any compressed streaming audio format, TrueSpeech's compression removes portions of the audio spectrum not usually associated with voice-only recordings. The idea is that with this excess baggage removed, the file is smaller and streams with less bandwidth. The tradeoff is that the reduction in audio fidelity can result in poor-sounding recordings (although if you stick to the rules, your encoded content should sound fine). Some types of TrueSpeech encoded music may sound acceptable, but most are painful to listen to, reminding you that the codec was really only designed for voice.

It is important to note that TrueSpeech has only one speed: 8.5 Kbps, unlike Xing Streamworks, RealAudio, and so on. A sampling of TrueSpeech clips can be found at http://www.virtualnoise.com/tsindex.htm, and a sample site can be found at http://www.alliance.net/lav/sound.html (see fig. 5.2).

FIGURE 5.2

*A TrueSpeech site on
the web.*

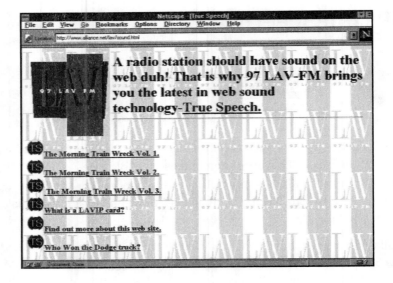

Players

DSP Group distributes the freeware TrueSpeech Internet Player plug-in,
which is also included with the NetManage browser and Microsoft's Internet
Explorer 3.0+. The player plays TrueSpeech-encoded .WAV files after a few
seconds of buffering as the files are downloaded from a website.

The controls are basic, as shown in figure 5.3, with VCR-like operation. The
player, however, lacks features such as stream statistics reporting or TCP/
UDP selection. The TrueSpeech Player uses the TrueSpeech 8.5 algorithm.

FIGURE 5.3

*The TrueSpeech
Player.*

Encoder

The TrueSpeech 8.5 encoder is built into Windows 95 and Windows NT.
Uncompressed .WAV files can be converted into TrueSpeech audio files by
using the Sound Recorder for Windows 95 and Windows NT. The Windows

Media player can then play back the files. If you are still using Windows 3.x, a free converter can be downloaded from `http://www.dspg.com/allplyr.htm`.

Bandwidth Requirements

At the time of this writing, TrueSpeech was available in only one data rate, 8.5 Kbps. Because TrueSpeech is optimized for speech-only applications, this design feature should not be considered a weakness in the product. A benefit of this limitation is that planning for your bandwidth needs is more straightforward than with other software. Table 5.3 provides a quick reference to help site designers provision enough bandwidth for the site.

TABLE 5.3

TRUESPEECH BANDWIDTH REQUIREMENTS	
Actual Throughput to the Internet, Excluding All Other Traffic	**TrueSpeech 8.5 Kbps**
Modem: 28.8 Kbps	3
Cable Modem: 28.8 Kbps	3
RF Cable Modem: 28.8 Kbps	3
Switched 56/Frame Relay: 56 Kbps	6
ADSL: 64 Kbps to 640 Kbps	7 to 75
ISDN: 128 Kbps	15
T-1: 1.54 Mbps	181
10BaseT/Ethernet: 7B (Overhead often lowers performance by 30%)	823
T-3/DS3: 45 Mbps	5,294
100BaseT/FDDI: 100 Mbps	11,764

With web server traffic, e-mail, ftp, and so on, your real-life throughput is likely to be significantly less than the figures listed in the preceding table, so treat those numbers as the absolute best performance possible and remember to subtract bandwidth you use for other traffic. See Chapter 13 for more details.

Servers

TrueSpeech does not employ an audio server, but is instead handled by
HTTP-type web servers as a MIME type in much the same way that
Macromedia's Shockwave is distributed. Like Shockwave, this creates a
relatively low-cost method for distributing low- to medium-volume website
audio content, and it lacks specialized monitoring, control, redistribution, or
other high-capacity Net broadcast tools.

VDOnet and TrueSpeech

The DSP Group has been busy spreading the use of the TrueSpeech family
of algorithms, including VDOnet (`http://www.VDO.net`—see fig. 5.4), which
licensed the base TrueSpeech algorithm for its WebPhone Internet telephone. In this application, the low-bit rate audio algorithm is used to
complement VDO's video streaming technology so that video and audio
can be on the same dial-up (or higher speed) connection.

FIGURE 5.4

*VDOLive: Low
bit-rate audio
plus video.*

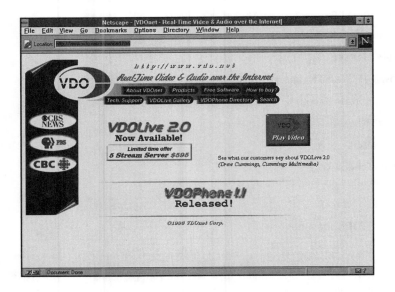

The VDOLive video server provides dynamic bandwidth scaling and is
designed to stream small and large (seconds to hours) files. VDOLive servers
are available for the following platforms:

- ◆ BSDI
- ◆ FreeBSD
- ◆ IBM AIX
- ◆ Linux (a.out and elf)
- ◆ SGI Irix
- ◆ Sun Solaris
- ◆ SunOS
- ◆ Windows NT

How to Create TrueSpeech Content

Creating TrueSpeech content is easy. First, create PCM encoded .WAV files with an 8 KHz sampling rate and 16-bit resolution. TrueSpeech is optimized for this configuration. SoundBlaster 16 or equivalent boards support this format. If you don't have this kind of equipment, or if you are converting pre-existing files, try using software tools such as Cool Edit (http://www.syntrillium.com) to convert the files to the optimal settings listed here.

To convert PCM-encoded .WAV files to TrueSpeech-encoded .WAV files, the DSP group recommends the Sound System of Windows 95 or Windows NT. The TrueSpeech format is built into these programs (see fig. 5.5).

FIGURE 5.5

Windows NT Sound Recorder TrueSpeech file conversion option.

In Windows 95, the Sound Recorder is located at

    START>PROGRAMS>ACCESSORIES>MULTIMEDIA>SOUND RECORDER

To convert your file by using the Windows 95 or Windows NT Sound Recorder, open the PCM encoded .WAV file, select the TrueSpeech format, and use Save As to create a new .WAV file. Select Convert, and a dialog box with a selection box for the file format pops up. Use the scroll bar to select DSP Group TrueSpeech and then save. The .WAV file has now been compressed by a factor of 15 into the TrueSpeech format.

If your client is using Microsoft's Internet Explorer 3.0 or compatible, a TrueSpeech .WAV file can begin streaming as soon as the web page is loaded by using the following HTML tag:

```
<BGSOUND src="myfile.wav" loop="Infinite">
```

How to Integrate TrueSpeech into Your Website

Website integration of TrueSpeech involves several steps.

1. Add MIME type to your web server mime table:
   `type/ext=.tsp, app=dsptype`

2. Acquire content.

3. Edit or digitally process content to prepare for encoding (see Chapters 9, "Sound Basics and Audio Theory," and 11, "Digital Audio Recording and Editing").

4. Use previously mentioned conversion utility or built-in Windows 95 or Windows NT sound recorder to convert the standard .WAV file to the TrueSpeech variant.

5. Copy TrueSpeech files to the appropriate web server directory.

6. Create MetaFiles for each of your TrueSpeech files, with the file extension of .TSP. These MetaFiles are plain text files that usually reside in the same HTML directory as the target web page. The MetaFiles contain a single line of text that redirects to the TrueSpeech file. For example

   `TSIP>>www.mysite.com/TrueSpeech/myaudio.wav.`

   in which `TSIP>>` takes the place of the more familiar `http://` tag.

7. Imbed HTML tags in your web page(s) linking to the MetaFiles:

   `<a href="www.mysite.com/TrueSpeech/myaudio.tsp">`

8. Your website is now TrueSpeech-enabled.

TrueSpeech Pros and Cons

As noted in the earlier section entitled "Servers," TrueSpeech is not well suited for a large scale broadcast of audio content. Players are fairly well distributed; with the launch of Microsoft's NetShow Internet multimedia streaming software, however, the future of Microsoft's involvement with TrueSpeech remains unclear. On the other hand, if your site and your budget are small, TrueSpeech is a great way to inexpensively add audio capabilities to your site.

Microsoft NetShow

Microsoft NetShow (`http://www.microsoft.com/netshow/`) is a server-based multicasting streaming audio package designed for Intranet and Internet operation. The client (listener) side receives the multicast stream via Microsoft Internet Explorer 3.0+ or another ActiveX-enabled browser that runs an ActiveX control that tunes to the multicast address and port and plays the audio.

NetShow is designed to use multicast networks, which means using the MBone (Internet Multicast Backbone). The MBone is a collective of individual multicast-enabled networks spread across the Net. In a multicast network, the broadcaster sends a single stream to the multicast network, and the network clones the stream for each client on that network that requests a stream.

If the client is not on a multicast-enabled network, an individual stream is sent to that client. This is accomplished by *tunneling*, in which streams that route across nonmulticast portions of the Net are sent as separate streams until they pass through the next multicast-enabled island.

At the time of this writing, Microsoft had released limited information on NetShow, which was in its first round of beta releases. As with any beta software, many significant features and options may change prior to the final commercial release of the software. As a result, the information provided about NetShow is intended to provide the reader with more of a sense of Microsoft's direction, than with the level of detail provided about other software within this book.

Player

NetShow is designed to be run on Intranets or Internets, on PCs running Microsoft Operating Systems. The minimum recommended hardware/software configuration is as follows:

◆ Ethernet adapter from a major manufacturer (DEC, Intel, 3Com)

◆ Microsoft Internet Explorer 3.0 (complete version)

◆ Multimedia PC with a 486/50 processor, Pentium recommended, with PCI or EISA bus, PCI recommended, 8 MB RAM (minimum) for Windows 95, 16 MB recommended, 16 MB RAM (minimum) for Windows NT, 32 MB recommended

◆ Sound Blaster 16 compatible sound card

◆ Windows 95, Windows NT Workstation 4, or Windows NT Server 4

Some models of Xircom PCMCIA Ethernet adapters may need updated software.

Server Requirements

The NetShow Server runs only under Windows NT Server and does not require specialized equipment. The minimum recommended hardware and software configuration is as follows:

◆ Minimum 486/66 MHz CPU, 90 MHz+ Pentium recommended

◆ PCI or EISA bus, PCI recommended

◆ Minimum 24 MB RAM, 48 MB recommended

◆ Creative Labs Sound Blaster 16 sound card

◆ Microsoft Internet Information Server

◆ PCI Ethernet adapter from a major manufacturer (DEC, Intel, 3Com)

◆ Windows NT Server 4 with IP networking installed

Figure 5.6 shows the wide range of formats, sixteen in all, available on the Microsoft NetShow Encoder. This broad level of encoding flexibility provides Net broadcasters with a wide range of content delivery options.

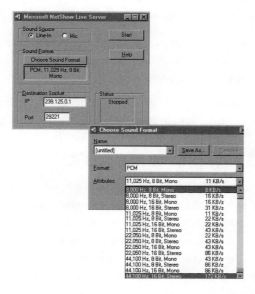

FIGURE 5.6

Microsoft NetShow Live Server.

Network Requirements

As mentioned previously, NetShow is designed to run on an Intranet rather than on the Internet. Operation requires an IP-based network, but no special network software patches or add-ons are needed. Because NetShow is designed for multicasting, your router needs to have multicasting turned on.

NetShow Server Setup

The NetShow Server runs under Windows NT Server 4 or later with the TCP/IP protocol installed. The hardware requirements are listed in the previous section, "Server Requirements," and, at the time of this writing, DEC Alpha NT does not yet appear to be supported.

If you are new to Windows NT Server, you should make certain that the installation correctly recognized your sound card. NT does not easily recognize some of the generic OEM-type sound cards that are bundled with many PC systems. If you have trouble with the card, check the Microsoft hardware compatibility list to see whether your card is listed or contact the card or PC manufacturer, as appropriate, for updated NT drivers.

After your Windows NT Server is installed and operational, you need to configure Internet Information Server (IIS) with appropriate permissions and a few web pages on which to begin testing.

After your system is ready, download NLASERVR.EXE from the Microsoft website. This is a self-extracting file. Then run NLARSERVR.EXE.

Microsoft NetShow Pros and Cons

As mentioned previously, NetShow was in early beta at the time of this writing. Many of the weaknesses of the product may be eliminated prior to final release, such as the lack of non-Windows client software. Overall, Microsoft seems to be covering a lot of ground with support for multicasting and a broad array of encoding options. The product's biggest strength may come with its integration (or lack of) with other Microsoft products. No secret has been made of Microsoft's intention to pound the Internet market from every angle. Its success or failure with NetShow remains to be seen.

IsoChrone isoAudio

IsoChrone's (`http://www.isochrone.com/`) isoAudio, like Microsoft's NetShow, is another new product not available in time for full coverage in this book. isoAudio enables websites to offer streaming music and speech over Intranets and the Internet at up to CD-quality sound. IsoChrone has provided high-end clustering features that enable server scaling, load balancing, and content replication. Notably, the codec technology behind isoAudio is provided by Lucent Technologies (`http://www.lucent.com/Bell/bell.html`) (formerly Bell Labs).

Player Requirements

The isoAudio player requires a minimum of a 486/66 Multimedia PC or faster, with a minimum of 12 MB RAM, running Windows 95 or Windows NT, and Netscape Navigator 2.0+ or compatible.

Server Requirements

The isoAudio Server requires a Pentium, 16 MB RAM, Windows NT or Windows 95. The SGI version requires IRIX 5.3, and the Sun SparcStation version requires Solaris 2.x.

Bandwidth Requirements

Table 5.4 describes how many streams can be simultaneously delivered for each type of bandwidth option.

TABLE 5.4

POSSIBLE DELIVERED STREAMS PER BANDWIDTH OPTION

Bandwidth to Internet or LAN/WAN	8 Kbps Audio Stream	16 Kbps Audio Stream	56 Kbps Audio Stream
Modem: 28.8 Kbps	2	1	0
Cable Modem: 28.8 Kbps	2	1	0
RF Cable Modem: 28.8 Kbps	2	1	0
Switched 56/ Frame Relay: 56 Kbps	7	3	1
ADSL: 64 Kbps to 640 Kbps	8	3	1
ISDN: 128 Kbps	15	7	2
T-1: 1.54 Mbps	185	80	25
10BaseT/Ethernet: 7B (Overhead often lowers performance by 30%)	875	388	125
T-3/DS3: 45 Mbps	5,600	2,500	800
100BaseT/FDDI: 100 Mbps	12,500	5,555	1,785

Encoding Options

IsoChrone has tapped into Lucent Technologies' audio codec engines to provide a wide array of encoding options, as described in the following list.

Lucent Technologies Elemedia's Fidelity Plus Speech Codecs

SX7300P — Mono

◆ Approximate data storage rate: 55 KB/minute

◆ 8 KHz sampling

◆ 7.3 Kbps (14.4 modem)

SX8300P — Mono

- ◆ Approximate data storage rate: 60 KB/minute
- ◆ 8 KHz sampling
- ◆ 8.3 Kbps (14.4 modem)

Elemedia's Fidelity, SX16000P — Mono

- ◆ Approximate data storage rate: 120 KB/minute
- ◆ 11 KHz sampling
- ◆ 16 Kbps (28.8 modem)

Lucent Technologies Elemedia's Fidelity Plus Music Codecs

AX56000P — Stereo

- ◆ Approximate data storage rate: 430 KB/minute
- ◆ Near CD quality
- ◆ 44 KHz/32 KHz sampling
- ◆ 56 Kbps (ISDN or better)

AX18000P — Stereo

- ◆ Approximate data storage rate: 135 KB/minute
- ◆ FM radio quality
- ◆ 44 KHz, 22 KHz sampling
- ◆ 18 Kbps (28.8 modem)

AX12000P — Mono

- ◆ Approximate data storage rate: 90 KB/minute
- ◆ 22 KHz sampling
- ◆ 12 Kbps (28.8 modem)

AX8000P — Mono

◆ Approximate data storage rate: 60 KB/minute

◆ 22 KHz sampling

◆ 8 Kbps (14.4 modem)

isoAudio Pros and Cons

IsoChrone's isoAudio Internet Broadcasting effort is too new to rate in this book. Teaming up with Lucent Technologies would seem to be a good move and may help draw attention to a company that might otherwise go unnoticed.

IBM Bamba

Developed by the IBM Research-Watson Center, Bamba (`http://www.alphaWorks.ibm.com/`) is a streaming audio/video product designed for clients with dial-up access to the Internet. The package contains the Bamba Audio, Bamba Live Audio, and Bamba Video plug-in players. The base rate for the audio stream is 6 Kbps, with the balance of the bandwidth used for the video stream. The video player plays prerecorded clips at data rates ranging from 10 Kbps to 300 Kbps.

Bamba is too new to describe in detail or rate in this book.

Shockwave

Macromedia's (`http://www.macromedia.com`) Shockwave for Director, like TrueSpeech, is a nonserver, web-based audio delivery system. When combined with Macromedia's powerful set of multimedia development tools, Shockwave adds an exciting audio component to any *Shocked* site containing animations and other visual effects.

Bandwidth Requirements

As noted in the later section, "Network Protocols," Shockwave exclusively uses TCP. Shockwave audio comes in two varieties: 8 Kbps (AM Radio) and 16 Kbps (FM Mono). Because no dedicated audio server exists and Shockwave uses HTTP-web servers to distribute its streams, the number of streams serveable from each server is limited due to HTTP resource consumption by the audio streams.

Web servers are designed to handle multiple simultaneous users who generally request HTML documents and associated graphics. After the files are sent, that resource opens up again for the next client. Because most of the files are relatively small, they can be distributed quickly and resources made available quickly for more simultaneous users.

Streaming audio never closes these resources, which, in some cases, can quickly choke a web server's capability to handle additional requests. As long as you are not trying to distribute to a large number of simultaneous users, the web server has a good chance of being able to handle the requests and still keep up delivery of HTML and other objects.

Table 5.5 lists theoretical audio distribution limits for Shockwave, although the higher numbers are not likely to be achieved with a single web server.

> With web server traffic, e-mail, ftp, and so on, your real-life throughput is likely to be significantly less than the figures listed in Table 5.5, so treat those numbers as the absolute best performance possible and remember to subtract bandwidth you use for other traffic. See Chapter 13 for more details.
>
> Due to Shockwave's HTTP-based distribution, achieving high numbers of simultaneous users will likely require the use of multiple, dedicated web servers.

Note

TABLE 5.5

	SHOCKWAVE BANDWIDTH REQUIREMENTS	
Actual Throughput to the Internet, Excluding All Other Traffic	**Simultaneous Shockwave 14.4 Listeners (8 Kbps Each) (Sounds Like AM Radio)**	**Simultaneous Shockwave 28.8 Listeners (16 Kbps Each) (Sounds Like FM Mono)**
Modem: 28.8 Kbps	3	1
Cable Modem: 28.8 Kbps	3	1
RF Cable Modem: 28.8 Kbps	3	1
Switched 56/Frame Relay: 56 Kbps	7	3
ADSL: 64 Kbps to 640 Kbps	8 to 80	4 to 40
ISDN: 128 Kbps	16	8
T-1: 1.54 Mbps	192	96
10BaseT/Ethernet: 7 Mbps	875	437
T-3/DS3: 45 Mbps	5,625	2,812
100BaseT/FDDI: 100 Mbps	12,500	6,250

Servers

Shockwave does not employ an audio server, but is instead handled by HTTP-type web servers as a MIME type. This creates a relatively low-cost method for distributing low- to medium-volume website audio content, and lacks specialized monitoring, control, redistribution, or other high-capacity Net broadcast tools.

Network Protocols

Packets are limited to distribution via TCP only, which can avoid some firewall problems. Streaming audio by using only TCP, however, exposes you to the inefficiencies of using TCP headers and TCP's biggest weakness: retransmissions. If the TCP packet does not show up, it is retransmitted again and again, clogging Internet bandwidth and resulting in audio drop-outs and other audio artifacts.

In its recent campaign against RealAudio, Macromedia claimed that RealAudio supported only UDP, which is inaccurate. RealAudio supports both UDP and TCP at the client's option within the RealAudio preference settings. UDP, however, is RealAudio's default protocol. VDOLive and Xing Streamworks also use UDP, as do new web standards, such as RSVP, RTP, and multicast solutions.

Buffering Shockwave Audio for Better Performance

As with any audio streamer, network delays and congestion can cause packet loss or out-of-order packets. If this happens, the player attempts to reorder or wait for these tardy packets. If the wait is too long, the player goes on without them, resulting in various audio artifacts such as skipping or other distortions.

Shockwave gives the broadcaster the option of increasing the lead-in buffer, which in many cases gives the player enough slack to let those late packets show up in time to eliminate the audio glitches. This feature is similar to RealAudio's PerfectPlay encoder option. The RealAudio PlayerPlus, however, has the additional option of controlling the buffer length from the listener end.

To set the Shockwave buffer, use the Lingo property called `the preloadTime`. With it you can set the number of seconds of audio that will be downloaded prior to player startup. The amount of delay experienced by the listener depends on the bandwidth throughput between the client and the source. Note that the number of seconds specified refers to the uncompressed play time experienced at the client end, not a real-time delay in stream reception.

Players

Controls on the Shockwave player are limited to basic start and stop. The appearance of the Shockwave player depends on the way it is implemented within the Director-created web page. As of the time of this writing, VCR-type functions such as fast forward, rewind, and pause have no support. Rewind is initiated by issuing a Stop command and then reissuing a Play command.

This is similar to the TrueSpeech, Streamworks, and VDOLive players, although the IWAVE RealAudio player does support these types of features.

Custom Interfaces

With Macromedia Director, you can create custom interfaces to enhance the visual experience of clients enjoying your content. An attractive example of using Director to create a visually appealing site is shown in figure 5.7. This site can be found at `http://www.macromedia.com/shockwave/epicenter/shockedsites/waterdragon/swa.html`.

FIGURE 5.7

Shockwave Director custom interface example.

Compatibility

Macromedia Shockwave is compatible with the following Windows and Mac systems and browsers:

Windows Operating Systems

◆ Windows 3.1x

◆ Windows 95

◆ Windows NT 3.51, Windows 4.0+

Windows Browsers

◆ Attachmate's Emissary

◆ Internet Explorer 3.0+

◆ Netmanage's WebSurfer

◆ Netscape Navigator 2.02 and 3.0+

Macintosh Systems

◆ Mac 68000, System 7.1.2+, 7.5.3 recommended

◆ PowerMac System 7.5.1+, 7.5.3 recommended

Macintosh Browsers

◆ Attachmate's Emissary

◆ Netmanage's WebSurfer

◆ Netscape Navigator 2.02+, 3.0+

How to Create Content

Creating content with Shockwave involves using Macromedia's extensive set of development tools. This impressive array includes

◆ Director Multimedia Studio: Director, SoundEdit 16 and DECK II, Extreme 3D, and xRes.

◆ FreeHand Graphics Studio: a set of tools for graphic arts and design includes FreeHand, Fontographer, Extreme 3D, and xRes.

◆ Backstage Designer Plus: an animation tool.

Use of these tools is a subject that could easily fill an entire book. This book does not attempt to cover the use of these sophisticated programming tools. Details on their use can be found at Macromedia's website: `http://www.macromedia.com/software/`.

Using the Macromedia toolset, you produce compressed multimedia objects directly linked to in your HTML with tags such as the following:

```
<EMBED SRC="myapp.dcr" width=250 height= 175>
```

The web server delivers the object along with your HTML, graphics, and so on. The client must have already installed the Shockwave plug-in for the site to work.

Shockwave Pros and Cons

Macromedia's line of multimedia content creation tools, combined with Shockwave audio streaming, is a relatively inexpensive route to a robust multimedia website. If you are interested in sophisticated animations and arresting visual effects, go no further.

The downside to Macromedia's product line is the lack of tools to control and widely distribute the audio streams. No tools replicate the audio among multiple, dispersed servers; no tools dynamically monitor current listenership; and no tools balance the audio stream bandwidth load among servers on multiple networks. On the plus side, HTTP-based audio streaming should work very well for small- to medium-sized sites.

Recently, Macromedia launched an aggressive campaign to compare Shockwave streaming audio to RealAudio and to directly compete in the audio arena. This would seem to pit Macromedia's weakest area against RealAudio's sole existence, especially with the release of RealAudio 3.0, in which RealAudio leapfrogged Macromedia in audio quality.

Ironically, the best combination for many websites might be using Macromedia's multimedia development tools to create dynamic visual effects, an area in which RealAudio has no presence, in tandem with RealAudio for the audio streaming, which supports Macromedia tools in the RealAudio SDK.

IWAVE

Vocaltec (`http://www.vocaltech.com`), the maker of the Internet Phone, leveraged its Internet Phone technology to create Internet Wave Audio. Like Macromedia's Shockwave (`http://www.macromedia.com`), IWAVE does not use a dedicated server and depends on HTTP-web servers for distribution.

Bandwidth Requirements

IWAVE exclusively uses TCP. Because no dedicated audio server exists, and IWAVE uses HTTP-web servers to distribute its streams, the number of streams servable from each server is limited due to HTTP resource consumption by the audio streams.

Web servers are designed to handle simultaneous users who request HTML documents and associated graphics. After the files are sent, that resource opens up again for the next client. Because most of the files are relatively small, they can be distributed quickly and resources made available quickly for more simultaneous users.

Streaming audio never closes these resources, which, in some cases, can quickly stifle a web server's capability to handle additional requests. As long as you are not trying to distribute to a large number of simultaneous users, the web server has a good chance of being able to handle the requests and still keep up delivery of HTML and other objects.

Table 5.6 lists theoretical audio distribution limits for IWAVE, although the higher numbers are not likely to be achieved with a single web server.

With web server traffic, e-mail, ftp, and so on, your real-life throughput is likely to be significantly less than the figures listed in Table 5.6, so treat those numbers as the absolute best performance possible and remember to subtract bandwidth you use for other traffic. See Chapter 13 for more details.

Due to IWAVE's HTTP-based distribution, achieving high numbers of simultaneous users will likely require the use of multiple, dedicated web servers.

TABLE 5.6

IWAVE BANDWIDTH REQUIREMENTS				
Actual Throughput to the Internet, Excluding All Other Traffic	**7.7 Kbps Speech (vsc77)**	**11.2 Kbps Some Music (vsc112)**	**15.4 Kbps Good Music (vsc154)**	**22.4 Kbps Better Music (vsc224)**
Modem: 28.8 Kbps	3	2	1	1
Cable Modem: 28.8 Kbps	3	2	1	1
RF Cable Modem: 28.8 Kbps	3	2	1	1
Switched 56/Frame Relay: 56 Kbps	7	5	3	2
ADSL: 64 Kbps to 640 Kbps	8 to 83	5 to 57	4 to 41	2 to 28
ISDN: 128 Kbps	16	11	8	5
T-1: 1.54 Mbps	200	137	100	68
10BaseT/Ethernet: 7 MB (Overhead often lowers performance by 30%)	909	625	454	312
T-3/DS3: 45 Mbps	5,844	4,017	2,922	2,008
100BaseT / FDDI: 100 Mbps (This is a LAN configuration)	12,987	8,928	6,493	4,464

Encoder Algorithms

IWAVE offers four encoding algorithms, as described in the following list:

◆ **VSC77:** 7.7 Kbps stream, sampling at 5.500 KHz+. Quality: Speech only.

◆ **VSC112:** 11.2 Kbps stream, sampling at 8 KHz. Quality: Good speech, AM radio level music.

◆ **VSC154:** 15.4 Kbps stream, sampling at 11.025 KHz+. Quality: Good speech, better music than VSC112.

◆ **VSC224:** 22.4 Kbps stream, sampling at 16 KHz. Quality: FM mono.

Servers

As noted previously, IWAVE does not use a dedicated audio server, but instead is distributed in the form of prerecorded clips by a HTTP-web server. To make your web server IWAVE-compatible, you must modify the MIME types to include configuration information for IWAVE.

Application Type	File Extension
application/vocaltec-media-desc	e.vmd
application/vocaltec-media-file	.vmf

In addition, if you want users to be able to Fast-Forward, you must install and use the CGI utility IWPOS on the web server. (Note that you need a Compiler.)

1. Locate the IWPOS.C file in the archive file from the IWAVE files you have previously downloaded from the `http://www.vocaltech.com` website.

2. Edit IWPOS.C.

3. Uncomment and update the HTTP_ROOT parameter with the web server document path.

4. Compile it (for example, cc -o iwpos iwpos.c).

5. Copy the executable into the CGI directory on your server.

6. Grant Execute permissions to the executable file.

7. When using the Internet Wave Encoder, enter the CGI in the BASE URL box, prior to the path to the audio files.

8. If your .vmd and .vmf files are in the document directory /myfiles, for example, the HTTP URL would read `http://my.audio.web.server/myfiles`; after the CGI utility is set up, the URL would look something like `http://my.audio.web.server/cgi-bin/iwpos?/myfiles/`.

9. Copy your .vmf and the .vmd files to your web server.

Network Protocols

IWAVE audio streams are distributed by a web server via TCP. TCP has the advantage of being a robust protocol and is designed to be routed all over the world—if that's what it takes to get to its destination. This robust-ness can also result in inefficiencies with TCP headers and TCP's biggest weakness: retransmissions. If the TCP packet does not show up, it is retrans-mitted again and again, clogging Internet bandwidth and resulting in audio dropouts and other audio artifacts.

Player

If the CGI utility described in the later section "Servers" is installed on the web server, the IWAVE player has several control features including Stop, Start, Volume, Play, Pause, Slow, Fast Forward, and Rewind. The control presentation is unique, with a blue ring that grows around the round player knob, coming to full circle when the clip is finished playing. You can click on and drag the knob to fast forward, rewind, or slow down the player (see fig. 5.8).

FIGURE 5.8

IWAVE Player.

The box in the middle right contains a depiction of the audio buffer (top), which fills with green as the buffer fills up with ten seconds of audio. Below the audio buffer is a thin dotted line that turns on whenever IWAVE is connected to the Internet. Beneath the Net indicator is the bandwidth availability level. That fills up when enough bandwidth is available to use IWAVE.

In a departure from some of IWAVE's more serious competitors, the lower right-hand box contains an animated Bozo used to show the current status, such as connecting, playing, pausing, and so on. When playing a file, the animation indicates whether it is music or speech (set by the creator of the audio file). The stick figure jumps up and down, carries a boom box, uses a tire pump to indicate that the network buffer is being filled, and so on.

How to Create Content

To create IWAVE content, you must first create your base sound files in .WAV format by using standard sound editing techniques (see Chapters 9 and 11).

After your .WAV files are ready, follow these steps to create IWAVE format files:

1. Start the Internet Wave Encoder, IWENCODE.EXE (see fig. 5.9).

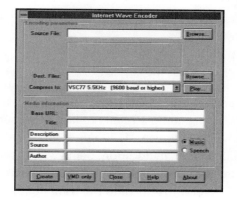

FIGURE 5.9

IWAVE Encoder.

2. Enter the .WAV file name in the Source File dialog box.

3. Enter the destination file name(s) in the Dest. Files dialog box.

4. The encoder creates both the compressed audio file (.VMF), and a MetaFile (.VMD), or *stub* file, that is linked to in your HTML.

5. Enter your web server's URL in the Base URL dialog box, such as `http://www.my.server.audio/myfiles/`. If you want to enable the fast forwarding/rewinding feature, and you have installed the CGI utility, the URL would look something like `http://www.my.server.audio/cgi-bin/iwpos?myfiles/`.

> It is recommended that the MetaFile (.VMD) and the corresponding .VMF file be located in the same directory on the web server. Tip

6. Fill in the Title, Source, and Author dialog boxes.

7. Select the compression type.

8. To encode, click on the Create button. After the encoder is finished, a message displays the names of the output files. If finished, click on Exit.

9. You are now IWAVE-enabled.

How to Integrate IWAVE into Your Website

Because IWAVE is distributed via web servers, all that needs to be done to activate your newly created content is to add appropriate HTML tags, such as

```
<a href="/myfiles/jazz01.vmd">Listen to my latest jazz single!</a>
```

IWAVE Pros and Cons

IWAVE presents an inexpensive way to add audio to your website. Like Macromedia's (`http://www.macromedia.com`) Shockwave, however, IWAVE lacks tools for distributing audio streams to large numbers of simultaneous listeners. As mentioned previously, TCP-only streaming has significant retransmission ramifications. In addition, being web-server based, significant numbers of simultaneous streams severely strain web server resources and limit both regular web server traffic and the total number of possible simultaneous listeners. Also, at the time of this writing, IWAVE lacked an SDK with which to create custom interfaces.

On the plus side, IWAVE is well suited for small- to medium-sized websites that do not plan to use *live* content—that is, IWAVE is a prerecorded, playback-only environment.

Voxware: ToolVox

Voxware (http://www.voxware.com), like IWAVE (http://www.vocaltech.com), has a product line that includes both an Internet telephone application and a voice-grade audio encoder and player (ToolVox). Like IWAVE and Macromedia's (http://www.macromedia.com) Shockwave, Voxware has no dedicated server and relies on web servers to deliver its streams.

Bandwidth Requirements

Voxware exclusively uses TCP. Because no dedicated audio server exists and Voxware uses HTTP-web servers to distribute its streams, the number of streams serveable from each server is limited due to HTTP resource consumption by the audio streams.

Web servers are designed to handle multiple simultaneous users who request HTML documents and associated graphics. After the files are sent, that resource opens up again for the next client. Because most of the files are relatively small, they can be distributed quickly and resources made available quickly for more simultaneous users.

Streaming audio never closes these resources, which, in some cases, can quickly stifle a web server's capability to handle additional requests. As long as you are not trying to distribute to a large number of simultaneous users, the web server has a good chance of being able to handle the requests and still keep up delivery of HTML and other objects.

On the plus side, Voxware's small bandwidth footprint, an estimated minuscule 1.3 Kbps, makes it attractive for many types of low-fidelity, speech-only, non-live (prerecorded) content.

Table 5.7 lists theoretical audio distribution limits for Voxware, although the higher numbers are not likely to be achieved with a single web server.

TABLE 5.7

VOXWARE BANDWIDTH REQUIREMENTS	
Actual Throughput to the Internet (Excluding All Other Traffic)	Theoretical Simultaneous Voxware Listeners 1.3 Kbps Each Highly Compressed Speech
Modem: 28.8 Kbps	22
Cable Modem: 28.8 Kbps	22
RF Cable Modem: 28.8 Kbps	22
Switched 56/Frame Relay: 56 Kbps	43
ADSL: 64 Kbps to 640 Kbps	49 to 492
ISDN: 128 Kbps	98
T-1: 1.54 Mbps	1,185
10BaseT/Ethernet: 7 Mbps	5,385
T-3/DS3: 45 Mbps	34,615
100BaseT/FDDI: 100 Mbps	76,923

Note

With web server traffic, e-mail, ftp, and so on your real-life throughput is likely to be significantly less than the figures listed in Table 5.7, so treat those numbers as the absolute best performance possible and remember to subtract bandwidth you use for other traffic. See Chapter 13 for more details.

Due to Voxware's HTTP-based distribution, achieving high numbers of simultaneous users will likely require the use of multiple, dedicated web servers.

Servers

As noted previously, VOX does not use a dedicated audio server, but instead is distributed in the form of prerecorded clips by a web server. To make your web server VOX-compatible, you must modify the MIME types to include configuration information for Voxware. The following shows the IWAVE MIME configuration.

Application Type	File Extension
audio/voxware vox	.vox
application/vocaltec-media-file	.vmf

After your web server's MIME table is updated and the changes have taken effect, your server is now VOX-enabled.

System Requirements

Voxware's minimum system requirements are as follows:

◆ 486DX-66

◆ Windows 95, Windows 3.1x, Windows NT 3.51+

◆ 4 MB RAM (16 MB RAM for NT)

◆ 2 MB hard disk space

◆ 8-bit sound card

◆ Plug-in capable Web browser, such as Netscape Navigator 3.0+

Voxware's recommended system configuration is as follows:

◆ Pentium PC

◆ Windows 95, Windows 3.1x, Windows NT 3.51+

◆ 8 MB RAM (16 MB RAM for NT)

◆ 2 MB hard disk space

◆ 16-bit sound card

◆ Plug-in capable Web browser, such as Netscape Navigator 3.0+

Encoders

Encoders are available for Windows 95/NT and the Mac (see fig. 5.10). Operation of the encoder is simple—just type the name of the .WAV file you want to convert and then enter the name of the output .VOX file you want to create.

FIGURE 5.10
VOX Encoder.

Players

VOX players are available for Windows 95, Solaris 2.5+, Windows 3.1+, and
the Mac. Controls are simple and include Start, Pause, Rewind, and a
slidebar to speed up or slow down the replay (see fig. 5.11).

FIGURE 5.11
VOX Player.

How to Create Content

To create VOX content, you must first create your base sound files in .WAV
format by using standard sound editing techniques (see Chapters 9 and 11).

> **Tip**
>
> Adjust the recording gain to create a file that is fully modulated but not clipped.
> The volume should have a wide range, but no static during the loudest portions
> of the clip.

The encoder processes uncompressed .WAV or .AIFF files and creates a
.VOX file with a compression ratio of 53:1.

Recommended content includes the following:

◆ One person speaking

◆ One person singing

◆ Multiple voices speaking or singing sequentially

Nonrecommended content includes the following:

◆ Music (musical instruments, and so on)

◆ Background effects

◆ Files under two seconds in real-time play length

After the content has been selected and recorded in a .WAV file, use the VOX Encoder, described previously, to create the .VOX file.

How to Integrate VOX into Your Website

Because VOX is distributed via web servers, all that needs to be done to activate your content is to add appropriate HTML tags, such as

```
<a href="/myfiles/story01.vox">Listen to a dramatic reading from my
➥novel</a>
```

This, however, causes the entire .VOX file to be downloaded prior to playback. To enable streaming, you need to use additional tags (Netscape 2.0 or later). To force the .VOX file to play, for example, after the page is first loaded and to display the player

```
<embed src="/myfiles/story01.vox" playmode=auto visualmode=player
➥height=82 width=160>
```

Playmode options include:

◆ **user:** User must initiate play by clicking on the Voxware icon or the Play button.

◆ **auto:** Playback begins automatically when the web page loads.

◆ **cache:** The entire .VOX file is downloaded. User must click on the Voxware icon or the Play button.

VisualMode options include the following:

◆ **embed:** The player is displayed on the web page.

◆ **player:** Same as embed.

◆ **auto:** Playback begins automatically when web page loads.

◆ **can click:** Users can turn on and off and change replay speed.

◆ **icon:** A Voxware icon is displayed on the web page. Users click on the icon to start and stop.

◆ **background:** Forces sound play; no player or interface on page.

◆ **float:** Player displays in separate window.

VOX Pros and Cons

Voxware presents an inexpensive way to add low-fidelity, voice/speech only, nonlive (prerecorded) audio to your website. Like Macromedia's (`http://www.macromedia.com`) Shockwave, however, Voxware lacks tools for distributing audio streams to large numbers of simultaneous listeners. As mentioned previously, TCP-only streaming has significant retransmission ramifications, and multiple, simultaneous audio streams can rapidly deplete web server resources.

Voxware lacks an SDK with which to create custom interfaces, but its extremely small bandwidth footprint, an estimated 1.3 Kbps, makes it highly suitable for adding voice capability to your website.

Conclusion

Traditional media companies, software manufacturers, and Internet infrastructure providers have high expectations for the long-term impact of the Internet on how entertainment, information, and other media is distributed around the world. Today's technology is embryonic, but everyone wants to be a player. Even though some have arrived late, such as Microsoft, IBM, and Lucent Technologies, their deep pockets should not be ignored—although examples such as Prodigy serve to remind us that deep pockets don't guarantee success.

With Internet video marketshare still limited by a tiny client base of users with adequate bandwidth, streaming audio dominates Internet multimedia. Progressive Network's RealAudio has the largest installed base of players and a strong following. Xing Streamworks MPEG-based technology has always been promising, although its installed base of players has lagged.

Macromedia has great multimedia development tools; Shockwave, however, suffers from a lack of high-end delivery and stream management tools.

Development of new players, servers, and streaming standards continue to be volatile and highly competitive. The technology companies involved are in the race for the long term, and the battle for technology marketshare will only grow more fierce as time goes by.

C H A P T E R

6

FILE/FORMAT CONVERSIONS

*If you have read chapters 2 though 5, you realize that many audio
formats are in use on the Internet and elsewhere. Some, such as
WAVE, AIFF, and RealAudio, are in widespread use across the audio
and computer communities, whereas others are proprietary and
highly specialized. Some are streaming, whereas others are static.
Some are for files on hard disks, whereas others are tape formats. No
matter what your application—be it new-age music or a weather
report—it is almost certain you will eventually need to convert
between some of these formats.*

Conversion between audio formats, both analog and digital, is the focus of this chapter. This chapter does not get into the details of why you should pick one format over another, because this is covered in some detail in Chapters 2 through 5. Instead, this chapter examines both practical conversion techniques and the underlying theory.

Conversion could involve a simple mode change in the same format. For example, you might need to convert a large 44.1 KHz, 16-bit WAVE file into a much smaller 22.050 KHz, 8-bit WAVE file. Conversion can also involve two different formats, such as WAVE and AIFF, between which there are potential incompatibilities.

Conversion is often as simple as the click of a mouse button. It can also be an elaborate process involving multiple iterations, several software packages, and audio hardware. Each of these methods is examined in this chapter, along with reasons for using them.

The meat of this chapter is divided between two sections. The first, "Conversion Methods," defines three practical methods of conversion between audio formats. The second section, "The Theory of Format Conversions," digs into some of the technical details of conversion, and explains why certain types of conversion have limitations.

Conversion Methods

In this section, three methods for performing format conversion are examined, each in its own subsection. The first method, Simple Conversion, discusses the use of a software utility designed specifically for format conversion. This is the simplest of the three methods. It is often adequate for many conversions, but it does have its limitations, as shall be explained in that topic paragraph.

The second method, Editing and Saving, takes conversion a step further and examines the use of audio editing tools (such as those described in Chapter 11, "Digital Audio Recording and Editing") as format converters. This is usually the preferred method for conversion because it allows changes and enhancements to be made to the audio during the conversion process.

When all else fails, the third method, Brute Force Conversions, can be used. This is actually a collection of techniques that can be used when conversion software is not available. It is the least preferred of the methods because it requires audio hardware, but it may be the only practical alternative when dealing with audio tapes or proprietary audio file formats.

Simple Conversion

Audio file format conversion utilities are widely available as freeware, shareware, or bundled with commercial audio production packages. To convert between formats, all that is needed is to supply the program with the location of the source file and to define the format of the destination file. The utility does the rest automatically. This is the simplest and easiest of the conversion methods discussed in this chapter.

Note

Two Audio Format Conversion Utilities

On a sunny Sunday afternoon, I decided to see what conversion utilities were available on the Internet. A brief search netted two such programs that are shown here as examples. These are Mac applications.

The first conversion utility I found is ConvertMachine by Rod Kennedy. It automatically recognizes the input format. You specify the output format by starting ConvertMachine, and use the Settings menu to specify format, sampling rate and other parameters. After that, you simply drag and drop the source file onto the ConvertMachine icon. This utility supports AIFF, WAVE, AU, Mac OS, and QuickTime formats. Various modes and compression methods are supported within these formats. Overall, this appears to be a friendly and useful program, well worth its $10 shareware registration fee. Its main limitation is that it cannot play the sounds, but Mr. Kennedy has a companion program, SoundMachine, for that purpose (for an extra $10). The home page for both SoundMachine and ConvertMachine is

http://www.anutech.com.au/tprogram/Software_ANUTech/welcome.html

The second utility is SoundApp by Norman Franke. SoundApp both plays and converts files. The list of input file formats is long and impressive, including WAVE, AU, AIFF, VOC (Sound Blaster), Sound Designer II, MOD, and others. Unfortunately the output format list is not nearly so long or impressive, including only WAVE, AIFF, NeXT, System 7 Sound, and Sound Suitcase. The

continues

interface is good; it supports a drag-and-drop motif. In my opinion, though, it is not quite as friendly as the less complex interface used for ConvertMachine. Even so, SoundApp is a well-designed, useful conversion utility for many applications. It is freeware, and can be found at

`http://www-cs-students.stanford.edu/~franke/SoundApp/index.html`

These conversion utilities are useful for conversion between similar formats or between different modes in the same format. They perform some (or all) of the following functions:

◆ Changing header format and content

◆ Transferring data, perhaps changing number system and addressing methods

◆ Truncating data, if going to a shorter word length

◆ Reducing or increasing sample rate

◆ Implementing an anti-alias filtering, if reducing the sample rate

◆ Interpolating new samples, if increasing sample rate

This list shows that the conversion utility has a lot of work to do. The utility does it all, without help from the user. Herein lies both the strength and the potential limitation of this method of format conversion. Very little effort is required on the part of the user; however, the user also has very little control over the conversion process.

Consider, for example, a conversion within the same format (WAVE, for example), in which the only change is to go from 16-bit word length data to 8-bits. What if the conversion utility simply picked the upper or low 8 bits of the 16-bit sample as the new 8-bit sample? This could cause soft passages in the audio to disappear, or loud passage to cause severe overloading.

A more sophisticated conversion utility might automatically adjust the gain to fit everything nicely into an 8-bit format. What happens, though, if the results are still not what you, the user, really wanted? These utilities are a take-it-or-leave-it proposition.

Fortunately, more often than not, the conversion utilities do a reasonably good job. On the occasions they don't, something more powerful is needed. This leads into the next topic, the use of audio-editing tools to perform format conversions. This method offers much more flexibility than the simple conversion method, at the expense of requiring that the user do a little more work.

Editing and Saving

The editing-and-saving method involves the use of audio-editing software to perform a format conversion, and optionally to modify the audio. The basic steps are as follows:

1. Import the source file into the editing program.

2. Perform any desired changes, such as equalization or the addition of special effects (reverb, echo, flanging, and so on).

3. Use the editing software's Export or Save-As function to create a destination file of the desired format.

The software must support both the source and destination formats. Editing and saving is the most sophisticated way to convert because it allows the most flexibility. Compression, equalization, and other signal processing functions can be applied to achieve desired effects and reduce adverse effects of the format conversion process.

The editing-and-saving method is useful when you don't have a conversion utility that supports the desired source and destination formats; when you want to merge several files; or when you want to modify or enhance the audio beyond just a simple format conversion.

Using Session™ for Format Conversion

This example shows how to convert between formats using Digidesign's Session audio editing software. This is done on the Mac version, but a Windows version is also available. Similar methods can be used with other audio editing tools, although the details vary from program to program. In this example, a WAVE (.WAV) file is used to create an equivalent AIFF format file. The steps are as follows:

◆ Session is started. A new editing session is created using the New Session command under the File menu. Session asks for a session name. "Converter" is used, but any unique name works just as well. After clicking the Save button, the Transport and Edit windows appears, indicating that Session is ready to edit Converter. (For those not familiar with this tool, these windows look like CD-player controls and oscilloscope displays, respectively.)

◆ Next, the Import Audio File command under the File menu is clicked. A dialog box appears that can be used to select one or an entire list of files to be imported. In this example, only one is picked, a WAVE file named TEST.WAV. Session automatically recognizes it as a WAVE file and knows the word length (16 bits) and the sampling rate (22.05 KHz). The Add button is clicked to add TEST.WAV to the list. The Finished button is clicked to tell Session that the import list is complete. Session imports the data from TEST.WAV, converting it into Session's internal format.

◆ Session doesn't automatically pull the converted file(s) into the editing window. This must be done manually by grabbing the file from the play list (located on the right side of the Edit window) using the mouse, and pulling it onto a track. It can be placed anywhere on any track. If other files had been imported, they can be placed on the same track before or after the audio from TEST.WAV, or they can be placed on other tracks.

◆ This capability to merge and manipulate audio data from different files demonstrates the power of using an editing tool for format conversions. Session can be used at this point for elaborate editing, including data manipulations, equalization, and other functions. Because this example is a simple format conversion, no such editing is done.

◆ The Solo button is pressed on the track containing the information from TEST.WAV. This makes the track active. Next, the Bounce Track command under the File menu is clicked. This brings up a menu that allows selection of the format of the bounce (output) file, the sampling rate, word length, and several other options. AIFF, 22.050 KHz sampling rate, and 16-bit words are selected. After clicking the OK button, a dialog box appears asking for the name of the bounce file and where to put it. TEST.AIFF is entered for the name, a folder is selected, and the OK button is clicked.

◆ Session creates the TEST.AIFF file as instructed. The Converter session is now abandoned, because it has no further use. TEST.AIFF is now tested by playing it through several audio players. It functions properly in all cases.

This example might seem like a lot of steps just to convert between two formats, but it's really very easy after you go through it a few times. Similar results can be obtained with other audio editing tools.

Converting with Cool Edit

Cool Edit is a hot digital sound editor for Windows. It supports many formats, including WAVE, raw audio, AIFF, AU and VOC. It also supports plug-in filter programs that expand the capabilities of the basic Cool Edit program. Filters are currently available for RealAudio, DiamondWare and MPEG. Compression and sound effects are supported during editing. Cool Edit is high-end shareware, competing with many commercial packages. Its home page is

```
http://www.syntrillium.com/cool.htm
```

Brute Force Conversion

The techniques described so far (simple conversion and editing and saving) are fine when software is available that supports both the source and destination formats. The following techniques should help you when you need to work with an odd file format or when you're dealing with digital or analog audio tape.

Complex Conversion

If you don't have a single piece of software that can do the complete conversion job, maybe you can accomplish the same thing with several programs. Suppose, for example, that a friend gives you a Sound Designer II (SDII) file, but you need the audio it contains in AU format for your Sounds-of-Unix page. You don't have an SDII-to-AU converter, but you do have an SDII-to-WAVE converter and a WAVE-to-AU converter. Your problem is solved, although it requires two programs to do it. You simply convert from SDII into

WAVE, then convert the WAVE file into AU. Other conversions could be more complex, requiring more than two steps. If you are doing this often, you might want to automate the conversion process using a batch or script file.

Analog-to-Digital and Digital-to-Analog Conversion

If you are dealing with analog audio tapes, vinyl records, or other sources of analog audio, you must convert the audio to digital form before you can store it in a desired digital file format. You need a sound card or the equivalent, audio cables, to connect the sound source to your sound card, and software running on your computer that can record digital audio directly to disk. The audio editing programs already mentioned in this chapter (Session and Cool Edit) are both capable of direct-to-disk recording. Other such programs are discussed in Chapter 11.

Turn off your computer and the analog audio source (the tape recorder, record player, and so on). Connect the audio cables between the line-level outputs of the sound source and the line-level inputs of your audio card. Turn on your computer and the sound source, and load the sound-editing software. Place the software in record mode, then start your analog recorder. You will probably have to experiment to get the levels right. After you have recorded the audio, perform any necessary editing and then save the digital audio in the format of your choice. You might need an additional format conversion utility if your audio editing program does not support the desired format.

Warning

Always make sure that the output of your tape recorder, record player, or other analog audio source is compatible with the audio inputs on your sound card or computer. Never connect outputs intended for driving speakers to your sound card. These outputs have high voltages that could damage your sound card or computer. Use only line-level inputs and outputs.

You can also use this process when going the other way—that is, from a digital audio file format to an analog format. Connect the line-level outputs of your sound card to the analog recorder's line-level inputs. Load audio player software that can read the source format file. Start the analog recorder, then the player. You will probably have to experiment to get the levels correct.

Digital-to-Analog-to-Digital Conversion

Digital-to-analog-to-digital conversion is a brute force technique used for converting between digital audio formats when no format conversion software is available. The digital source is run through a player, thus converting it to analog audio. This audio is then rerecorded using a computer or other recorder that supports the destination format.

Note that this requires either two computers, or a computer and a recorder of some sort. Drawbacks of this method are the need for this extra hardware and the resulting addition of noise due to the conversion processes.

The advantage is that this might be your only choice in cases such as the conversion of a tape format to a file format or when you are using a proprietary format that is not well supported with converters and other software.

Aliasing

If any of the techniques just described that use analog audio result in the addition of an odd "swooshing" sound in the output file, you might have an aliasing problem. Aliasing is caused by high frequencies in the audio that are higher than half the sampling rate. This can be prevented by filtering these high frequencies out of the analog audio using an equalizer or low pass filter.

This filtering must be done before the analog audio is converted to digital form. It will not work after the conversion. Aliasing is discussed later in this chapter and also in Chapter 9, "Sound Basics and Audio Theory."

The Theory of Format Conversions

This section examines the concepts of information, data, and compression and how they relate to format conversions. This section gets a bit technical, but it is worth reading if you're having trouble converting between two formats and don't understand why the results don't work as expected.

If you do not have a basic understanding of concepts such as dynamic range, signal-to-noise ratios, dynamic range and aliasing, you should skip ahead and read Chapter 9 before attempting this section.

Information, Data, and Compression

Information is not the same thing as data. *Information* is meaningful content. *Data* is information plus noise, redundancy, and everything else. For example, an odd book that contains nothing but the letter "A" repeated two million times has a lot of data, but very little information. The data in that book is easily *compressed* into a much tighter form. An English phrase such as "A repeated two million times," or a code such as "A:2000000" contains the same information and can be stored in a tiny fraction of the memory or disk space required for uncompressed storage.

Although this example is obviously contrived, real-world data, including audio, also has a certain amount of redundancy. Over the years, algorithms have been developed that can efficiently remove the extraneous data, leaving only the useful information. This process of removing redundancy in data is called *compression*. As a computer user, you are familiar with compression programs such as PKZIP or StuffIt Deluxe and how useful they are in saving disk space or the time it takes to transfer a file over the Internet.

Practical compression algorithms are also widely used in audio work. Many audio formats support compressed and uncompressed modes. Compression is based on removing as much redundancy from the data as possible, while destroying as little of the information as possible.

Tight compression is essential for transmitting sound over the Internet. Static format files take much less time to download when they are tightly compressed. Streaming-format files convey much information in relatively little bandwidth because they are well compressed.

> The concepts of information and data help explain why compression software such as PKZIP or StuffIt can only compress a file so much. When these programs reach the point in which all that is left is pure information, no further compression can occur without the loss of content. How closely these programs actually come to achieving this theoretical limit is a matter of algorithm design and how well hidden the information is in the data.

Special compression algorithms designed for audio, or even for certain narrow types of audio, can achieve better results than these general-purpose programs—and often do it in less time.

Some audio file formats support compression, whereas others do not. AIFF, for example, does not support compression, but AIFF/C does. Thus, it is better to use an AIFF/C format file on your website because it can be much smaller.

Information Loss

Converting between two formats, or applying compression, is either *lossless* or *lossy*. These terms refer to whether information (not data) is lost. If the conversion or compression is lossless, all information in the original audio is preserved. The original audio can be re-created perfectly.

However, if the conversion or compression process is lossy, some information in the original audio is sacrificed. Errors will exist, of course, and these errors usually translate into noise. Almost all audio compression algorithms tolerate a certain amount of loss to gain higher compression.

Because of the relatively low bandwidths of most Internet connections, webmasters usually prefer to post relatively low-resolution, highly compressed audio files. A deliberate sacrifice is made in audio quality to achieve a much smaller file size. This is done by converting original files with high sampling rates, 16-bit words, and multiple tracks into a low-sampling rate, 8-bit mono format wherever possible.

An important point to remember is that *after information is lost, it cannot be recovered!* Remember this when you are preparing audio files for your website. Although the audio file you post should be as small as possible, you should also keep an offline copy of the high quality original. In general, you want to maintain the highest possible quality in any audio you create, until the final step, in which you convert to a lower-quality format. You may need this high quality at a later date for making changes to the audio, or for high-bandwidth applications.

During a format conversion, if both the source and destination formats are uncompressed and support the same word length and sampling rate, the conversion can be lossless. Exceptions exist, however. A format that uses u-law (logarithmic) encoding is inherently noisier than a linear format of the same word length, but the u-law format has a wider dynamic range.

Conversions that reduce word length or sampling rate are always lossy. This leads into the next two topics.

Word Length and SNR

Converting from a 16-bit audio format to an 8-bit audio format causes information loss. Information that made the difference between telephone-quality audio and CD-quality audio is gone forever.

In technical terms, the SNR (signal-to-noise ratio [see Chapter 9]) of digitized audio drops whenever the word length is shortened. The best possible SNR for 8-bit data is approximately 48 DB. It rises to 96 DB for 16-bit data. The best possible SNR for a particular format is approximately equal to the number of bits in the word length times 6.

This SNR of 6 DB per bit is an inherent limit of the format itself. It isn't related to the stored audio, except to serve as an upper limit. For example, suppose that a digital audio source has a 70 DB SNR. This means that the desirable audio is 70 DB stronger than the noise. Suppose that digital audio is then stored in a file using a 16-bit format. Because the maximum possible SNR of the 16-bit format is 96 DB (6×16), the digital audio is not degraded. It retains its 70 DB SNR.

Suppose that this 70 DB digital audio had instead been stored in an 8-bit format. The maximum possible SNR of an 8-bit format is 48 DB. The stored audio would be degraded to this maximum SNR of 48 DB. In practical terms, this means that the 70 DB audio requires at least a 12-bit format to store it without degradation (70/6=11.67). Putting it into an 8-bit format requires truncation and the resulting reduction of SNR.

Now suppose that the 48 DB SNR audio in the 8-bit format file is converted to a 16-bit format. What is the new SNR of the converted audio?

The answer remains 48 DB. Although the maximum possible SNR in a 16-bit file is 96 DB, the actual SNR of the data is never better than the source. During the conversion from the original 70 DB audio to the 8-bit, 48 DB version, some information was lost. This loss is permanent—it cannot be recovered by putting the 8-bit data back into a longer format.

Word Length and Dynamic Range

Word length also determines the dynamic range (see Chapter 9) of a format. Longer formats can support a wider range of loudness levels than can short formats. Faint sounds that can be heard quite distinctly when playing a 16-bit format sound file can be reduced to nothing but a blank spot in an 8-bit format. At the other end of the scale, an 8-bit format also can saturate on very loud sounds. The result is an extremely irritating buzz.

Several techniques can reduce the adverse effects of the smaller dynamic range encountered in short formats. One is to use a "sliding window" during the conversion from the longer format. For example, suppose that a 16-bit audio file is to be converted to an 8-bit format. The simplest approach is to use the upper or lower 8 bits of the 16-bit format (or perhaps something in the middle) to build the 8-bit file. A more sophisticated approach is to allow this 8-bit window to move around, selecting a different 8-bit sequence depending on the signal level. During soft passages, the window moves toward the lowest 8 bits. As the signal becomes stronger, the window moves up.

Some of the more sophisticated format conversion software packages support this moving-window approach or use a similar method to reduce the dynamic range. This can also be done, somewhat more laboriously, with sound-editing software that supports gain automation. In this approach, the fader (gain) level for the audio is manually adjusted to compensate for different loudness levels. The editing software then remembers these settings and uses them as the sound is played back and stored in a short word length format.

Another way of making audio work better in a short format is compression (in the audio sense; see Chapter 10, "Audio Equipment Basics"). The audio is compressed using a hardware compressor/limiter or special software that reduces the dynamic range. This produces better effects than the sliding window method, but it requires more sophisticated processing.

Both the moving window method and the compression method have their limits. The resulting sound is not as pleasing as the original sound with its full dynamic range. Even so, it is far superior to blank spots and loud buzzes.

Sampling Rate and Frequency Response

Dropping the sampling rate also loses information. If done properly, it does not add noise like a reduction in bit length would. Instead, it reduces the high-frequency response, which may be just as bad.

For example, reducing the sampling rate from 44.1 KHz to 22.05 KHz halves the maximum frequency of the audio that can be stored. It drops from 20 KHz to only 10 KHz. See Chapter 9 for a discussion of basic digital audio and how the sampling rate relates to frequency response.

The effects of a reduction in sampling rate cannot be reversed later because the necessary high-frequency information is gone. Converting from a 22.05 KHz sampling-rate format to a 44.1 KHz format does not improve the frequency response of the stored audio; it just pads the extra space with averages of available data points.

Aliasing

Any format conversion that reduces sampling rates introduces the possibility of aliasing (see Chapter 2, "Static (Downloadable) File Formats"). *Aliasing* occurs any time an audio signal contains frequencies that are higher than half the sampling rate. The result can be "swishing," "glimmering," and other undesirable noises that are not in the original audio.

Even if you are not interested in the high frequencies that cause aliasing, the effect occurs. A low-pass anti-aliasing filter must be used to remove these higher frequencies. The pass band of an ideal low-pass filter extends from half the sampling frequency downward to zero. In practice, the pass band is usually set about 10 to 20 percent lower, and a less sharp filter is used to prevent phase distortion (see Chapter 9).

When using a software program to convert an audio file to a reduced sampling rate, the software must perform the anti-aliasing filter function. Note that this works only if the data in the source file is not already aliased. If a digital audio file contains aliased data, an anti-aliasing filter does not remove it.

For this reason, original recordings require the anti-aliasing filter be implemented in hardware before the signal is sampled. A dedicated filter in the digital recorder or a separate equalizer must be used to remove high-frequency components (see figure 6.1).

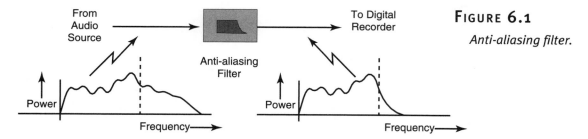

FIGURE 6.1

Anti-aliasing filter.

Summary

Three practical methods of format conversion were presented in this chapter, along with a theoretical discussion of the conversion process. Although some of the theory seems complicated, it becomes second nature as you use it. If you have doubts about this, the best thing to do is to jump in and start experimenting.

When a file containing digital audio data is converted to a different format, information is sometimes lost. If the sampling rate is reduced, the maximum frequency of the stored audio is also reduced. Reducing the word length has the same effect as adding noise. Compressing the audio can also increase the noise, depending on the compression algorithm.

Such losses in quality are not always bad. They are actually desirable for Internet use because they also shrink the file size. This reduces the time required to download an audio file from your Web site. These losses are permanent—you should always keep an offline copy of the original, high-quality audio.

C H A P T E R

7

DISTRIBUTION ARCHITECTURES/ SERVER IMPLICATIONS

When you explore all the options for Net broadcasting—and try to determine which option will outlast your fiscal year—your biggest concern is not necessarily which technology is best. You first need to decide which solution provides the most widely distributed audio player within your target audience.

If you are broadcasting to an internal audience (as in a corporate Intranet), this is a factor you actually have some control over. But if your audience is on the Internet, keep in mind that the bulk of new users connecting to the Net have no idea how to download and install a player—even if it's distributed free of charge. The player that is prebundled on most browsers is probably going to win, although this can change overnight with the release of new browser versions.

The other primary issue is deciding which option provides the lowest cost per listener. The factors in this equation are the following:

◆ The cost, for bandwidth, for each stream.

◆ The cost, for multicasting, of reserving address space on multicast-enabled segments of the Internet.

◆ The cost of each server and its operating system divided by the number of simultaneous connections it can support.

◆ The cost of the audio streaming server software for each server.

◆ The cost of support staff. For example, Windows NT servers may require less experienced support personnel than Unix servers due to the ease of use of the Windows' interface. If you already have staff members who can handle such support, this may be a moot issue.

Table 7.1 shows that the cost per stream often decreases as you benefit from economies of scale. The example does not include tech support staff costs, which can vary depending on which solution you choose. If your organization must support a network (or networks) with high-capacity Internet connections, for example, you need staff who have specialized training and who demand higher salaries. Also, the cost of bandwidth varies widely depending on several factors, including city, proximity to a local fiber loop, and the availability of high-capacity (especially DS3), long-distance circuits out of your city to the Net. (Note the increasing expense of network routers as bandwidth rises.)

TABLE 7.1

AUDIO STREAMING SOFTWARE ANNUAL COST-PER-STREAM ANALYSIS									
Number of Streams	Cumulative Discount	Total Software Cost	# of Servers Needed	Cost of Servers	Band-width Type	Router Costs	Bandwidth (per Year)	1st Year Cost per Stream
10	5%	$950	1	$2,500	ISDN	$800	$1,200	$545
100	10%	$9,000	1	$2,500	T1	$3,000	$12,000	$265
1000	30%	$70,000	2	$5,000	1/4 of DS3	$40,000	$75,000	$190
10000	50%	$500,000	15	$37,500	2.25 DS3s	$80,000	$675,000	$129

You can express your cost per stream in several ways. The one-year approach might not fit your needs; it should, however, give you an idea of the kind of analysis you must perform to competently compute the project's return on investment, fill out your business plan, compute your advertising rates, and do all the number crunching needed to make your enterprise a success.

The one-year approach should also help you decide which of the available technologies is the most cost-effective. If you have narrowed your choices, the cost per stream can be the tie-breaker you need to move your project forward.

General Hardware Considerations

No matter the website sound solution you choose, you are bound to face some hardware considerations that are independent of your operating system or hardware platform. First, hard disk performance is of increasing importance as the amount of content on your site and the number of simultaneous users climbs. The second area of concern surrounds the reliability of your equipment and appropriate precautions regarding backup power supplies for uninterrupted operation.

Hard Disk Storage

Broadcasting audio files requires continuous, long duration, hard disk access against multiple files. Most of today's PCs use an IDE-type controller to manage their hard drive and CD-ROM. Many improvements have been made in the IDE standard that have extended its life and vastly increased its popularity.

IDE hard drive manufacturers often list "burst" (short-term, non-sustained) external transfer rates that go as high as 16 or 17 MBps, but your actual, sustained, heavy-use performance is probably closer to 4 or 5 MBps. If you have many concurrent users who request different audio files, your performance drops due to the limitations of an IDE hard drive's heads to keep up. This can, for example, limit the total number of simultaneous 20 Kbps streams to the very low hundreds or possibly much lower—depending on a variety of factors. These factors include the relative size (length) of your content and the distribution pattern by which your listeners access files of different sizes.

High-performance PCs and servers have long used the more robust SCSI format. A standard FAST SCSI-2 controller can control up to seven internal SCSI or SCSI-2 devices and seven external SCSI or SCSI-2 devices, for a total of 14 devices. A multichannel SCSI card can handle as many as 30 devices. In recent years, manufacturers have made SCSI vastly easier to install and support, and it has remained a standard in high-end equipment. 16-bit FAST-SCSI-2 has a base external transfer rate of 20 MBps. Multichannel Wide SCSI has a base transfer rate of 40 MBps. Adaptec's (http://www.adaptec.com) 3940UW for the Power Mac supports up to 30 devices and has a transfer rate up to 80 MBps. If that isn't fast enough, FiberChannel can boost data transfer rates to a blazing 100 MBps.

For the ultimate in overall performance and reliability, a RAID drive array cannot be beat. Several recognized RAID levels include the following:

◆ **RAID 0**   Data spread across all attached drives. No fault tolerance.

◆ **RAID 1**   Data on one disk is *replicated*, or mirrored, on a second disk. Can also apply to multiple disks being replicated on the same number of alternate disks. If a disk fails, the controller uses the other drive for data recovery and continues operation. Provides good data protection and fast performance.

◆ **RAID 2**   Not available on file-server-level commercial systems.

◆ **RAID 3**   Data is *striped* across two or more drives. A separate drive stores the parity information, which can be used for data reconstruction in the event of a drive failure. If the parity drive fails, however, some array systems face serious problems. Provides very good performance and reliability.

◆ **RAID 5**   Similar to RAID 3, except data is transferred via independent read/writes (not parallel), and the parity information is spread across all the drives, with no separate parity drive. If configured with a hot-spare, RAID 5 systems automatically repair themselves—with a configurable performance hit during rebuild. Performance is a little slower than RAID 3, however; when configured with a hot-spare, this approach is more fault-tolerant.

For your audio server, configure a RAID 3 or RAID 5 configuration for optimal performance and reliability. Some drive array systems have optional, hot-pluggable power supplies and even hot-pluggable controller cards. Storage capacities range from double-digit gigabytes to the terabyte range. If you begin with the best controller cards and software, you can continue to add capacity almost indefinitely.

Naturally, these options increase the cost of the array system. As with any risk analysis, you must weigh the costs of system down time against the cost of reliable hardware and software.

CPU Cabinet

If your system will be running continuously and down time is not an option, ensure that the CPU cabinet has at least two internal cooling fans. If the system has only one fan (which might cost two dollars) and that fan dies, your computer can literally cook itself to death. If the computer does not come with two fans, consider adding another one or installing a FanCard (http://www.asiansources.com./tsmicro.co).

One more thing about CPU cabinets: If you are a hobbyist (or if you work from home), you should consider the answer to the following question: Do you have kids? If you place your computer on the floor, the power switch is probably at the perfect height for toddlers or other hazards. Some cabinets have a door or piece of plastic that slides down to shield the switches from accidental use. If yours does not, you might want to consider improvising one or moving your server to a safer altitude.

Equipment Warranty and Support

If you are part of a large corporation that has a large technical staff and corporate computer support agreements, you might not need to worry as much about computer warranties and service. If you are with a small company, a startup company, or are a hobbyist, the issue hits closer to your wallet. In any case, the first question you should ask yourself is this: How much system down time can I afford?

Your servers, like any complicated equipment, eventually need service. Count on it. Would you want to buy a big screen TV that required you to find the original packing material, ship it back to the manufacturer, and wait for weeks or even months to have it repaired? That's not unusual in the PC world. Even if you purchase your computer from a retail store, it might only have a 30 day in-store warranty. After that, the manufacturer warranty takes over. Some manufacturers provide on-site warranties, but the terms may vary depending on what and when you buy. For example, it might cover the CPU and not the monitor.

Ask for the fine print. What does the warranty cover and not cover? What about returns? Some stores charge a hefty restock fee if you bring the computer back for a refund. After you figure out what kind of computer you want, shop around and compare warranties. You might want to consider extended or store warranties. Some stores charge you $60–70 for an extra year or two of warranty. It might be worth it, but where will the repairs take place, and will they happen any faster than if you do not shell out the extra cash? In addition, what happens if they do not repair it within the time stated? Is there a time period stated? Are there penalties, and do you have recourse?

Does the warranty state that parts will be replaced with new, rather than used parts? Does the warranty cover labor and parts? Most cover both up to a cutoff point. Then you pay for labor to a second cutoff. After that, you are on your own. Even companies that offer two or three year on-site warranties often bill you for a trip charge of at least $100.

If you cannot afford down time, look for a manufacturer that offers a four-hour response time service agreement. This costs you a few hundred dollars a year, but the manufacturer commits to stockpile parts and usually brings complete new motherboards, cards, hard drives, and so on and simply swaps out—rather than attempting to repair—the suspect components.

If you are spending only two or three thousand dollars on your system, you simply might want to buy two of them and stick the second unit in a closet as a backup unit.

Uninterruptable/Backup Power Supplies

Perhaps even more important than the warranty is what you plug your multithousand-dollar investment into. Computer equipment can be damaged or destroyed by surges, spikes, dips, and other electric power anomalies. If you plug a power analyzer into your AC socket, you will probably be distressed to see how much your power fluctuates. This fluctuation can be caused by turning on a washing machine, the air conditioner, a power saw in the garage, and so forth. In an office, surges are caused by copier machines, AC units, and any number of other types of heavy equipment and equipment operated by other tenants.

The power can even fluctuate before it gets to your building. The reasons power can be disrupted are myriad: storms; ice; wind; birds; animals; cars running into telephone poles; cars running into high power transmission lines, knocking the high power lines onto residential lines; and so on.

"OK," you say, "So my power is not safe. What do I do about it?" The first thing is to invest in $10 surge suppresser power strips and make sure any electrical equipment is plugged into them or ground-fault-protected AC outlets. If your building is struck by lightning, and it does not have a lightning protection system, the powerful surge will probably fry anything not plugged into a protected circuit. These surges have been known to blow air conditioning control boxes off walls, blow out televisions, and more. Usually, even a $10 surge suppresser protects your equipment, which is pretty cheap insurance (although it is not 100 percent effective). (By the way, if this happens to you, throw away your surviving surge protectors. They might appear to work, but they have probably lost the capability to protect your equipment.)

Surge protectors are last-ditch protection against catastrophic power surges; however, even at that task, they are not completely effective. For your server equipment, you need a more effective solution, one that includes keeping your equipment running even during a power outage. When you buy your computer or server, you should also buy a backup or uninterruptable power supply (UPS).

Recommended UPS suppliers include the following:

◆ Carrollton, Texas-based Para Systems, Inc. (http://www.minuteman-ups.com/) makes the MinuteMan line of UPSs.

◆ Necedah, Wisconsin-based Best Power (http://www.bestpower.com/) a unit of General Signal Power Systems, Inc., manufactures a wide range of UPS products, including the highly regarded premium line of Fortress UPSs.

◆ West Kingston, Rhode Island-based American Power Conversion (APC) (http://www.apcc.com/) produces a highly successful line of power protection products that are widely available in retail computer outlets.

Basically, UPSs are rechargeable batteries with automatic switches. When the power drops, dips, or spikes, the UPS continues to send your PC clean power by switching you to the battery. When the AC power stabilizes (assuming your battery does not run out first), you are switched back to the regular AC feed. More expensive models provide continuous, uninterrupted power (instead of switching to the battery when a problem is detected). The switching versions are often good enough for basic protection needs; however, the more expensive models do protect against a more diverse set of electrical problems.

Which UPS is the most appropriate for your needs? More to the point, how long do you want the UPS to keep your computer, router, and so on running in the event of a power outage? If your answer is several hours, you have narrowed your selection of UPSs to the higher end of the market, and the UPS will probably be in the $800 to $2,500 range. If you need to maintain power longer than that, you probably need to buy a backup power generator.

A few other things you should remember about power protection include the following:

◆ Power surges can travel along computer cables, such as printer or modem cables. That means your printers, modems, and so forth should be plugged into your UPS or power strip.

◆ The telephone lines going into your modem or fax machine should be routed through a surge protector that includes modular jacks for telephone and fax lines. Power surges can travel down telephone wires through your modem and zap your computer.

◆ Do not plug your printer into the same UPS as your computer. Most people do not need to print during a power outage, so you might want to leave your printer on a good-quality surge protector or separate, low-end UPS. Printers pull a lot of power and dramatically shorten the battery life of your UPS, often bringing down your entire system in seconds rather than the minutes or hours your computer would have otherwise stayed up.

Computers Near Windows and Floor Mats

All computer equipment and peripherals are sensitive to static electricity, even in small amounts. Hard plastic floor mats are notorious for generating static electricity. If you use floor mats, you should regularly spray them with antistatic spray or replace them with nonstatic mats that have conductive filaments embedded in them with a ground wire. If you do not take this precaution, your computer equipment or peripherals can become damaged if you touch them while they are "charged" with static electricity.

Computers located near windows are often subject to higher levels of static discharge than PCs located away from windows—especially in high-rise buildings in dry climates. In these areas, it is wise to treat the floor with an antistatic spray. You can also purchase a small keyboard mat that has a ground wire attached to it. The idea is that when you rest your wrists on the mat, you are grounded.

The problem with static electricity is real. Static discharge on computer equipment (the result of a person walking across a room and touching the CPU cabinet) is a low-cost-to-avoid, high-consequence problem that should never come between you and your audience.

Server and Network Implications for Streamed or Static Content

Static audio formats, such as .WAV files, have a lot in common with streaming formats that depend on HTTP-web servers. Web servers are designed to handle multiple, simultaneous users who request HTML documents and associated graphics—most of which are relatively small. After the files are sent, the web server resource is made available for the next client.

Non-server-based streaming audio, as well as static downloadable formats, do not close web server resources until the file has finished streaming or downloading. This situation can quickly choke a web server's capability of handling additional requests. As a consequence, these formats probably perform best in low- to medium-volume environments.

Although it will not necessarily increase the number of supportable listeners, setting up a dedicated web server to handle audio files frees up your primary web servers to handle standard HTML traffic. Response time on your regular web traffic substantially improves (unless the audio is consuming all your bandwidth), and the administration of HTML updates and audio file updates is simplified by virtue of being on separate machines.

Distributing static or streaming audio with a web server substantially increases the server horsepower requirements. Failure to compensate for the increased load may likely result in significant performance reduction, and in some cases, increased server instability. Depending on the amount of audio traffic, requisite upgrades can include processor or multiprocessor upgrades—and additional memory.

How much RAM do you need, and how fast does the processor need to be? Regardless of the audio server software you run or the platform it runs on, the equipment you'll need will probably be in the mid to high range of what is available. Microsoft's NetShow, for example, requires as a *minimum* a 90 MHz Pentium with 32 MB of RAM running one of the Microsoft operating systems. Xing Streamworks runs on Windows, Macintosh, or X-Windows platforms on Intel, Mac, SGI, Sun Sparc, and Linux boxes. RealAudio runs on Macs, PowerMacs, DEC Alphas, HP RISC boxes, Intel Pentium, Sun Sparc, and SGI boxes running a litany of operating systems.

These platforms have a few things in common, including the following:

◆ Adequate processor performance

◆ High-performance hard disk input/output

◆ High-performance network interface input/output

Processor requirements are specified by the software manufacturer, although sometimes the recommendations are a bit lower than is realistic. Hard disk performance that leaves the network interface was discussed earlier in the section "Hard Disk Storage".

Assuming that you have adequate network bandwidth (see Chapter 13, "Bandwidth and Cost Considerations"), you need to make sure your server(s) can maximize the delivery of your audio content to the available bandwidth. For example, if you have a 45 MBps, DS3 connection, it would be foolish to install 10BaseT (10 MBps) network interface cards in your server(s). In this scenario, the obvious choice is to use the next step up: 100BaseT or one of the competing standards.

Other issues to be aware of include competing network protocols on your LAN. If at all possible, you should segment your LAN to maximize the amount of bandwidth you are willing to commit to your audio streams. This means that other traffic, such as Netbui, IPX, or AppleTalk, should be on a different

LAN segment than your audio servers, which would optimally have a clean, IP-only segment with a straight connection to the port on your switch or router, and beyond.

Note

The maintenance and support of high-speed, high-performance networks requires careful attention to the design, layout, and implementation of your network infrastructure. The expertise to perform these tasks well can be hard to find and, in many cases, expensive. Conversely, without this expertise, your mistakes can be even more costly in terms of poor network performance, disappointing service to your listeners, lost support from your advertisers and sponsors, lost revenue, and lost opportunities.

Multicasting

Multicasting is a technological understudy that might soon have an opportunity to enter the main Internet broadcasting stage. (See Chapter 13 for a complete discussion on multicasting.) As the core network bandwidth providers and ISPs figure out how to cope with the changes that widespread multicasting brings, you might be faced with planning for that uncertain future.

How much will the choices you make today affect your future viability in a multicasting world? A great deal, if your software provider isn't prepared to support that environment *before* it becomes widespread. If you are not sure of the effect, ask your prospective software manufacturers. Will they support RSVP or any of the multicasting implementations making the rounds? Hopefully, they will support any or all of them. If not, they had better have a convincing explanation, or you might want to seriously consider voting with your feet and going elsewhere.

In general, as multicasting hits the Net and evolves, there will probably be a significant period of coexistence with unicasting (with unicasting remaining dominant in the face of the growing multicasting rollout). Eventually, multicasting will likely outstrip unicasting as the dominant distribution mechanism for streaming multimedia, with unicasting continuing to survive to service remaining nonmulticasting-enabled portions of the Net.

It remains to be seen how you will manage, bill for, and be billed for the use of multicasting resources, and, as mentioned earlier, that is part of the reason for its slow acceptance and implementation. Chances are, multicasting resources will not make your job any easier, and unless you are very lucky, it promises to be a complex administrative task for organizations to track and validate charges. If multicasting "islands" somehow report back to your server their usage, the maintenance and analysis of your server logs will take on heightened—even crucial—importance to your organization. This increased database support might require some organizations to establish high-performance, relational databases to monitor the logs and make sure these remote services are not overbilling.

Of critical concern to those being billed for multicasting reservations is the possibility of illegitimate use of the multicasting addresses for which they have paid. It would be an easier challenge to hijack these ports and addresses than to tunnel into an organization's bandwidth and send streams back out through its pipes. In any event, those providing multicasting services will face a significant challenge in securing these resources.

Multicasting proponents gratefully embrace the promise of a reduced need for large bandwidth pipes to Net broadcaster facilities. Instead of maintaining these high-capacity connections, they look forward to allowing the ISPs and MCIs of the world to worry about the stream distribution and simply waiting for the multicasting reservation monthly bill.

Reality will probably be somewhere between that picture and where you are today. You will probably continue to need significant amounts of bandwidth (for unicasting purposes) for a long time to come. Therefore, it appears that your bandwidth investment of today will not be in vain. On the contrary, if the familiar pattern of technological innovation continues, something else will expand to fill the void.

What are the server implications for multicasting? Stay the course, and be prepared to continue unicasting in transition to a future dominated by multicasting and other new technologies.

Firewalls

Corporate firewalls pose a significant challenge to all websites, sound-enabled or not. For example, some firewalls are configured to filter out Java applications. The promise is that any website feature that is perceived as unnecessarily consuming corporate bandwidth resources will be filtered out. After all, corporate networks are not a public resource; they are bought by the company for official company business. Excessive web traffic on company local area networks can hurt productivity and result in lost jobs and loss of stockholder confidence.

Firewalls can also prevent employees from receiving valuable information or services. For example, attending a conference by listening to it over the Internet can actually save a company money and *increase* productivity.

How do you reconcile the legitimate need for responsibly conserving corporate network bandwidth with the real and perceived value of taking advantage of various Internet broadcasts and other resources? This question is reminiscent of the early days of personal computers when MIS organizations argued that users could do anything they needed on dumb terminals connected to central computers, running centrally maintained and controlled programs. PCs were toys people used to play games instead of do work.

No easy answers can be found, and many pitched battles between the self-proclaimed forces of employee freedom and the priestly protectors of corporate resources will occur. Meanwhile, streaming multimedia software manufacturers are working closely with firewall manufacturers to make their products more firewall-friendly, and at the same time, adding client features that help users bypass firewall problems.

For example, one of the issues facing software manufacturers is how to allow clients to send status updates back to the server, with instructions such as stop and restart. Clients attempt to send these update packets to one or more of a range of port addresses. This can conflict with the security built into firewalls; thus, the software manufacturers are working with the firewall manufacturers to establish mutually agreeable standards.

Dominating Platforms of Internet Multimedia

Before you jump to the usual conclusion that the dominant platform has to include Sun, Unix, or SGI, think again. These popular platforms play a crucial role in Internet multimedia, but many have overlooked another platform—one now beginning to be called *Wintel* (short for Windows/Intel and, in the case of Internet multimedia, Windows NT and Intel).

Indeed, Wintel servers have been so successful at chewing away at the traditional Unix workstation market that companies such as Silicon Graphics have been working hard to revamp their server lines to better compete with the NT onslaught.

The relatively low cost of the Intel platform and the ease of use of Windows NT's familiar Windows interface create a low-cost combination in hardware, software, and training that is hard to beat. Organizations are finding it easier and less expensive to operate and maintain Wintel servers than their counterparts such as Silicon Graphic's Indy or similar workstations.

The nature of the Internet, with its thousands of websites and an ever-growing population of audio broadcasters, makes the prospect of quantifying an answer to who dominates Internet multimedia almost as difficult as trying to figure out how many people are actually *on* the Internet, a topic that could itself easily be the subject of an entire book.

The competition is fierce, and it increasingly includes Microsoft and Intel. For example, AudioNet (`http://www.AudioNet.com`) is, many times over, the largest broadcast network on the Internet. AudioNet uses Intel Pentium and Pentium Pro computers running Windows NT on its huge network of servers located around the world. For those who have not taken the Wintel platform seriously for Internet multimedia, this is a bold statement about the effectiveness and viability of this Microsoft/Intel combination.

Keeping Your Upgrade Path Clear

No matter which hardware and software platform you choose, one thing is certain—it will soon be obsolete. When planning which hardware you'll use, make sure that you take the opportunity to configure enough extra capacity to exceed your growth expectations. Upgrading in-production systems is often time consuming and disruptive to your operations. Worse, delaying upgrades to avoid service disruption can lead to performance problems and can degrade the quality of your broadcasts.

When the time comes to perform an upgrade, plan it in advance of when it is really needed. If you wait to increase capacity or speed until after you need it, your operations will suffer during the period of time that your systems are overloaded. Mistakes are often made when upgrades are performed under stressful situations, such as when the network or system is already overloaded.

When upgrade plans are combined with other proactive network and organizational strategies, the stress level is lowered and more time is available for advance system testing and configuration. The extra time will also provide an opportunity to more thoroughly explore new features, technologies, and capabilities.

C H A P T E R

8

MIDI

If you want to post instrumental music on your website, consider

MIDI. Maybe all you want to do is brighten up your home page with a

little background music. Or maybe you are a musician or a composer

and want to feature your musical creations as the centerpiece of your

site. MIDI provides an efficent means of accomplishing either goal.

MIDI, the *Musical Instrument Digital Interface*, began as a serial interface bus designed to connect electronic musical instruments with each other and to computers. First proposed in the early 1980s, MIDI has since grown into the music-industry standard for this purpose.

Now the term MIDI also refers to a file format (usually with the .MID extension) that can be used to store MIDI command codes as might be found on a MIDI bus. These files can be used to control a MIDI-compatible system with synthesizers, samplers, and other MIDI devices. These devices emulate musical instruments of various types and are discussed in more detail later in the section "MIDI-Compatible Hardware and Software."

Of more importance to most Internet users, MIDI files can also be played by using a *MIDI player*, which is a software program that mimics musical instruments. Such players are almost universally available. They come bundled with sound cards for PCs. They also come as an operating system extension for the Mac or as plug-ins for web browsers, such as Netscape.

MIDI files are widely used on the Internet to distribute instrumental music. These files are compact and require no special server software. They can be posted on a website like any other binary file and downloaded for playing. Web browsers, if properly configured, automatically call up a MIDI player when a MIDI file is downloaded.

MIDI files do have their limitations. They support only instrumental music, not vocals or nonmusical audio. The next section, "MIDI Files," discusses the reasons for this.

This chapter examines the MIDI bus, the hardware it supports, and MIDI files. Topics include the following:

◆ The MIDI file and how it is used

◆ Strengths and weaknesses of MIDI files

◆ The MIDI bus and MIDI-compatible hardware

◆ Creating a MIDI file

MIDI Files

MIDI provides a powerful way to create and distribute instrumental music on the Internet. MIDI-compatible hardware and software are widely available for creating music and MIDI files.

A major strength of MIDI files is their compact size. The Classical MIDI Archives (`http://www.prs.net/midi.html`), a large, award-winning website, boasts over 3,000 MIDI song files. This totals 80 megabytes (MB), or an average of only 26.7 kilobytes (KB) per file. Although 80 MB is a lot of data, it's only enough to store about 7.6 minutes of uncompressed, CD-quality audio. The files on this site represent many hours of music. A single selection, picked at random from the Mozart page, ran for 1,242.5 seconds (over 20 minutes), and yet required only 100 KB of disk space.

The secret of a MIDI file's compactness is that it contains no audio. Instead, it is a sequence of commands containing instructions on how to generate music—electronic sheet music of a sort. Calling it sheet music oversimplifies it a bit, but states an essentially correct concept.

Ironically, a MIDI file's greatest strength (its compactness) is also its most severe limitation. Because it stores only musical notes and other commands and not audio, it cannot be used to generate arbitrary sounds. A MIDI file cannot be used to transmit a news or stock market report, or even the vocal portion of a song. MIDI is useful for instrumental music only. To record or distribute something else, you need to use an audio format. Audio formats are discussed in detail in Chapters 2 through 5.

The commands in a MIDI file must be interpreted by hardware or software that can translate those commands into audio. The sheet music analogy holds true. Sheet music can graphically represent the instrumental portion of a song. For the music to be heard, however, the sheet music's directives must be played on one or more musical instruments. The sheet music itself is not sound, just as a MIDI file is not audio. When you think of MIDI, think of electronic sheet music.

This raises an interesting (and crucial) point about MIDI. Like sheet music, MIDI commands can be interpreted in many different ways. Although a MIDI-formatted song may have been composed for one set of musical instruments, nothing prevents playing it on entirely different instruments. (The *instruments* in this case are synthesized, not actual instruments.) A song written for a piano, snare drums, and a flute might be played on an electric guitar, bongo drums, and an oboe. The interpreted result can differ greatly from the original, and may or may not be pleasing to the ear.

A MIDI player, synthesizer, or sampler supports various patches. A *patch* is a setup that creates the characteristic sounds of a musical instrument such as a piano or guitar. The term patch comes from early synthesizers; patch cords (audio cables) were used to connect various tone generators and effects generators to create a specific sound. Physical connections such as these are no longer necessary because the processing is done digitally, but the term has lingered.

MIDI has 128 *patch numbers* or *programs*, which are codes that identify musical instruments. A *patch map* is a table used by a MIDI device to determine which instrument sound is assigned to which patch number. A patch map may assign program 17 to a drawbar organ, for example, program 31 to a distortion guitar, and program 42 to a viola.

Originally, there were no standards defining which patch number should correspond to what instrument. The need for this and other standards led to the creation of the General MIDI standard, which is the next topic.

General MIDI

A MIDI file does not define what a program is. It does not say, for example, that program 42 should be a viola. This was a major problem in early MIDI applications; nothing guaranteed that a work written for specific instruments would be played on those same instruments.

The *General MIDI* (GM) specification (see the [INTMIDI] reference at the end of this chapter) was written to address this problem and other MIDI-standardization issues. Among other things, it defines a set of standard programs. The following table summarizes these programs.

TABLE 8.1

GENERAL MIDI PATCH MAP SUMMARY

Program Numbers	Instrument Types	Examples
1–8	Pianos	1=Acoustic Grand, 7=Harpsichord
9–16	Chromatic Percussion	10=Glockenspiel, 14=Xylophone
17–24	Organs	19=Rock Organ, 23=Harmonica
25–32	Guitars	25=Acoustic Guitar (Nylon)
33–40	Bass	33=Acoustic Bass
41–48	Strings	41=Violin, 43=Cello
49–56	String Ensemble	49=String Ensemble 1
57–64	Brass	57=Trumpet, 61=French Horn
65–72	Reed	65=Soprano Sax
73–80	Pipe	73=Piccolo, 76=Pan Flute
81–88	Syth Lead	81=Lead 1, 82=Lead 2
89–96	Synth Pad	89=Pad 1 (New Age)
97–104	Synth Effects	97=FX 1 (Rain), 102=FX 6 (Goblins)
105–112	Ethnic	105=Sitar, 106=Banjo, 111=Fiddle
113–120	Percussive	113=Tinkle Bell, 116=Woodblock
121–128	Sound Effects	123=Seashore, 126=Helicopter

As shown in the table, GM defines a total of 128 musical instruments and sound effects. Although no single list could contain all musical instruments, the set provided by the GM patch map is more than adequate for playing most musical works.

Almost all MIDI players, including popular packages for the PC and Mac, support the GM patch map, or at least a subset. You can use a different patch map than that defined in GM, but it's not a good idea for use on the Internet. Songs based on a non-GM patch map will probably not be played correctly. Most people downloading MIDI files do not have the knowledge, or even the software, to use anything other than the GM-compatible patch map built into the MIDI player that comes with their sound card.

Exceptions occur, of course. If you are creating a website aimed at musicians, you can expect a more sophisticated user of your MIDI files. You might want to post not only MIDI files, but samples of musical instruments you have defined. The later section, "Samplers," discusses the use of samples and MIDI samplers.

MIDI Audio Quality

The title of this section is an oxymoron. MIDI has nothing to do with the basic tonal quality of the audio it can be used to generate. The same MIDI file can be played on a crude player with noisy 8-bit audio, or on an elaborate arrangement of MIDI synthesizers and samplers that produce brilliant highs, rich mid-ranges and thundering bass. Whether a bass drum sounds like something off your best CD or a soup spoon thumping on an oatmeal box is not a MIDI function.

Again, the sheet music analogy applies. The Boston Pops Orchestra is going to sound a lot better than the marching band at the local junior high school, even though both groups are playing the same piece of music.

Of course, the quality of the composition itself is important too. Even the best MIDI system cannot make an uninspired or downright bad song sound good.

MIDI-Compatible Hardware and Software

If you are merely posting a few existing MIDI files to your website, you need no special hardware other than your computer. MIDI files can be uploaded and downloaded like other binary files. As was mentioned in the introduction to this chapter, Netscape and other web browsers support plug-in MIDI players that can be used to play MIDI files automatically after they are downloaded.

If you want to create your own MIDI files, you need extra hardware—and some musical talent. The rest of this chapter is dedicated to providing a survey of basic MIDI equipment, explaining how it is used, and outlining how MIDI files are created.

Basic MIDI equipment includes *sequencers*, *synthesizers*, and *samplers*. MIDI sequencers generate MIDI commands. Synthesizers or samplers turn these commands into audio. The following sections discuss these devices.

Synthesizers

A *synthesizer* (synth) is a piece of electronic hardware (or equivalent software running on a computer) that can combine and manipulate multiple tones in complex ways to create musical notes. The first synthesizers were analog, but most modern units are digital.

The basic functions of a synthesizer are shown in figure 8.1. As shown in the figure, digital tone generators produce simple tones and other basic waveforms. These are processed to create effects or to change the shape of the waveforms. The resulting complex waveforms are then merged and converted to analog form to create audio. The entire process is under the control of a MIDI bus.

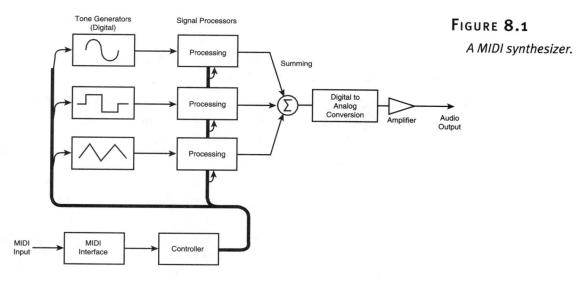

FIGURE 8.1

A MIDI synthesizer.

Some synthesizers are specialized, emulating a single type of musical instrument, such as a guitar or piano. Others are more flexible and can mimic an entire orchestra of instruments. Many of these more versatile synthesizers also support the General MIDI standard.

Some synthesizers allow great flexibility and experimentation, giving the user the ability to create new musical sounds. Others support predefined functions only. Selecting the best synthesizer depends greatly on one's musical needs and tastes.

MIDI-compatible synthesizers take their commands from a MIDI interface connected to a computer or other MIDI sequencer. In response to commands, the synthesizer *plays* one or more notes on one or more instruments simultaneously, generating audio that can be recorded or transmitted. This audio does not go through the MIDI bus. It is taken out of the synthesizer on conventional audio jacks separate from the MIDI connector.

Some sound cards, such as some of the SoundBlaster series from Creative Labs, have basic built-in synthesis capability.

More sophisticated synthesizers, designed for professional musicians, produce better quality sound, can generate more simultaneous notes, and provide more flexibility in the generation and control of the sound.

The terms *multitymbral* and *polyphonic* are used to describe synthesizers. Multitymbral means that the synth can emulate more than one musical instrument at a time. Polyphonic means that the synth can play more than one note at a time on the same instrument.

A multitymbral synthesizer can be used to emulate a small band or even a small orchestra, depending on its capabilities. A polyphonic synth can generate chords (simultaneous playing of multiple notes).

Synthesizers that are both polyphonic and multitymbral are sometimes rated in terms of the number of simultaneous notes they can produce. A 64-note synthesizer, for example, can produce 64 simultaneous notes in any combination. This could be used to emulate an entire orchestra of 64 instruments if each instrument produced only a single note at a time. This is not very practical, though. A single piano requires at least 8 simultaneous notes to create its complex chords. A guitar might need up to 6 notes. Thus, the 64-note synthesizer can emulate about 10–15 real instruments.

Samplers

Synthesizers create music by combining and manipulating tones and other basic audio elements generated entirely inside the synthesizer. Samplers take a different approach. A set of short, externally generated sound samples are loaded into the sampler's on-board memory. These samples can be any digitized sound. Usually they originate from a real musical instrument, but they can be something more exotic, such as a singer's voice or even a dog's bark. Figure 8.2 shows a basic sampler in schematic form.

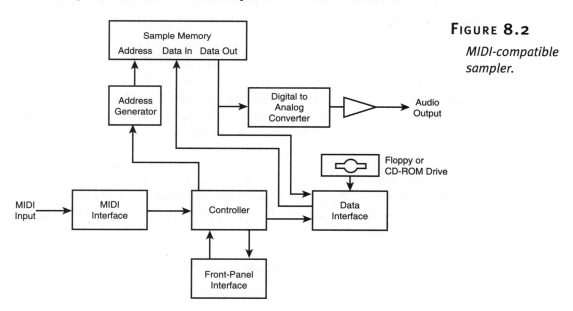

FIGURE 8.2

MIDI-compatible sampler.

A controller interprets MIDI commands, causing an address generator to sequence through a section of the sample memory. Digitized samples from the memory are then converted to audio. This unit also has a disk drive for loading and saving sound samples. A front-panel interface enables the user to edit samples.

Samplers usually provide sound-editing capability so that the sound samples can be adjusted for length, pitch, frequency content, and so forth. More complex sample editing can be done on a computer by using sound-editing software (see Chapter 11, "Digital Audio Recording and Editing").

When a sampler receives a MIDI command, it executes it by playing one or more samples at a pitch and duration defined by the command. Other functions such as distortion are also supported by some samplers.

A few software-only samplers exist as well, the best known being Apple's QuickTime Musical Instruments Extension, a Mac OS extension that contains 30 MIDI sound samples from Roland, a major manufacturer of samplers. This basic, software-only sampler supports a subset of the General MIDI patch map.

Many samplers are available, with different capabilities. Like synthesizers, they vary in terms of the number of notes and samples that can be played simultaneously.

Some samplers are ROM- (Read-Only Memory) based. Their memories are preprogrammed with a set of instruments and cannot be changed. A common example of a specialized, ROM-based sampler is the *drum machine* available from various manufacturers. It contains preprogrammed samples of various types of drums. It is optimized for this purpose and has enhancements such as drum pads for manual control.

RAM- (Random-Access Memory) based samplers use writable memory so that new samples can be loaded at any time. Although generally more expensive, these RAM-based samplers are much more versatile than their ROM-based cousins.

Samplers Versus Synthesizers

Both samplers and synthesizers have their place in electronic music. Many musicians use both—and sometimes even multiple—units to emulate the type and number of instruments needed for their work.

Samplers can produce more realistic music, complete with minor defects such as fret, pick, and breath noises. They are also more flexible in the sense that any sound that can be recorded can be used as a sample to generate music. Samples from a great performance artist can be used to create high-quality notes. On the lighter side, you have probably heard novelty songs such as pigs squealing "Jingle Bells" or dogs barking a popular tune. These songs were created using a sampler.

Synthesizers were once relegated to the somewhat dubious realm of surrealistic *electronic music* because early models did not sound like conventional musical instruments. Synthesizers can still be used to create this sort of spacey, high-tech music. New "virtual instruments" can be created using synthesizers, opening the door to many possibilities.

Modern synthesizers also produce sparkling, pristine simulations of real musical instruments. This can represent a significant savings in cost and size. Even diehard advocates of "real" acoustic instruments must admit it's a lot easier to take a band on tour with several 8-pound keyboard/piano synthesizer units than it is with an equivalent number of 800-pound pianos.

Modern digital technology creates constant advancement in sampler and synthesis technology. Both functions can now be found in a single box, somewhat blurring the distinction between them.

MIDI Sequencers

The control center of any MIDI system is the *sequencer*. It generates the commands sent to synthesizers and samplers to generate the music. A sequencer can involve dedicated hardware, or it can be implemented in software on a computer. No matter how it is implemented, the sequencer function is essential in a MIDI system. In simple terms, the sequencer is what plays the music, although it doesn't actually generate the audio. (That's what the synthesizers and samplers do.)

A sequencer can perform other functions as well, such as recording and editing MIDI commands. Multiple channels, the MIDI equivalent of audio tracks, can be recorded separately and later edited and time synchronized. They can then be played back simultaneously, emulating an entire band of instruments.

Sequencers take many forms. Computer-based sequencer software is responsible for reading a MIDI file and sending the appropriate commands over a MIDI bus. Some sequencers provide even more functions, such as the automatic generation of rhythmic accompaniment.

When a MIDI file is played on a computer without an external sampler or synthesizer, the computer must be sequencer, sampler, and synthesizer all in one.

MIDI Keyboards and Other Midi-Compatible Input Devices

Musical instruments have been around for thousands of years. As such, it is no surprise that some of the devices used for generating MIDI commands during live performances should emulate the function and sometimes even the appearance of traditional musical instruments. These devices, MIDI controllers, supplement or even replace the sequencer function during live performances.

A MIDI keyboard looks very much like a piano or organ keyboard. Such keyboards are the most common devices for generating MIDI commands during live performances or studio recording sessions. Pressing a key generates a MIDI Note-On command. (For a brief description of this and other MIDI commands, see the next section, "Inside the MIDI Bus.") Releasing the key produces a Note-Off command. Depending on the sophistication of the design, the keyboard may also measure the speed by which the keys are struck and generate appropriate MIDI velocity codes that control the loudness of the note.

MIDI guitars are also available. They start life as a conventional acoustic or electric guitar. A special pickup device is then installed, either at the factory or as an aftermarket product. This pickup connects to a digital signal processor in a separate box. Playing notes or chords on the guitar causes the processor to generate corresponding MIDI codes.

Even MIDI wind instruments are available. Played like a woodwind instrument, they contain sensors that measure breath pressure and detect when valve keys are pressed. Corresponding MIDI codes are generated.

Inside the MIDI Bus

A MIDI bus ships data in one direction at 31.25 Kbps. A MIDI connector has five pins, but only three of them are used. One of these three is a ground. Data is sent over a MIDI bus in 8-bit bytes.

Up to three bytes are needed for a MIDI command. Although this is only one physical bus, the MIDI protocol supports 16 separate logical *channels*.

Multiple samplers and synthesizers, each on its own channel, can be connected to a single controller or sequencer on one bus in a daisy-chained configuration. Figure 8.3 shows an example. Each device obeys commands on its assigned channel and ignores all others.

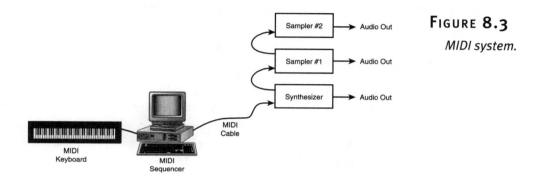

FIGURE 8.3

MIDI system.

A computer-based sequencer generates MIDI commands to control this simple system. A synthesizer and two samplers are controlled by a single daisy-chained MIDI bus. Each of these three devices has its own dedicated channel, enabling individual control by the sequencer.

Channels are sometimes reserved for specific instruments. Channel 10, for example, is usually used for percussion. This is not an absolute requirement, though. Some MIDI instruments support only a specific channel; others can be programmed to reside on any channel.

MIDI messages are divided into two types: channel voice messages and channel mode messages.

Channel mode messages are for controlling the status of the hardware. A channel mode message, for example, might tell a synthesizer that it is assigned to channel 8.

Channel voice messages actually play the music and constitute most of the MIDI bus traffic. A Note-On command from a MIDI musical keyboard, for example, has fields to select a channel, to define which key on the keyboard was pressed, and to define how hard the key was pressed. To stop the note, a separate command (Note Off) must be sent to the synthesizer. This would be done automatically by the keyboard. There is no special MIDI command to play a chord (three or more simultaneous notes). Instead, multiple Note-On commands are sent in rapid sequence.

MIDI also supports *SMPTE time codes* to keep everything synthesized. These codes are sent as system messages to all devices in the MIDI chain. Like an electronic metronome, SMPTE time codes can be used to control when notes start and end. This is critical in large MIDI systems where multiple synthesizers and samplers are in use.

A MIDI bus is a one-way serial interface. It operates at the relatively slow rate of 31.35 Kbps. Because it is so slow, delays can accumulate when a MIDI bus is daisy-chained between several instruments. Larger MIDI systems use several MIDI buses for this reason. In those larger music systems, a MIDI interface box is used to supplement a computer as a sequencer, to provide SMPTE timing, and to provide patching (routing) of MIDI signals.

For those familiar with network design, note the similarity between the MIDI digital music system and a LAN. Messages are passed between different nodes. An interface box serves as a router. This similarity has not gone unnoticed. MIDI has its limitations, and will some day be replaced with a faster, more capable system. This might be based on LAN technology, or at least borrow some of the hardware. This is not something, however, that will likely happen in the near future. MIDI in its current form has years left in its lifetime.

A MIDI System

Figure 8.4 shows such a fairly sophisticated MIDI system in schematic form. MIDI-controlled sampling and synthesis are supported. MIDI buses also control some of the audio hardware, such as an effects box.

Synthesizer and sampler audio outputs are sent to a mixer, for combination with other audio sources. The mixed audio is then recorded on a computer that serves as a direct-to-disk recorder, sound editor, MIDI editor, and master MIDI sequencer. A DAT (Digital Audio Tape) drive is also available for audio recording.

To provide timing information and tighter control over the system, a MIDI interface is used to supplement the computer in controlling the MIDI buses.

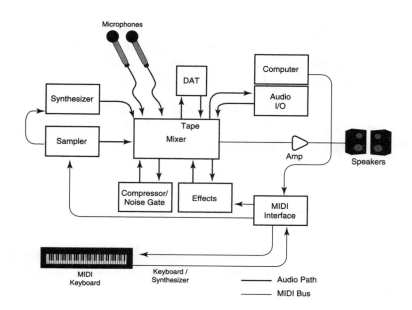

FIGURE 8.4

MIDI-controlled system for perfor-mance and recording.

Creating MIDI Files

A MIDI file, suitable for posting on the Internet, can be created by either of two methods: music composition or MIDI scoring.

Using music composition software, music can be entered manually, one note at a time. Although assisted by a computer, this is not fundamentally different from the method composers have used for centuries. Upon completion, the composer enters a command to save the composition as a MIDI file. The software can also print sheet music or save the composition in other formats.

MIDI scoring takes a very different approach. In this case, MIDI-scoring software is used to record a stream of MIDI commands generated by a MIDI keyboard, guitar, or other input device. (Refer back to figure 8.3. It shows a system that could be used for such a purpose.) By playing the piece, a musical score is automatically created and recorded. This method is often preferable to musicians and *organic* composers who would rather spend time performing their music than writing it down. The software can then be used to save the work as a MIDI file or in another format. The software can also print sheet music.

More advanced MIDI software can combine both the composition and scoring functions in one package. A product such as Steinberg's Cubase can record and play back MIDI, enable manual composition, and even record, edit, and play back the audio generated by MIDI devices.

The hardest part of creating a MIDI file is having or developing the musical talent to create the work in the first place. With modern software, the recording and editing process is relatively simple.

Summary

MIDI sound files provide the most efficient means of instrumental music delivery on the Internet.

MIDI will continue to be dominant in the digital music industry for years to come. MIDI-based instruments and processors continue to grow in sophistication and features.

Further Reading

See the references at the end of Chapter 10, "Audio Equipment Basics." [HUBER1] and [BARTLETT] provide fairly extensive discussions of MIDI. [HUBER2] and [NARDAN] also provide information. Another reference includes [INTMIDI].

[INTMIDI] - A copy of the Level 1 Specification for General MIDI may be obtained from the following address:

International MIDI Association
5316 West 57th Street
Los Angeles, CA 90056
Telephone: 213-649-6434

The fee for this specification is $5 as of late 1996.

CHAPTER 9

SOUND BASICS AND AUDIO THEORY

Whether it's a song, a dramatic reading from a popular book, or live coverage of a heated political race, sound must be converted to electronic form (that is, audio) and processed before it can be used on the Internet. Except for live broadcasts, it must also be recorded and edited to eliminate mistakes and enhance the quality of the final product.

Many newbies assume that recording and editing sound require the skills of a professional audio engineer and the resources of a studio full of outrageously expensive equipment. Hit records and sound tracks for major motion pictures may indeed require this treatment. Fortunately, most audio projects don't require anything near this level of sophistication.

Very good audio, worthy of any website, can be created by the serious amateur with a modest collection of equipment. You may already own the most expensive component of an audio recording and editing system in the form of a well-equipped Macintosh or PC. This and the following two chapters explain how to record and edit your own audio.

This chapter examines the basic properties of sound and audio and defines many of the terms of the audio trade. Some of this material can get a bit technical. For this reason, sidebars are included for the benefit of those readers concerned more with the practical essentials than the technical details. If you want only the bare essentials, read only the sidebars. If you need details, dig into the text.

Chapter 10, "Audio Equipment Basics," is a brief survey of the audio equipment necessary to make a recording. Chapter 11, "Digital Audio Recording and Editing," puts everything together, describing how to integrate the equipment into a practical, cost-effective recording system, make and edit a recording, and set up a simple home or small-business recording studio.

Sound Versus Audio

Strictly speaking, *sound* refers to acoustic energy—waves of varying pressure that travel through the air. *Sound pressure* refers to minute pressure fluctuations caused by these waves when they strike an object, such as human eardrums or the diaphragm of a microphone.

Microphones work by converting the vibrations caused by sound pressure into an electrical signal. *Audio* refers to these electrical signals (or after conversion, digital data) that are an abstract representation of sound. Just as a photographic image is a representation of a real, three-dimensional object, audio is an "image" of real world sound. This concept is discussed in more detail later in this chapter in the section on microphones because it helps you understand why something as simple as a different microphone placement can have a profound effect on audio quality, even though the sound is unchanged.

Sound, Audio, and the Decibel

Sound is what you hear; it travels through the air as waves. Audio is an electronic signal that represents sound; it travels through wires or resides in digital form on a computer. A microphone, for example, converts sound into audio.

The loudness of sound and audio are both measured in decibels, which are abbreviated as DB. Decibels are logarithmic. This means that for every 6 DB increase, the sound or audio is twice as loud. A 20 DB sound, for example, is twice as loud as a 14 DB sound, which in turn is twice as loud as an 8 DB sound.

The difference between the loudest and the faintest sound or audio signal is called the *dynamic range*. For example, a tape recorder with a 120 DB dynamic range could handle a 120 DB difference between the faintest signal it could detect and the loudest signal it could tolerate before overloading. The dynamic range of an audio signal must not exceed the dynamic range of a piece of audio equipment because overloading or dropouts result.

The term sound is also used collectively (and less precisely) to include both acoustics and audio. Even the authors are guilty of this collective use in the title of this book, *Website Sound,* and the title of this chapter, "*Sound* Basics and Audio Theory." This distinction between audio and the varied meanings of sound shall be emphasized when it is important.

Sound Loudness

Human ears are sensitive to an extremely wide range of sound loudness. The difference between the loudest and the faintest sounds may be as much as ten trillion to one (10,000,000,000,000 : 1). This difference between the loudest and faintest sounds is called the *dynamic range* of a sound source.

Because of this wide dynamic range and the way human ears are sensitive to sound, engineers often use a decibel (DB) scale as a convenient way to express loudness.

A ten-to-one increase in loudness is represented on the decibel scale as an increase of 20 DB. Conversely, a ten-to-one decrease in loudness corresponds to a decrease of 20 DB. For example, a 40 DB sound is ten times louder than a 20 DB sound and a hundred times louder than a 0 DB sound. If you are mathematically inclined, you may have noticed that the decibel scale is logarithmic.

To show that a loudness measurement is associated with sound rather than audio, the prefix SPL (for Sound Pressure Level) is usually added after the DB. For example, the faintest sound a person with normal hearing can detect is 0 DB SPL.

A faint sound of –20 DB SPL cannot be heard with unaided ears, but it can be detected with a sensitive microphone and a high-gain amplifier. A quiet library may have 30 DB SPL background noise. Normal speech comes in at about 60 DB SPL. A loud rock band can generate 120–130 DB SPL. The *threshold of pain*, the point in which sound is loud enough to make a person's ears hurt, occurs at about 130 DB SPL.

It is worth noting that long-term exposure to sounds far less than 130 DB SPL can cause permanent hearing damage. Unfortunately, many musicians and sound engineers develop serious hearing loss and *tinnitus* (ringing in the ears) due to such prolonged exposure.

High sound pressures represent a more immediate danger. A jet aircraft on takeoff may produce 150–160 DB SPL. Exposure to a 150 DB sound pressure level for even a short period of time can cause permanent deafness. Sailors on the flight decks of aircraft carriers must wear special hearing protection. Without it, they could lose consciousness in minutes. NASA has conducted experiments with 210 DB SPL sound generated by massive concrete and steel towers with voice coils carrying many thousands of watts. Sound this loud can punch holes in sheet metal. [EVEREST] reports that a somewhat less energetic level of 194 DB SPL can be measured 10 feet away from the explosion of 50 pounds of TNT!

Audio Signal Levels

Because audio signals are electric representations of sound pressure levels, they share the same wide dynamic range. Whereas sounds are measured as pressures, audio signals are measured in volts or watts.

As is the case with sound, it is convenient to measure audio signals on a decibel scale. One such scale, the DBV scale, uses 1 volt as the 0 DBV level. Another scale, the DBu scale, uses 0.775 volts as the 0 DBu level.

Do not confuse electrical and acoustic DB levels. It is highly unlikely that a sound with 0 DB SPL will produce a 0 DBV signal in an audio system. The exact relationship is arbitrary, depending on design of the audio system, microphone efficiency, and room acoustics. It is only important that the two are proportional. That is, a 10 DB increase in sound pressure levels should cause a 10 DB increase in audio levels.

Several audio DB scales exist, and they differ only in their 0 DB references. This plethora of DB scales may seem confusing, but in practice it is rarely a problem. The 0 DB references are not that far apart, ranging from about .775 to 1.226 volts, depending on the DB system.

Understanding the fact that different references are used helps explain why one piece of equipment may seem slightly loud compared to others at the same settings. It is simply calibrated using a different reference. Data sheets for the equipment almost always define their reference point for 0 DB.

The absolute range of audio signal levels a system is designed to handle is called its *dynamic range*. Recall that this term is also applied, in a similar manner, to sound pressure levels. For example, a microphone capable of detecting sound pressure levels from 16 to 136 DB SPL without distorting has a dynamic range of 120 DB.

Amplifiers

An *amplifier* (or amp) is used to boost an audio signal (see figure 9.1). The output of an amplifier matches the input in shape, but has increased voltage and power. Amplifiers are the most common and useful of all active audio circuits. *Active* simply means that an external power source is used as a source of energy to boost the signal. (For reference, *passive* circuits have no power source, except for the signal itself, and can only *attenuate*, or weaken, the signal.)

Amplifiers come in many forms, either as simple amplifiers or as part of a more complex circuit. A *preamp* is an amplifier designed to boost a low-level signal (such as a microphone output at a few hundred micro-volts) up to line level (roughly 0 DBV peak). A *power amp* is designed to drive heavy loads, such as speakers. Large power amps can generate peaks of a kilowatt or more.

> **Amplifiers and a Question of Balance**
>
> An *amplifier* is an electronic circuit used to boost (amplify) an audio signal. Amplifiers of one type or another are found in all audio equipment. They range in size and power from the extremely sensitive microphone preamps to the large power amps used to drive speakers. The capability of an amplifier to boost a signal, the *gain*, is measured in DB.
>
> The inputs and outputs of an amplifier are said to be either balanced or unbalanced. Unbalanced inputs and outputs are simpler and cheaper to build, but are more noise-sensitive. Balanced signals need an extra wire, and there-fore use a different type of cable than unbalanced signals.
>
> Balanced amplifiers are normally used for low-level signals that would be easily swamped out by even a little noise. The most common example of a balanced amplifier is a microphone preamp.

Amplifiers with single inputs and outputs, as shown in figure 9.1, are called *single-ended* or *unbalanced*. They are best used on line-level signals (signals at a level of roughly 1.0 volt), although they can be used with lower-level signals in situations in which noise can be controlled.

The most important amplifier specification is its *gain*. Gain can be adjusted on most amplifiers. For example, an amplifier with a gain of 40 DB (100x) could be used to boost a –56 DBV signal from a microphone up to a –16 DB level (–56 + 40 = –16).

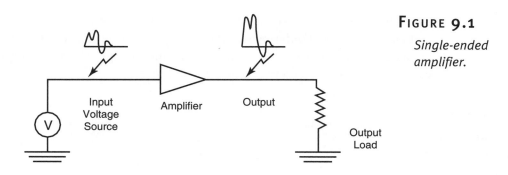

FIGURE 9.1

Single-ended amplifier.

Balanced Amplifiers

Some amplifiers, such as microphone preamps, are called *differential* amplifiers because they amplify the voltage difference between two input signals. The signal lines and the amps are said to be *balanced*. Figure 9.2 shows such an amplifier connected to a microphone output.

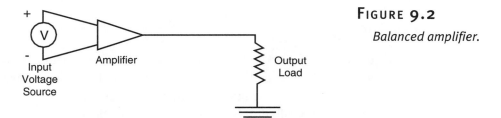

FIGURE 9.2

Balanced amplifier.

An audio signal from the microphone appears as a voltage difference (a few hundred microvolts to a few millivolts) across the preamp's input terminals. Some types of noise, such as hum, often appear on both terminals at the same voltage levels. This is called a *common-mode* voltage. The signal is amplified and the noise is rejected because the amplifier is sensitive to voltage differences, not the absolute, common-mode voltage.

Balanced amplifiers and lines are prized for this noise-canceling capability. A well-designed balanced amplifier can pull a millivolt signal out of several volts of common-mode noise. Balanced amps are commonly used with low-level signals, such as microphones outputs, in which even a few microvolts of noise are catastrophic.

Some amplifiers also have balanced outputs (see figure 9.3). The output voltage appears as a difference in the voltages across the two outputs. An unbalanced (single-ended) amp has only a single output, with the output voltage being referenced to ground.

FIGURE 9.3

Amplifier with balanced inputs and outputs.

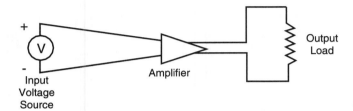

Until recently, balanced amps and lines were uncommon in low-end pro audio, except for microphone preamps and cables. This trend is changing as hardware costs drop and the low-noise benefits of balanced amplifiers become better known to musicians and other users.

Feedback

Figure 9.4 shows a condition known as *feedback*. A portion of the output of an amplifier is returned (fed back) to the input. If conditions are right, the amplifier chases its own tail, resulting in *oscillation*. An example of feedback and resulting oscillation is the electronic howl heard in public address systems when the microphone is placed too close to the speaker.

FIGURE 9.4

Feedback.

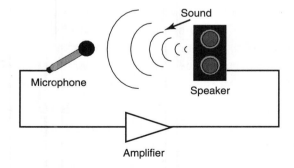

Frequency

An *oscilloscope* is an electronic instrument that plots an electrical signal on a cathode ray tube or computer screen. The result is a display of voltage over some period of time. An audio signal might look something like figure 9.5.

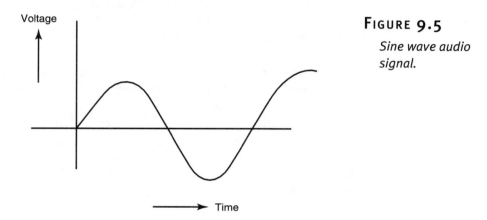

Voltage

Time

FIGURE 9.5

Sine wave audio signal.

This figure shows a very simple audio signal called a *sine wave*, a pure tone. Note that the signal repeats at regular intervals. The time required to make one full cycle is called the *period* of the signal. Another way to look at this is to count the number of cycles that can be completed in a second or other length of time. This is the *frequency* of the signal. The frequency and period of a signal are reciprocals:

period = 1/frequency

The period is measured in seconds. The basic unit of frequency is the hertz (Hz), named after the 19th-century German physicist and mathematician, Heinrich Rudolf Hertz. A hertz is identical to one cycle per second. Because frequencies can vary over a wide range it is often convenient to use larger units of frequency such as kilohertz (KHz), megahertz (MHz) and even gigahertz (GHz). Respectively, these represent one-thousand, one-million and one-billion hertz.

Sounds can have a frequency range from a tiny fraction of a hertz to well up in the gigahertz region, but human hearing is only sensitive to a range from 20 to 20,000 Hz. Even this limited range is optimistic because high-frequency hearing slowly deteriorates with age. *Subsonic sound* is sound below 20 Hz; *ultrasonic sound* is sound above 20 KHz.

Frequency

Frequency is essentially the same thing as pitch, although its precise definition is rooted in complex mathematics. A shrill whistle has most of its sound energy at high frequencies. The sound from a bass drum is concentrated at low frequencies.

A single-frequency sound is a pure tone. Real-world sounds and the corresponding audio are made of many frequencies. The study of the frequency content of sound is called *spectral analysis*.

The basic unit of frequency is the hertz, abbreviated Hz. A 1-hertz audio signal or sound repeats itself once every second. Humans can hear sounds ranging in frequency from 20 Hz to 20,000 Hz. A range of frequencies is called a *band*. An amplifier capable of amplifying signals in the range of 1 KHz to 5 KHz has a bandwidth of 4 KHz.

The term *bandwidth* is used to describe the range of frequencies contained in a signal. Audible sound has a nominal bandwidth of 20 KHz (actually, it's 19.980 KHz for those people particular about decimal points). A signal consisting only of frequencies in the range of 2 KHz to 5 KHz has a bandwidth of 3 KHz.

Sound engineers often refer to octaves or decades when discussing frequency bands and bandwidth. An *octave* represents a doubling (or halving) of frequency. For example, 20 KHz is one octave higher than 10 KHz. A decade represents a 10 times increase (or decrease) in frequency. Two decades are between 17 Hz and 1700 Hz.

Spectral Analysis

Very few sounds are pure tones. Voice and music consist of complex combinations of many frequencies. The 18th-century French mathematician Joseph Fourier showed that any arbitrary function (an audio signal, for instance) can be decomposed into an infinite series of sine waves. His work forms the basis of *Fourier analysis*, a branch of mathematics widely used in the design of audio circuits and in digital signal processing.

Fourier analysis can be used to derive the spectrum of an audio signal. In simplest form, a *spectrum* is a graph of the amplitudes of the frequency components of an audio signal. Figure 9.6 shows several spectrums. Each signal has its own unique spectrum, and a spectrum has its own unique signal. A spectrum is another way of looking at an audio signal. Such a view is said to be in the frequency domain, as opposed to the more familiar time domain.

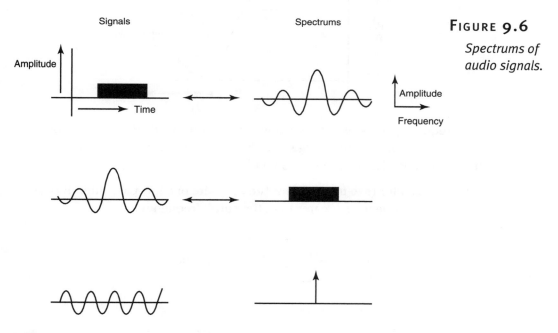

FIGURE **9.6**

Spectrums of audio signals.

Filters

Filters are circuits designed to either boost or attenuate selected audio frequencies. Filters are extremely important in audio work and are widely used to enhance audio, to create special effects, and to remove certain types of noise and feedback.

A low-pass filter (see figure 9.7) accepts only frequencies below its *cutoff frequency*, which is the highest frequency it passes without attenuation.

Higher frequencies are rejected. These higher frequencies are said to be in the *stop band*, the range of frequencies that the filter attenuates. Conversely, those frequencies passed are said to be in the *pass band*.

FIGURE 9.7

Low-pass filter.

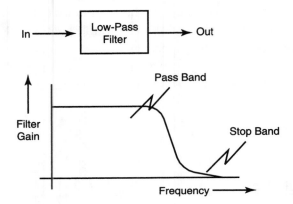

The frequency response curve shown in figure 9.7 is idealized. Real-world filters have more rounded edges, gradual rather than steep cutoffs, and nonzero transmission in the stop band.

A high-pass filter (see figure 9.8) is the opposite of a low-pass filter. It passes only those frequencies greater than the cutoff frequency.

FIGURE 9.8

High-pass filter.

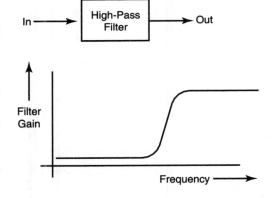

A band-pass filter (see figure 9.9) is an optimized combination of a low-pass and a high-pass filter. It passes only frequencies between an upper and a lower limit.

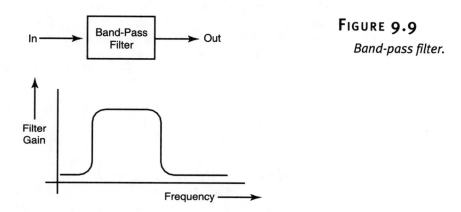

FIGURE **9.9**

Band-pass filter.

A notch filter (see figure 9.10) is the opposite of a band-pass filter. It passes all frequencies, except those in a stop band.

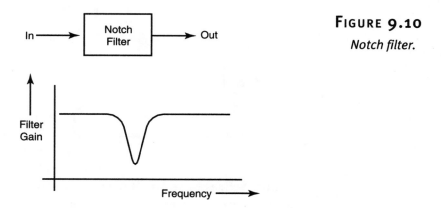

FIGURE **9.10**

Notch filter.

A shelf filter is used to apply a constant attenuation above or below a cutoff frequency. The name comes from the shape of the response curve, which resembles a shelf (see figure 9.11).

Note

Filters

As was discussed in the last sidebar and in the main text, real world sounds (and audio) are composed of many frequencies. During recording or processing audio, it is often desirable to boost the loudness of some frequencies and decrease (*attenuate*) the loudness of others. This enhances desirable sounds and helps hide problems. For example, *stage rumble*, a low frequency noise problem often encountered during live recording, can be prevented by removing frequency components below 100 Hz.

An electronic circuit that changes the frequency content of a signal is called a *filter*. Computer algorithms that can perform equivalent functions on digital audio are also filters.

A *high-pass* filter is a filter that passes high frequencies and blocks low frequencies. A *low-pass* filter is just the opposite, passing low frequencies and blocking high frequencies. *Band-pass* filters pass frequencies only between upper and lower limits. The opposite of a band-pass filter is a *notch* filter.

FIGURE 9.11

Shelf filter.

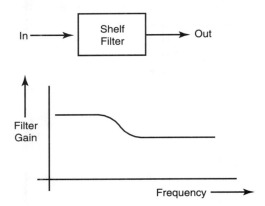

Filters can be either active or passive. *Passive* filters can only attenuate (weaken) a signal. *Active* filters are capable of both attenuation and amplification. Common application of active filters include equalizers and anti-aliasing filters (discussed later in this chapter, in the section "Digital Audio").

Passive filters are often used in applications involving high power. Common applications include crossover networks for speaker systems and EMI/RFI filters that block high frequency noise from AC power lines.

Phase

Figure 9.12 illustrates another important property of an audio signal: the phase. Although the two signals in this figure have the same amplitude and frequency, they are not identical. One signal is a fraction of a cycle ahead of the other. These signals are said to be *out-of-phase*.

Phase is the position on a cycle relative to some reference point. Phase is usually measured in degrees. A complete cycle is 360 degrees.

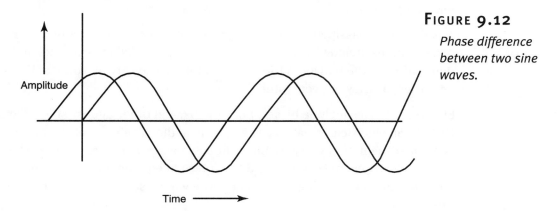

FIGURE 9.12

Phase difference between two sine waves.

The *phase angle* is a measurement of how far out of phase two signals are. A phase angle of 0 degrees means the signals are exactly in phase. If they are added together, the result is the sum of their values.

A phase angle of 180 degrees means they are exactly opposite. Such signals cancel each other out when added. Intermediate values of phase angles are possible too.

Phase has many practical implications. When hooking up a set of stereo speakers, for example, it is important that the speaker wires be connected so that the speakers reinforce each other. If connected out of phase, sound from one speaker partially cancels sound from the other.

Noise

Noise is the nemesis of the sound engineer. It can take the form of an inconsiderate neighbor's blaring stereo, the hiss on an analog tape, or an objectionable hum from a poorly designed amplifier. Simply put, *noise* is any unwanted sound or audio, regardless of the source. (In a strict engineering sense, this definition is too broad, but it serves the purposes of this book.)

Noise is as fundamental as sound itself. Noise can be reduced to an arbitrarily low level (for an arbitrarily large sum of money), but never completely eliminated. Billions of dollars are spent every year reducing noise. Companies have made their fortunes and reputations on effective noise reduction techniques and equipment. Various aspects of noise are discussed throughout this chapter, along with techniques for minimizing noise problems.

Noise may be classified as either environmental or electronic. Environmental noise sources include the neighbor's stereo, a plane flying overhead, and the dull roar from the blower in the air conditioner. They are all sounds. You can hear them as they are generated.

Electronic noises include hisses, pops, hums, and other undesirable effects that are all electrical in nature. They are all audio, all electrical signals. You can't hear them until you play them though speakers or headphones. The level of electronic noise generated by a piece of equipment is an important consideration in selecting audio gear. More will be said on that later in this section.

The most common form of electronic noise is the hiss that can be heard when an amplifier is turned up to full volume with no input. This hiss is called *thermal noise*, and it is caused by heat. Any electronic device operating at a temperature above absolute zero (about 459° F below zero) produces thermal noise. Well-designed equipment minimizes it, but it cannot be eliminated.

Because of thermal and other noises, a signal cannot be amplified indefinitely. More noise is added at each stage of amplification until there is more noise than signal.

Electronic noise can also be picked up from outside sources through *inductive* coupling. This coupling occurs when varying magnetic fields induce (generate) a small voltage in wires or electronic circuits. If you run a microphone cable too close to a power cord, you may induce hum. Placing a sensitive preamp near a transformer or electric motor may also induce noise.

Noise and Distortion

For the purposes of this book, *noise* is defined as any unwanted sound or audio signal. It takes many forms, including pops, crackles, hums, and hisses. Preventing, reducing, and eliminating noise is a major concern in recording and broadcasting. Too much noise can ruin an otherwise good recording or broadcast.

The absolute amount of noise present in an audio signal is much less important than the signal-to-noise ratio (SNR). Measured in DB, SNR indicates the overall noise content of an audio signal. An audio signal with an SNR of 50 DB sounds scratchy when played. 70 DB is fairly quiet. 80 DB is excellent. Theoretically, digital CD-quality audio can achieve an SNR of 96 DB, although 85–90 DB is more common.

Audio equipment usually has an SNR rating, indicating how much noise is added by the equipment. Good equipment has an 80 DB or better SNR rating. Digital equipment should be higher, at least 90 DB.

Distortion is an effect closely related to noise; it is any defect introduced into an audio signal by a circuit. For example, high peaks in the input signal of an amplifier might not appear at the output because the amplifier could not reach a high enough output level. The output signal is therefore a distorted version of the input.

Another noise-producing effect is *capacitive* coupling. This is similar to inductive coupling, except that the source of the noise is a stray electric, rather than magnetic, field. Crosstalk between channels on a mixer or multichannel amplifier is often partly due to capacitive coupling.

Both inductive and capacitive coupling are short-distance effects, rarely extending more than a few yards from the source. They are sometimes lumped together under the term EMI, or electromagnetic interference. Radio-frequency interference (RFI), a closely related effect, can act over long distances because it propagates in the form of radio waves.

How does one reduce noise? All noise reduction methods involve one or more of the following techniques:

◆ Reduce the noise at its source.

◆ Move away from the noise source.

◆ Filter out the noise.

◆ Hide the noise by increasing the signal level.

Except for noise that is above or below the audible range, filtering usually involves signal degradation. For this reason, filtering is probably the least practical of the four methods outlined above, except in special situations. It is far better to avoid recording noise than it is to try to filter it out later.

The effectiveness of the last method, hiding the noise, is measured by an important figure of merit called the *signal-to-noise ratio*, or SNR. Usually expressed in DB, SNR is a critical parameter in the selection of audio equipment. An SNR of 50 DB or less is usually considered poor, 60 DB is acceptable, and 70 DB or better on analog equipment is excellent. Some digital equipment can achieve an 85 DB SNR or better.

Recalling the discussion on DB, note that a 70 DB SNR means that the signal *power* is 10,000,000 times stronger than the noise power. Alternately, the signal *voltage* is over 3,100 (the square root of 10,000,000) times higher than the noise voltage.

Distortion

Another undesirable effect often encountered in recording and broadcasting is *distortion*, the corruption of an audio signal. An amplifier (or other audio circuit) is designed with a broad *linear* region, in which a change in signal input strength results in a corresponding increase in output voltage (that is, doubling the input voltage should double the output voltage).

Outside the linear range, a change in input does not produce a corresponding output, and the signal is corrupted. This distortion is usually most severe at the high end of the scale, where an overly strong input signal overloads an amplifier. This overloaded amplifier does not have the *headroom* (output voltage range) to accommodate such a large signal.

Much smaller amounts of distortion actually occur throughout an amplifier's range due to minor imperfections in the design. Various distortions of this type, such as Total Harmonic Distortion (THD) and intermodulation distortion, are often specified as a percentage of the signal strength. Any amplifier, no matter how low its distortion specifications, produces severe distortion when overloaded.

Cables

An audio cable seems such a simple device—nothing more than a length of copper wires and plastic—yet few things can cause more problems if not used correctly. Fortunately, it is not difficult to learn how to select the right cables for an audio job and how to use them properly.

> **Cables**
>
> Cables for connecting audio equipment should be durable, relatively heavy, and well shielded. Shielding consists of a layer of fine wires or foil inside the cable. Shielding reduces noise by keeping out unwanted electrical fields from fluorescent lamps, motors, and other sources of electrical noise. Double-shielded cable is the best, although a braided wire shield works reasonably well. For balanced circuits, shielded-twisted pair cables are the best.
>
> No matter which type of cable is in use, it is best to keep it as short as possible. Long cables are harder to drive and may cause the amplifiers in your audio equipment to distort the signal.

Cable Basics

A wire is composed of a metallic central *conductor* and an outer *insulator* (see figure 9.13). A cable is nothing more than two or more unconnected wires, bundled together with an insulating covering. *Connectors* at one or both ends make it quick and easy to attach and remove the cable from audio equipment. The most common connectors used on professional audio cables are quarter-inch phone plugs; phono plugs, or RCA plugs; and XLR plugs (widely used on microphone cables).

As shown in figure 9.13, the usual function of a cable is to efficiently deliver electrical energy from a *source* (a microphone, for example) to a *load* (such as the input to a preamp).

FIGURE 9.13

Electrical cable.

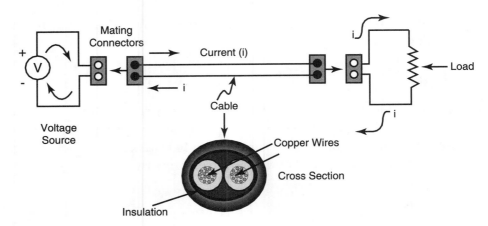

A *current* of electrons flows through the wire because of a small *potential* (voltage) difference between the ends of a wire. Note that two conductors are always required to complete the circuit. One conductor is the *hot* side, and the other side is the *ground return*, or simply the *ground*. Their names come from the common safety practice of tying one side of a high-voltage electrical system to a ground rod, driven deep into the ground.

The relationship between voltage and current follows:

$$V = IR$$

This equation is known as Ohm's Law, after the German physicist Georg Simon Ohm. First defined in 1826, the law states that the voltage (V) across the wire is equal to the current (I) through the wire times the resistance (R) of the wire. The units of voltage, current, and resistance are, respectively, the volt, ampere, and ohm.

The diameter and length of a wire and the material of its construction determine its resistance. Wires are selected for a particular application to keep the resistance (and therefore the voltage drop from end to end) at acceptable levels. A short piece of heavy speaker wire might have only a few milliohms of resistance, giving a voltage drop of only a few millivolts for every ampere. Such wires are efficient conductors of electrical energy. They deliver almost all of that energy from the source to the intended load, rather than dissipating the power in the wire itself as heat.

Long, thin wires can also be efficent conductors, but only if the current is kept at a low level. A microphone cable, for example, carries only a few microamps.

Alternating Current in Cables

Ohm's Law is an accurate model of electrical activity in a wire or cable—up to a point. It works fine for direct current (DC) and low-frequency alternating current (AC) electrical signals, but it begins to break down as the frequency rises or the cables become longer. This was first discovered in the latter half of the nineteenth century when the first submarine telegraph cables crossed the Atlantic, linking North America and Europe. Strange effects were seen that could not be explained simply by the resistance of the cable.

James Clerk Maxwell, a 19th-century Scottish physicist, along with other scientists, eventually discovered the cause of the problem. A current flowing through a wire creates a magnetic field around the wire. Due to voltage differences between the wire and the ground, an electric field also exists. Energy is required to create these fields. This energy is drained from the signal traveling down the wire. Conversely, as the fields collapse, they return their energy to the signal. The net result is much like inertia in a mechanical system in that there is a tendency to keep the voltage and current at a constant level.

In engineering terms, the wire or cable is called a *transmission line*. Elaborate mathematical models of this transmission line allow accurate estimates of the cable's electrical behavior at any frequency. In simplest form, a modified form of Ohm's Law is used:

$$V = IZ \text{ (AC form of Ohm's Law)}$$

As before, V and I are the current and voltage, but a new term, Z, the *impedance*, replaces R, the *resistance*. Z is a complex number (complex in the mathematical sense, having both a real and imaginary part) containing terms for resistance, inductance, and capacitance. *Inductance* is the electrical effect due to the magnetic field, and *capacitance* is the electrical effect due to the electric field. Impedance is measured in ohms, as is resistance.

Any circuit trying to drive a cable must be capable of delivering sufficient current to overcome inductance and capacitance effects. If it cannot overcome these, sufficient energy to drive the cable at high frequencies does not exist. The result is distortion. High-impedance microphones cannot drive long cables for this reason. This is another reason why it is desirable to keep a cable as short as possible.

Shielding

A cable carrying an electrical signal as part of a circuit could be nothing more than two insulated wires bound together. Such a cable is simple and cheap and is often used in audio equipment for carrying strong, high-level signals or power. Speaker cables are one example; power cords are another.

These simple, two-wire cables are not suitable for low-level signals. Electrical and magnetic fields coming from outside the cable can generate noise voltages in the cable. Conversely, the fields generated by the cable can be picked up as noise in nearby cables and circuits.

A practical method of reducing the effects of the magnetic field is to twist the two wires tightly together. In use, the wires in this twisted pair carry equal currents in opposite directions. Thanks to the tight coupling created by the twisting, a magnetic field generated by one wire is canceled by an equal but opposite magnetic field from the other wire. The result is no external magnetic field to corrupt the signals in other nearby wires. Also, any external magnetic field induces the same voltage in both wires. This common-mode voltage can be canceled out by a differential amplifier with balanced inputs.

To control electric fields, an extra conductor is added to the cable in the form of a continuous sheath, wrapping the other wires (see figure 9.14). An electric field cannot penetrate a conductor, so the sheath forms an effective shield to keep in the internal field and keep out any external fields. To be effective, the shield must be grounded. Inner conductors therefore "see" a constant DC electric field from the sheath itself.

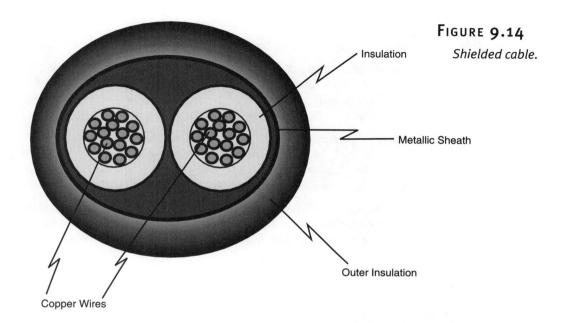

FIGURE 9.14

Shielded cable.

Insulation

Metallic Sheath

Outer Insulation

Copper Wires

Sheaths are made of various materials. The sheath in cheap shielded cable is made of fine stranded wire wrapped around the inner conductors. Gaps in the sheath are easily formed by bending or kinking the cable, thus reducing the effectiveness of the shielding. Shield impedance is also relatively high.

A braided sheath, although more expensive, does not form gaps and is a better shield. Aluminum foil can also be used as a shield. It is continuous and resistant to gaps, but its resistance is higher than a braided shield.

Double-shielded cable combines aluminum foil and either braided or wrapped stranded wire. This high-quality cable is more effective, but also more expensive.

An unbalanced cable has only one inner conductor. The shield forms the other conductor, and current flows in it. A balanced cable has two inner conductors, and the sheath carries no current (ideally).

High-quality balanced audio cables combine twisted pair inner conductors with shielding.

Note

Cable Hype: Let the Buyer Beware

Double shielding, heavy-duty wires, and quality connectors make a quiet, reliable cable. Such cables fetch a fair price, but are usually well worth the money. Unfortunately, some manufacturers take matters to extremes and produce grossly overdesigned cables at an exorbitant price.

Overdesigned, overpriced cables may have impressive technical specifications, but they really are no better in the vast majority of applications than lesser cables costing a fraction of the price. It's much like buying a car that can do 300 MPH for going to the grocery store and back.

A few unscrupulous cable vendors even make outrageous claims that defy the laws of physics. If someone trying to sell you a cable claims that your old cables will not work properly because they have developed a memory problem, walk away. Better yet, run.

Digital Audio

The sound and audio discussed in this chapter up to this point have been analog quantities. They are *continuous*. This means they can take on any arbitrary value, such as 45.23123445962 DBV, and they have no discontinuities or breaks over time. Digital quantities are *discrete*, taking on only specific values (see figure 9.15). Analog quantities can be approximated only in digital form.

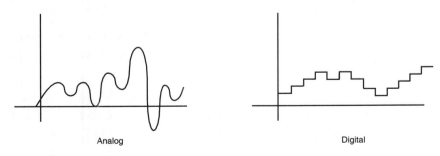

Analog   Digital

Suppose that a digital voltmeter is used to sample an analog audio signal. For the sake of illustration, this voltmeter has only two significant digits and requires a tenth of a second to make a measurement. If readings are taken at regular intervals, such as a second apart, and recorded in a notebook, the audio has effectively been *digitized*. The voltmeter is an *analog-to-digital converter* (A/D converter, or A/D).

Many problems accompany this crude approach. Although the analog signal could take on any arbitrary value, the voltmeter has only two significant digits. A 0.72482352 volt signal would be recorded (at best) as .72 volts. It also takes a tenth of a second to make a measurement, thereby introducing further error because the signal could change during the measurement. Collectively, these problems are called *quantization error* and are equivalent to introducing noise.

The sampling rate is much too slow also. The signal has been *undersampled*. At one sample per second (a 1 Hz sampling rate), almost none of the information has been captured from an analog signal that has a 20 KHz bandwidth. If the sample data points were converted back to audio and then to sound, nothing but a few clicks could be heard. Plotting the samples on a graph would show a signal varying at a frequency no faster than 0.5 Hz! This gross mismeasurement of frequency due to undersampling is called *aliasing*.

Using a faster voltmeter with a higher resolution decreases the quantization error. Increasing the sampling rate decreases the aliasing effect. As more resolution is added and the sampling rate is raised, the results get better. Eventually, a point comes when the digital approximation to the analog audio becomes nearly perfect. It can be used to reproduce an analog signal that is, for all practical purposes, identical to the original signal. After this point, adding more resolution or increasing the sampling rate has no benefit and is wasted effort.

Where is this magic point? How fast and with what resolution must the A/D take samples to avoid adding extra noise? Without delving into the complex Fourier mathematics, it turns out that the sampling frequency must be twice the maximum frequency of the audio signal. This is called the *Nyquist rate*, after the engineer who originally derived the associated theorem.

Because audio signals can contain frequency components in the range of 20 to 20 KHz, they must be sampled at 40 KHz (2 times 20 KHz) to prevent aliasing. In practice, actual sampling frequencies are slightly higher, either 44.1 KHz or 48 KHz in most digital audio equipment.

This slightly higher sampling rate provides a safety margin against aliasing caused by ultrasonic noise. This raises the interesting point that aliasing can be caused by frequencies that are not of interest and are not even audible!

It is common to place an anti-aliasing filter in front of the A/D converter to minimize high-frequency components. It is a low-pass filter with a pass band below 20 KHz. This filter is not extremely sharp, to avoid phase distortion. As a result, some high-frequency signal still gets through, and the extra safety margin of a higher sampling rate is still needed.

To get back to the original discussion, where is the "magic" point at which the sampling rate and resolution are high enough to reproduce analog audio accurately? As has been explained, the sampling frequency must be twice the highest audio frequency (plus a small safety margin), but what resolution is needed?

The resolution—that is, the number of bits in each sample—must be high enough to reduce quantization error to negligible levels. To achieve this, the quantization error must be below the noise floor of the audio to be digitized. The *noise floor* is the background noise level.

This can best be shown with an example. Suppose that an analog audio system introduces thermal noise and hum into an audio signal at a level of –60 DBV (which is not very good). Even when no input signals exist, this system produces a constant, noisy output at a level of –60 DBV. –60 DBm is the noise floor of that mediocre system. To avoid adding significant noise when digitizing an output from this system, equivalent quantization noise must be somewhat less than –60 DBm.

Note

Digital Audio

Audio signals must be converted into digital form so they can be processed on a computer or stored on an audio CD or other digital media. Digital audio is really nothing more than a series of measurements of the audio voltage taken at regular intervals. These measurements are represented as a series of binary numbers.

Each of these numbers, or samples, has the same number of bits. The number of bits in a sample is important because it defines both the dynamic range and the SNR of the digital audio. The more bits, the better, at least up to a point. CD-quality audio uses 16 bits and has a maximum SNR of 96 DB. This is more than enough for most audio applications, including most anything on the Internet. To save space, 8-bit audio is commonly used. It has a noisy, but usable SNR of 48 DB.

The rate at which samples are taken is also critical. The more samples per second, the higher the maximum audio frequency that can be digitized. In theory, the sampling rate must be twice the maximum frequency present in the audio that is to be digitized. In practice, the sampling rate must be slightly higher. CD-quality audio is digitized at a 44.1 KHz sampling rate. It is capable of reproducing a maximum audio frequency of 20 KHz.

If audio is digitized at a sampling rate that is less than twice the maximum audio frequency, a condition known as aliasing occurs. Aliasing introduces false readings and can be heard as odd sounds when the audio is played. To prevent aliasing, you must raise the sampling frequency or use a low pass filter before digitization to remove the high frequencies. This filter is called an *anti-aliasing filter*.

Determining the resolution needed is simple using SNRs, rather than absolute noise values. If the analog audio system in the example operates at a nominal signal level of 4 DBm, its SNR is 64 DB (4 minus –60 = 64). Using Table 9.1, it can be seen that a 12-bit A/D converter (with a 72 DB SNR) or better is needed to avoid degrading the 64 DB SNR signal.

In real-world systems, A/D converters do not quite achieve the ideal SNR values shown in Table 9.1, although they can come close. This is because no A/D is ideal, and noise sources exist inside the analog circuitry surrounding the A/D. A practical digital tape recorder with 16-bit resolution might achieve 85– 90 DB SNR.

In the example, a real 12-bit A/D is probably still okay, even though its SNR may be more like 65 DB, rather than 72 DB.

TABLE 9.1

	QUANTIZATION ERRORS FOR IDEAL A/D CONVERTERS		
Bits	**Worst Case Quantization Error for a 1 Volt Maximum Signal (Volts)**	**SNR (Linear Scale)**	**SNR (DB)**
1	0.5	2	6.02
2	0.25	4	12.04
3	0.125	8	18.06
4	0.0625	16	24.08
8	3.906×10^{-3}	256	48.16
10	9.766×10^{-4}	1,024	60.21
12	2.441×10^{-4}	4,096	72.23
14	6.104×10^{-5}	16,384	84.29
16	1.526×10^{-5}	65,536	96.33
18	3.815×10^{-6}	262,144	108.37
20	9.537×10^{-7}	1,048,576	120.41

Summary

You have now been exposed to the basics of sound and audio theory. This information should help you understand many of the concepts and terms presented throughout *Website Sound*. It should also give you a basic foundation for understanding how audio equipment works and how audio is digitized for use on the Internet and other purposes.

That leads into the next two chapters. If you intend to record your own audio for use on the Internet, these chapters will tell you how to do it.

Further Reading

For in-depth discussions of the topics introduced in this chapter, consult the following references:

[BARTLETT] "Practical Recording Techniques" by Bruce and Jenny Bartlett. Sams, 1992. ISBN 0-672-30265-9. Paperback, 511 pages.
Less technical than [HUBER1] or [NARDAN], but still a solid treatment of equipment and recording techniques.

[EVEREST] "The Master Handbook of Acoustics" 3rd. ed. by F. Alton Everest. TAB Books, 1994. ISBN 0-8306-4437-7. Paperback, 452 pages.
An authoritative, technical reference on all aspects of acoustics related to performing and recording, including sound physics, hearing, and studio design.

[HUBER1] "Modern Recording Techniques" 4th ed. by David M. Huber and Robert E. Runstein. Sams Publishing, 1995. ISBN 0-672-30639-5. Paperback, 496 pages.
An excellent, moderately technical treatment of audio equipment, basic studio acoustics, and recording techniques.

[HUBER2] "Hard Disk Recording for Musicians" by David Miles Huber. AMSCO Publications, 1995. ISBN 0-8256-1433-3 (In UK, ISBN 0-7119-4353-2). Paperback (large format) 192 pages.
A specialized text focusing primarily on computer-based sound, music, and multimedia production. Despite the title, the majority of the book is also of interest to nonmusicians who use direct-to-disk recording. Huber takes a somewhat less technical approach in this book than in [HUBER1].

[NARDAN] "Sound Studio Production Techniques" by Dennis N. Nardantonio. TAB Books, 1990. ISBN 0-8306-3250-6. Paperback, 293 pages.
Not as thick a book as [HUBER1], but still a very good, moderately technical survey of acoustics, audio equipment, and recording techniques.

C H A P T E R

10

AUDIO EQUIPMENT BASICS

This chapter examines audio recording and processing equipment. It attempts to describe all the basic equipment needed to set up a cost-effective home or small-business sound recording studio that can produce audio for the Internet.

Equipment coverage includes the following:

◆ Microphones and accessories

◆ Amplifiers

◆ Wires and cables

◆ Equalizers

◆ Control consoles (mixers)

◆ Signal processors

◆ Effects processors

◆ Recorders

◆ Equipment racks and cases

◆ Monitor speakers and headphones

The gear in this list is often classified as pro audio equipment, as opposed to consumer audio equipment. Pro audio equipment is designed for high-quality recording and live performances.

Further coverage of audio equipment is provided in Chapter 8, "MIDI," and in Chapter 11, "Digital Audio Recording and Editing."

Audio equipment from various manufacturers is shown throughout this chapter as examples. Please note that this does not constitute an endorsement for these products, not is it a guarantee that a particular piece of audio gear is suitable for your application. The authors have received no compensation from the manufacturers, nor are they in any way associated with them.

Before buying equipment, the reader is strongly encouraged to read the section entitled "Consumer Tips for Buying Pro-Audio Equipment" near the end of this chapter, and the section "Integrating an Audio System" in Chapter 11.

Microphones

If any type of audio gear is the most important, it would have to be the microphone. It is the first stage in the audio chain, that long string of amps, recorders, computers, networks, players, and other gear that leads from a performer to a listener. The microphone limits the ultimate quality of the finished work. Even the best, most sophisticated signal processing and editing cannot compensate for a bad microphone or the incorrect use of a good microphone.

Sound is an extremely complex phenomenon. As an example, consider a four-piece band with a lead singer. The sound from the front of the drums is not the same as the sound from the back. The singer's voice is projected more forcefully in the direction she is facing. The band sounds different in a room with a wooden floor than in one with carpeting. Sounds mix and interact as they bounce, refract, and become absorbed by the room and objects in it. Sound is three dimensional.

Audio, by comparison, is simple. It is created by sampling sound at discrete points in space with microphones. Audio is one dimensional. Just as a video camera creates visual images of real-world objects, microphones create audio "images" of the sounds around them. What the camera sees depends on where it is pointed, the focal length of the lens, and so forth. What the microphone "hears" depends on its directionality, sensitivity, and frequency response.

These factors are discussed in some detail in the following sections. Understanding them will help you improve the quality of your audio projects and enhance your ability to achieve desired effects.

Microphone Sensitivity

Sensitivity is a microphone's capability to pick up faint sounds. Expressed more scientifically, sensitivity is the microphone's voltage or power output level for a given sound pressure level (that is, sound loudness. See Chapter 9, "Sound Basics and Audio Theory"). The sensitivity of the Audio-Technica DR-2700HE microphone, for example, is specified as –56 DBV at 94 DB SPL.

Microphone Directionality

Directionality is a microphone's capability to reject unwanted sounds coming from off-axis directions (the sides, top, bottom, and rear). This capability to reject unwanted sound greatly improves the quality of the audio.

The directional response of a microphone is often specified using a polar pattern as shown in figure 10.1.

FIGURE 10.1

Polar pattern (omnidirectional).

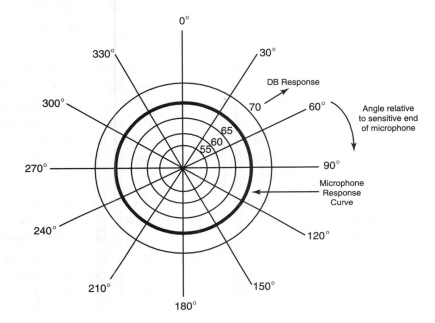

Reading a polar pattern is fairly simple, but it does take a little thought. Imagine the pattern blown up to a larger size and a microphone laid on top of it, with the sensitive end of the microphone pointing along the 0° line. Now imagine a sound source of constant loudness moving around the outer circle and the relative response (voltage output) of the stationary microphone being marked on the pattern. The farther out on the pattern, the higher the microphone output (in DB) for that angle.

The polar pattern in figure 10.1 is *omnidirectional*, meaning that it is equally sensitive to sound coming from all directions. Figure 10.2 shows a microphone with a *cardioid* response curve. A cardioid response is *unidirectional*, meaning it is more sensitive to sounds coming from the front than to sounds coming from the side or rear.

A supercardioid microphone is unidirectional like a cardioid microphone, but even more so. This is taken a step further in the hypercardioid microphone shown in figure 10.3.

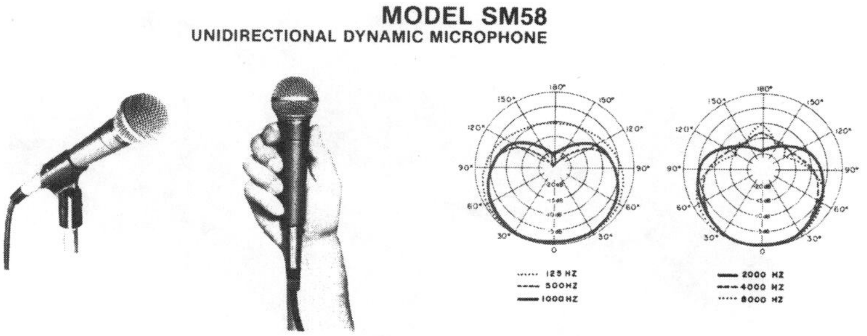

MODEL SM58
UNIDIRECTIONAL DYNAMIC MICROPHONE

······ 125 HZ
----- 500HZ
——— 1000HZ

——— 2000 HZ
--- 4000 HZ
······ 8000 HZ

FIGURE 10.2

*Cardioid microphone
(Shure SM-58).
(Courtesy Shure
Brothers.
Copyright 1996)*

audio·technica.

DR-2700HE

Hi-ENERGY® Hypercardioid Dynamic Vocal Microphone

Polar Pattern

FIGURE 10.3

*Hypercardioid
microphone
(Audio-Technica
DR-2700HE).
(Courtesy Audio-
Technica.
Copyright 1996)*

Note that as the response becomes more directional, a small side lobe begins to grow at the back of the polar pattern. This translates into a slight sensitivity to sounds coming from behind the microphone; therefore, a cardioid has better rear rejection than a hypercardioid, although its side rejection is not as good.

The pattern shown in figure 10.3 takes directionality to an extreme. This is the pattern for a shotgun microphone. The name comes from the extremely long sound tube that at least vaguely resembles the barrel of a shotgun. Shotgun microphones (see fig. 10.4) are useful for isolating a sound source in noisy, uncontrolled situations, such as outdoors or in a crowd. This is why shotgun microphones are often used when recording sound for movies and television.

FIGURE 10.4

*Shotgun microphone
(Shure SM89).
(Courtesy Shure
Brothers.
Copyright 1996)*

Microphone Frequency Response

As shown in figure 10.5, a frequency response curve defines how sensitive a microphone is to different frequency sounds.

FIGURE 10.5

*Frequency response
curve for CAD E-100.
(Courtesy CAD/CTI
Audio, Inc. Copyright
1996)*

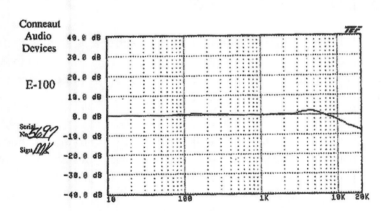

A "perfect" microphone would respond equally well to all audio frequencies of the same sound pressure level. Such performance is difficult to achieve, particularly in unidirectional microphones. In many applications this is not even desirable because a slight boost or dip at certain frequencies helps reduce noise and improve sound quality.

Vocal microphones are designed primarily to respond to human voice. They typically have a frequency response curve that trails off around 15 KHz to 17 KHz. Voice has little content at higher frequencies, so a wider frequency response is only an opportunity to pick up high-frequency noise. Purists argue this fine point, insisting on vocal microphones with a full, flat 20 Hz–20 KHz response.

Dynamic Microphones

Dynamic microphones are the most common type of professional microphone. All microphones work by *inductance*. Move a loop of wire through a magnetic field, and a small voltage is induced in the wire (see fig. 10.6). In effect, dynamic microphones are tiny generators. A major benefit of dynamic microphones is that they are self-powered, requiring no external power source.

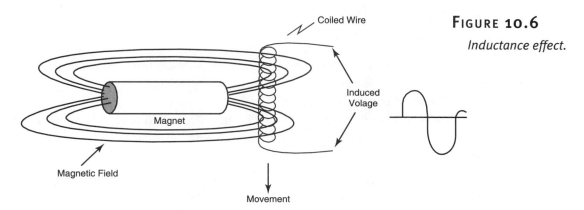

FIGURE **10.6**

Inductance effect.

Moving-Coil Dynamic Microphones

By far the most common type of dynamic microphone is the moving-coil dynamic microphone. Construction details vary considerably, but the capsule (the active element of a microphone) consists of a tiny coil of wire fastened to a thin, moving diaphragm, mounted over a stationary permanent magnet. This is shown schematically in figure 10.7.

FIGURE 10.7

Schematic view of a dynamic microphone.

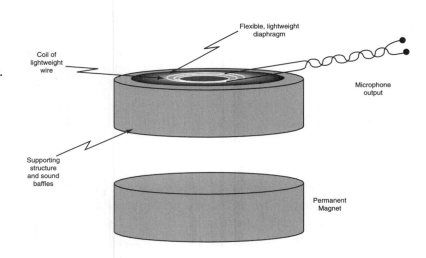

Sound entering the microphone housing strikes the diaphragm, causing it to vibrate. The coil, riding on the diaphragm, passes though the magnetic field from the magnet. The result is a voltage across the coil that is proportional to the sound.

This simple, reliable design has existed for decades, but it has been through many refinements in recent years. Strong, lightweight plastics have been used to reduce the thickness and weight of the diaphragm, making it more responsive to sound. Coils have been lightened also, using materials such as copper-plated aluminum wire that maintains good electrical properties while reducing weight.

Neodymium (known as rare-earth) magnets have also been used in recent designs to produce a much stronger magnetic field than ordinary magnets. The advantage is that higher output voltages can be achieved without increasing noise. This produces a higher signal to noise ratio (SNR—see Chapter 9) than an equivalent microphone with ordinary magnets. The disadvantage is that some preamps were not designed to handle this stronger signal and could overload.

Some sources also claim that neodymium magnets are somewhat brittle, making them more susceptible to damage from dropping or other abuse than ordinary magnets. Shock mountings inside the microphone reduce the chance of damage and also serve to isolate the microphone from noises caused by moving the microphone cord or bumping the housing. (Note: Shock mountings are used in many types of microphones, not just neodymium models.)

Dynamic Ribbon Microphones

An alternative to the moving-coil design is the dynamic ribbon microphone (mic). A metal ribbon replaces both the coil and the diaphragm. The ribbon is extremely thin (only a few microns) and made of a lightweight metal, such as aluminum. It is usually corrugated to increase flexibility and maximize surface area.

Compared to a moving coil, a ribbon reduces mass and improves frequency response at the expense of output level. Ribbon mics have been around for decades, but new materials such as titanium ribbons are now used to further improve performance. Ribbon mics are often prized for their "warm" sound.

Ribbon microphones tend to be more delicate than their moving-coil cousins, because the ribbon is so thin. The fragile ribbon can be torn or overstressed by loud noises or wind. Special baffles inside many ribbon microphones provide protection against such damage.

Ribbon microphones have traditionally been considerably larger than moving coil designs. Some recent ribbon mic designs have been reduced in size to no larger than a moving-coil design.

Hum-Bucking Coils and Magnetic Shielding

As has already been described, the moving coil or ribbon of a dynamic microphone generates a small electrical signal as it moves through a static (constant) magnetic field from a small permanent magnet.

This is not the only way to generate a voltage in the coil or ribbon. A voltage is also generated if the coil or ribbon is stationary and the magnetic field varies with time.

Unfortunately, this sensitivity to a time-varying magnetic field is the way a dynamic microphone picks up hum from nearby electric wiring, fluorescent light ballasts, and other common electrical devices. The degree of sensitivity to external magnetic fields is an important measure of the quality of a dynamic microphone.

Unintentional magnetic coupling can be eliminated in two ways. Both methods are used, sometimes in the same microphone design. The first is magnetic shielding. Surrounding the microphone capsule with a magnetic material, such as a steel screen, shields the capsule from externally generated magnetic fields, thus reducing hum.

The second method is a hum-bucking coil. This coil, located inside the microphone, has magnetic pickup properties closely matched to those of the coil or ribbon in the capsule. The hum-bucking coil is not allowed to move, however, so it is not sensitive to sound. Both coils "see" the same external magnetic field and are wired so they cancel (buck) each other and eliminate most of the hum.

Condenser Microphones

Condenser microphones work by the electrical effect called capacitance, rather than inductance. If two metal plates are separated by a *dielectric* (an insulator, such as air), the resulting device can be used to store an electric charge (see fig. 10.8.) This device was once commonly called a condenser, but the modern name is capacitor. Even so, the term *condenser* is still used to describe microphones that work via *capacitance* effects.

FIGURE 10.8

Capacitor (condenser).

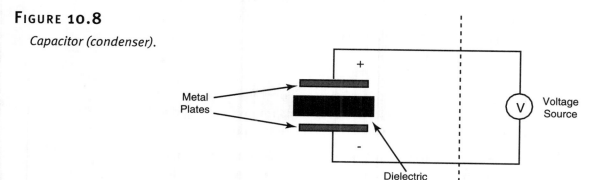

Inside a condenser mic, a thin, moving diaphragm vibrates when struck by a sound wave. This part is much like a dynamic mic, except with no coil or ribbon. Instead, the diaphragm is conductive, forming one plate of a capacitor. The second plate of the capacitor is stationary and separated from the first by an air gap. As the moving plate vibrates, it changes its distance from the stationary plate in proportion to the sound striking it. This change in distance changes the capacitance, which in turn causes a voltage change across the capacitor that is proportional to the sound. A condenser microphone is shown schematically in figure 10.9.

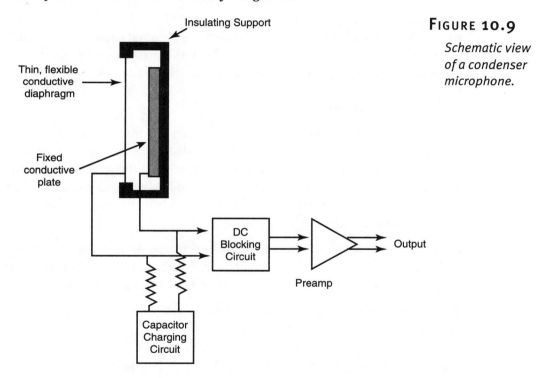

FIGURE 10.9

Schematic view of a condenser microphone.

The output of a dynamic microphone's voice coil may be connected directly to a preamp, but the output of a condenser mic must be amplified and the DC (direct current) component of the capacitor's voltage removed. This amplification and DC removal is done by a special circuit built into the microphone body. To keep the capacitor charged and the circuit working, electrical power must be supplied to the microphone. This power can come from either a built-in battery or from *phantom power* supplied by an external preamp or mixer with this capability. A phantom power supply can deliver approximately 48 volts DC at a few milliamps or more.

Compared to dynamic microphones, condenser microphones generally have better frequency responses and higher sensitivity, but they are also easier to overload with loud sounds (that is, they have less dynamic range.) They are also immune to hum pickup from stray magnetic fields.

Electret Condenser Microphones

A special type of condenser microphone is the electret condenser microphone. An *electret* is essentially a permanently charged capacitor. Although no external power source is required to keep the capacitor charged, this microphone does require phantom power for the built-in circuitry.

Tube (Valve) Microphones

A tube microphone is actually a condenser microphone with a built-in vacuum tube ("valve" in the UK) amplifier instead of a solid state circuit. (An exception is that a few tube amps are based on a dynamic mic element instead of a condenser.) Vacuum tubes, considered an obsolete technology after the introduction of the transistor, have made a comeback in high-end professional audio electronics in recent years.

People who use such microphones or other vacuum-tube equipment often profess a liking for the "warm" sound vacuum tubes impart to the audio even though this warm sound is actually a form of distortion or coloration.

Tube mics require a special power supply, usually provided in a separate package and connected to the mic by a cable.

Vocal, Instrument, and Studio Microphones

Microphones, whether dynamic or condenser, are often classified as being either for *vocal* or *instrument* use (see fig. 10.10). Vocal microphones typically have a bulbous wind screen to reduce breath noise and an upper frequency response that drops off around 15 KHz to 17 KHz. Better vocal mics also have built-in shock absorbers to reduce mechanical noise when the mic is hand-held. Most vocal mics for stage work use a dynamic moving coil design because of its inherently rugged construction.

Figure 10.10

Vocal microphone (Audix OM-7). (Courtesy Audix Corp. Copyright 1996)

Instrument microphones (see fig. 10.11) have less prominent cylindrical wind screens and may extend upper frequency response to 20 KHz. Many are condenser mics, used to achieve the flattest possible frequency response. Dynamic microphones are also used as instrument microphones, particularly in applications in which cost is an issue or in which a wider dynamic range is needed, such as for micing drums.

Figure 10.11

Instrument microphone (Audix D2). (Courtesy Audix Corp. Copyright 1996)

Some microphones are designed for general use with both vocals and instruments in a studio. These studio mics are often large and boom-mounted, such as the one shown in figure 10.12. Their large size makes them impractical for most stage work, but the audio quality of the better units is exceptional.

FIGURE 10.12

FIGURE 10.12

Studio microphone (Conneaut Audio Devices E-200). (Courtesy CAD/CTI Audio, Inc. Copyright 1996)

Microphone Stands, Booms, and Goosenecks

Microphone stands are essential in most recording and broadcasting applications. They eliminate noises caused by handling the microphone and also free the performer's hands.

Figure 10.13 shows three upright microphone stands. All of these stands are adjustable in height. The stand on the left has a traditional round, weighted base. The stand in the middle has a tripod base, providing moderately better stability than a round base. The longer the legs of the tripod, the more stable the stand. Stands with five legs instead of three are even more stable. The stand on the right has a boom. A *boom* tilts and telescopes, further increasing the stand's usefulness in positioning a microphone at the best location. Booms and stands may be sold separately or as a unit.

Booms are less likely to tip over a stand when the weight of the boom and microphone is counterbalanced by careful adjustment of the boom or by small counterweights on the light side of the boom.

A more stable stand can also be used to prevent the booms from tipping. In a pinch, a five-pound bag of fine gravel laid on the stand's base or legs adds extra stability. Gravel is preferable to sand because it's less of a mess if the bag breaks.

An alternative to a boom is the gooseneck, as shown in figure 10.14. *Goosenecks* are flexible, spiral-wound metal tubes with enough stiffness to retain a shape. They are easier to use than booms, but they cannot carry as much weight and also do not have the long reach of a boom. When selecting a gooseneck, the stiffer the better. Limp goosenecks cannot support even the weight of a larger microphone.

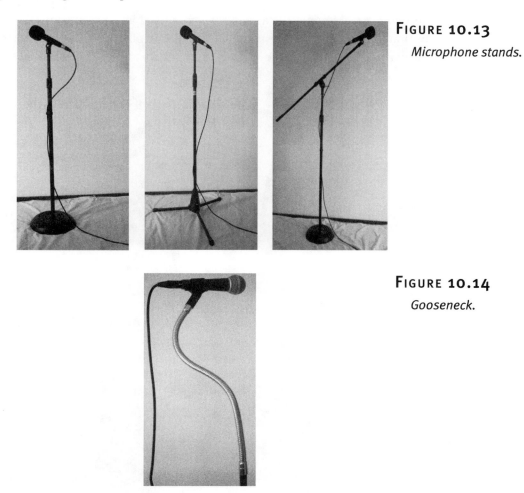

FIGURE 10.13
Microphone stands.

FIGURE 10.14
Gooseneck.

Small microphone stands are popular for tabletop use. Various models are available that support either small or large microphones. Simple mounting adapters are also available. These are screwed or bolted to a tabletop or control console and allow a gooseneck to be screwed into it.

Wind and Pop Screens

A *pop screen* is a simple mechanical filter that reduces undesirable breath and mouth noises caused when performers work close to the microphone. The screen consists of one or two layers of thin nylon mesh tightly stretched across a metal hoop. This assembly is mounted on a small gooseneck. For optimum performance, pop screens should be positioned an inch or two away from the microphone. Figure 10.15 shows a pop screen mounted in front of a microphone.

FIGURE 10.15

Pop screen.

A foam wind screen (see fig. 10.16) is a low-cost, somewhat lower-performance alternative to a pop screen. Made of low-density, open-cell foam rubber, it slips over the end of a microphone. Foam wind screens can be used when large pop screens are impractical.

FIGURE 10.16

Foam wind screen.

Microphone Cables

Virtually all professional microphones have detachable cables with XLR connectors (see fig. 10.17). This versatility enables cables of various lengths to be easily selected for different applications and also greatly simplifies repair if a cable is damaged.

FIGURE 10.17

XLR connectors on microphone and cable.

Balanced outputs are used on almost all professional microphones to prevent picking up electrical noise. Balanced outputs have three conductors: two inner conductors carrying the microphone signal and a third conductor acting as a shield. See Chapter 9 for a further discussion of the benefits of balanced lines for noise reduction.

Selecting Microphones

Anyone serious about sound recording should expect to build a small collection of microphones. There is no "best" microphone; each type has its own strengths and weaknesses. Experimentation and demos are the best way to learn about microphones and to test new microphones before purchasing.

Technical specs and application notes from manufacturers are also helpful. These can be obtained through your local dealer or in some cases through the microphone manufacturers' websites. See the list of manufacturers' home pages in Appendix C, "Website Audio URLs."

The first factor to be considered in microphone selection is directionality. When it is important to isolate a sound source from its environment, go for a highly unidirectional microphone such as a hypercardioid or a supercardioid. In extreme cases, especially outside, a shotgun mic may be necessary.

Cardioid microphones, although directional, have some width to their sensitive area. They are useful for recording several sources that are close together and on the same side of the microphone, such as a trio of backup singers.

Omnidirectional microphones are useful for recording "in the round" with the microphone at the center of a group of performers. They can also be used to capture ambient sound.

The price range for microphones is phenomenal, ranging from a few dollars for a cheap piezoelectric unit, to $2,500 or more for a top-of-the-line, large-diaphragm studio mic with adjustable directional response and an elaborate shock-isolation mounting. Obviously the $2,500 unit is going to outperform the cheaper one, but how much should one expect to spend on a good microphone?

No firm answer to this question exists. Cost alone is not a universal metric because a microphone must be matched to the application. A good vocal mic is not an ideal instrument mic, just as a good instrument mic is not an ideal vocal mic. Personal preferences may dictate a "warm" tube mic for a vocal, or perhaps a "gutsy" dynamic would be more to one's tastes.

The $20–50 microphone will almost certainly be disappointing and may even lack basic features such as a balanced output and a removable cable. Fortunately, many excellent dynamic microphones are available in the $100–$300 range. You are likely to find especially good prices if you buy a microphone during sales and other promotions.

Microphones in the $300–$500 dollar range should give higher sensitivity and flatter frequency-response curves than cheaper models. You can find many good condenser microphones within this price range.

$500–$1,000 buys a condenser or ribbon microphone with features such as adjustable polar pattern and near-perfect frequency response (for the condenser) out to 20 KHz.

Microphones costing more than $1,000 are generally the studio-quality mics and the special-purpose mics such as the shotgun mics.

More is usually better in the case of microphones, but please note that every rule has exceptions. It is not uncommon to find a moderately priced microphone with better performance than a unit that costs much more.

New microphone designs are constantly being introduced. New designs and new technology improve performance and add features. High technology is not cheap, at least not at first. Fortunately, prices drop rapidly as production methods improve, sales volumes increase, and other companies introduce competing models. An innovative, new-technology microphone introduced at $400 may sell for half that price a year later.

Equalizers

During a recording session, it is often desirable to selectively boost or attenuate certain frequencies in an audio signal. For example, boosting the higher frequencies makes a sound "brighter," while attenuating frequencies below about 100 Hz reduces stage rumble (low-frequency feedback). An equalizer is a device commonly used to make these types of frequency corrections.

An *equalizer* is a bank of filters that split an audio signal into a number of frequency bands, then recombine them into a single signal. The filters are individually adjustable so that the gain in each band can be set as desired.

Figure 10.18 shows a schematic diagram of a typical equalizer. It is a three-band equalizer—it has three independent filters, splitting the audio spectrum into a high-, medium- and low-frequency band. Such simple equalizers are common in mixers (see the next section).

Graphic equalizers allow for more precise control. These devices split the audio spectrum into as many as twenty bands (six to ten is more common, though), which gives very precise control over frequency content. Graphic equalizers got their name because the positions of the sliding faders (gain controls) map directly to points on the equalizer's frequency response curve.

FIGURE 10.18

Equalizer schematic.

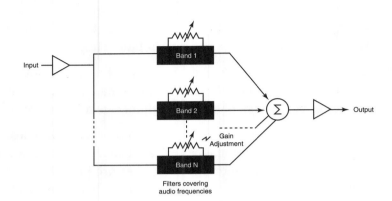

Most equalizers are based on shelf filters (see Chapter 9). Frequency response across each band is dropped or raised by an amount set by each adjustment.

A parametric equalizer takes a different approach. A parametric equalizer offers more control than an equalizer with shelf filters. Both the gain and the frequency response of each filter can be adjusted to some extent within its assigned band. Many parametric equalizers also have Q controls that define the sharpness of the filter. Graphic equalizers are often used to "tune" audio that is played aloud so that it can be adjusted to the room's specific acoustics. Parametric equalizers are more often used for fixing specific frequency-related problems, such as nulling out an unwanted resonance or boosting the bass at a specific frequency.

When using equalizers, it is a good idea to test the resulting audio in its intended application. Something that sounds good when played over an expensive speaker system does not necessarily sound good when played over small computer-grade multimedia speakers.

Control Consoles (Mixers)

Control consoles are the heart of an audio recording system. They are used to combine, amplify, equalize, monitor, and route audio signals to and from all parts of the system.

They are more often called *mixers* or *mixer boards* instead of control consoles because they "mix" the audio. "Mixer" is also easier to say than "control console." Strictly speaking, this term is not exactly correct because a true mixer's only function is to combine two or more signals. A control console does much more.

Control consoles are available in sizes and prices ranging from tiny to tremendous. Figure 10.19 shows a small, portable unit suitable for many home or small business applications. It has four mono input channels with balanced microphone inputs, plus four stereo input channels. Each input channel has a preamp, a two-band equalizer, a pan control, a post amp, and fader (gain) controls for the amp.

FIGURE **10.19**

Portable control console (Spirit Folio Lite). (Courtesy Spirit by Soundcraft. Copyright 1996)

The main mix output is stereo. The console also provides two mono auxiliary mix outputs and a stereo monitor output. Other features include a fast-reacting LED level meter and inserts (taps points in the audio chain) for adding external effects boxes or signal processors (see the section "Signal Processors and Effects Boxes" later in this chapter).

Figure 10.20 shows a much larger control console with twenty-four input channels and eight outputs. Four-band equalizers and multiple pan controls are provided for each channel.

FIGURE 10.20

*Studio control console
(Spirit 8). (Courtesy
Spirit by Soundcraft.
Copyright 1996)*

Mixer users have developed their own terminology. A *fader* is a gain control, usually controlling the gain of a signal-mixing circuit. Some faders adjust with a linear, rather than a circular, motion.

The *solo* button (or PFL [Pre-Fader Look] button if the console was designed in Great Britain) is a switch that enables the signal from a single channel to be routed to a monitor output without adjusting any settings of the overall mix. This is useful when setting up for recording to test each channel. It varies where the solo or PFL function is tapped and how it works, but the basic function is to enable a channel to be examined separately without changing its settings.

The block diagram in Figure 10.21 shows the functions of a typical mixer console. Although details vary greatly by manufacturer and model, each channel usually has the following features:

◆ An input (balanced or unbalanced, stereo or mono)

◆ A preamp with its own (premix) gain control

◆ An insert jack at the preamp output

◆ An equalizer covering two or more frequency bands

◆ Several auxiliary faders controlling how much of the signal is added to one or more auxiliary outputs

- A pan control (adjusts balance between left and right channels)
- A main fader controlling how much of the signal is added to the main mix
- A solo (PFL) button

Other more-or-less standard mixer features include the following:

- Two or more mix outputs with master (postmix) gain controls
- One or more auxiliary outputs with gain controls
- One or more VU or other level meters
- A switchable monitor output with gain control
- Inserts on the main mix outputs

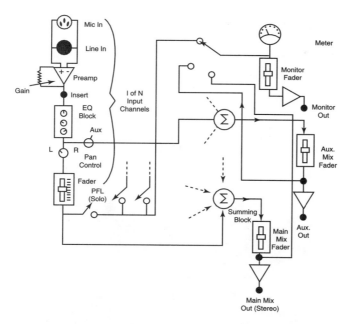

Figure 10.21

Control console block diagram.

Digital Control Consoles

Mixers have traditionally been analog devices full of op-amps, active filters, potentiometers and mechanical switches. This is starting to change with the slowly but steadily growing availability of reasonably priced digital mixers.

Digital mixers generally offer all the features of analog mixers plus lower noise, the capability to accept digital inputs and outputs, and electronic signal switching. They might also have extra features such as built-in effects processors and the capability to be controlled remotely by an external computer.

An example of a digital mixer is the Yamaha ProMix 01, as shown in figure 10.22. In addition to basic mixer functions, it includes many high-end features including but not limited to the following list:

◆ Eight balanced XLR mic inputs with phantom power

◆ Eight separate balanced TRS inputs

◆ Stereo input and output

◆ Digital output

◆ Auxiliary 3 and 4 outputs

◆ MIDI Interface

◆ Motorized faders for gain automation

◆ Parametric EQ

◆ Two programmable effects processors

◆ Three stereo compressor/limiter/gates

◆ Memory for storing control parameters

FIGURE 10.22

Yamaha ProMix 01 Digital Mixer. (Courtesy Yamaha Corp. of America. Copyright 1996)

As of late 1996, digital mixers are less common than their analog counterparts. This is expected to change in the near future, as prices drop and users become more familiar with the benefits of using digital mixers. High performance digital mixers such as the Yamaha ProMix 01 and its big brother, the Yamaha O2R, will probably be the norm in a few years.

Selecting a Mixer

When buying a mixer, look for the following features:

◆ Enough input channels and balanced mic inputs to handle the largest recording session you anticipate in the next few years. If you are buying a large mixer for serious recording, consider an expandable unit that will grow with your needs.

◆ Enough outputs to handle your needs. Eight output channels are more than enough for most personal and small business applications. A stereo output plus one or two auxiliaries can be expected from a smaller mixer.

◆ Low noise design. Some mixers designed for live performances are noisy, making them unacceptable for recording. A minimum acceptable SNR is 85 DB, but more is preferred.

◆ Two-band or three-band equalization. Parametric equalization is a plus.

◆ At least one stereo level meter that can be switched between channels. A bank of meters is useful on the larger mixers and is often available as an add-on option.

◆ Main mix, monitor, and auxiliary outputs.

◆ Effects inserts on each input channel and on the mix outputs.

Monitor Speakers

Monitor speakers (monitors) are usually not used during recording. Their main use is playback after recording and during editing, or for live performances at concerts, clubs, and theaters. Monitor speakers are often housed in rugged enclosures that double as carrying cases. Some also feature an angled design so they can be easily pointed in directions other than horizontal. Studio monitors, designed for a less physically demanding environment, tend to look more like conventional home-stereo speakers.

Compared to consumer-grade speakers, monitors generally have flatter frequency response curves and are better protected against overloads. Features vary by manufacturer and model, but some monitors are capable of withstanding high-energy audio surges that can destroy an ordinary set of stereo speakers. Note that this shouldn't be used as a license to abuse monitors. Long-term or severe abuse damages them.

These differences don't mean that ordinary speakers can't be used as monitors in the home or small business recording studio. It simply means that care must be taken not to overdrive them. Unprocessed audio from synthesizers might contain large, low-frequency components that could damage woofers. Severe distortion and feedback (common problems encountered when adjusting amplifiers and mixers) might contain powerful high-frequency components that can damage unprotected tweeters.

Most monitors, and some of the better home-stereo speakers, have special protective circuits built into their crossover networks to reduce the chance of damage. Equalizers and other audio equipment often have filters to block low frequency noise. Perhaps the best way to avoid damage is to test a new setup at low volume levels before turning up the power. This helps to keep monitors in good working condition for many years.

Power Amps

Power amps are designed to drive monitor speakers. One of the characteristics of most audio is that the peaks are much greater (by roughly 10–20 DB) than the average levels. Power amps must have the *headroom* (margin) to accommodate these peaks, or distortion occurs.

For this reason, it is not uncommon to use power amps rated at 3–10 times the average power needed for an application. Depending on intended use, some sacrifice in power-handling capability and the quality of the resulting sound can be taken to reduce cost. What is not acceptable for a live band performance might be acceptable for monitor speakers for home recording for Internet use.

Headphones

During recording, it is common practice to provide performers and audio technicians with headphones. Headphones allow them to listen to the audio mix rather than ambient sound. Headphones are also widely used during edits for sound isolation and to hear audio without adding room acoustics that are heard with monitor speakers.

Headphones are available in a wide range of performance and price categories. Not only must they sound good, but they must feel good so they don't cause discomfort during long recording sessions. Features to look for include the following:

◆ Large, well-padded ear pieces using a *closed-cup* design that helps screen out external sounds

◆ Stereo capability

◆ Adjustable headband

◆ A frequency response that is acceptable for the intended use

For example, figure 10.23 shows the Sony MDR-V600. These low-cost stereo headphones are comfortable, have moderate sound isolation, and have excellent frequency response (8 Hz to 35 KHz). Their performance is more than adequate for most amateur and professional audio applications. Other features include neodymium magnets, copper-plated aluminum wire in the voice coils, a coiled cord, and a clever frame design in which the headphones can be folded to save space during storage.

FIGURE **10.23**

Sony MDR-V600 headphones.

More expensive professional monitor headphones may provide features such as better sound isolation and higher power handling capabilities. These range in price from about $250 to $1,000. These high-end units are usually unnecessary for all but the most demanding applications.

Headphone Amplifiers

During a recording session, each performer and technician needs a set of headphones. Although it is possible to drive several headphones from a single amplifier, it is not desirable. Users want to adjust headphone volume levels according to environment, personal preferences, and the characteristics of their headphones.

A headphone amp is the solution (see fig. 10.24). A typical unit has a single mono or stereo input and a number of outputs, each with its own headphone jack and volume control. A master volume control that affects all channels is useful, as is a mono/stereo switch.

FIGURE 10.24

Headphone amp.

The number of outputs is usually around five, but some units have an extra line-level output (usually on the back, with no volume control). This output enables two or more headphone amps to be linked together to produce as many outputs as needed. This feature simplifies future upgrades.

Signal Processors and Effects Boxes

Audio signal-processing equipment is readily available. These boxes can increase or decrease the dynamic range of a signal, reduce noise, and perform other useful functions.

Effects boxes are closely related to signal processors. Their function is to add special effects such as reverberations, echoes, and voice transformations.

Some of these signal processors and effects are discussed in this section. This is not meant to be an exhaustive list because new devices are constantly being introduced.

During this discussion, the terms *wet* and *dry* are used to denote, respectively, processed and unprocessed audio.

Compressors

Many sound sources, including the human voice, have extremely wide dynamic ranges. For example, during the recording of a radio play, an actor might whisper one line, then shout the next.

This wide dynamic range causes several problems. At the quiet end of the range, a whisper might be so soft that it is hard to detect. If you turn up the gain to correct this problem, you run the risk of saturating amplifiers and other equipment when the sound levels become louder, thus introducing severe distortion.

Constantly adjusting the gain controls works, but it is inconvenient and prone to error. The solution is a *compressor*, an electronic gain control that automates the process. Inserted into the audio chain, a compressor automatically reduces the gain as the signal gets louder.

The level at which compression begins (the threshold) and the amount of compression (the compression ratio) are adjustable on most units. Other controls such as attack and release are also generally available. The attack knob controls how quickly the compressor goes into action as a signal changes from soft to loud. The release knob controls how long the compressor waits before turning off compression after the signal becomes less loud.

Nothing is free, and compression has a cost. At high levels of compression, the signal begins to sound unnatural. Because of this, compressors generally work best when the compression ratio is kept as low as possible while still achieving the desired effects. Voice compression seems to work best with a maximum compression ratio of 3 or less. Optimum control settings on a compressor are best determined by experimentation. Instructions packaged with the compressor might also provide some guidance.

While you experiment with a compressor, use the same types of sounds that are used during recording. Control settings that are best for voice are not the best for drums. The settings that are best for drums are not the best for guitars, and so forth.

Some compressors have an additional input known as a side chain insert. This allows an external signal to be used as the reference for controlling compression. One application of this feature is shown in figure 10.25. A signal is split, going into both a compressor and an equalizer. The output of the equalizer then feeds into the compressor's side chain input.

FIGURE 10.25

Frequency-sensitive compressor.

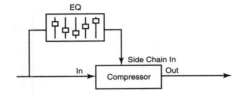

This configuration forms a frequency-sensitive compressor. Among other uses, it can function as a *de-esser* to remove excessive sibilance (hissing sounds) from vocals. Purpose built de-essers are also available.

Another application of a side chain input is *ducking* (see fig. 10.26). Feeding a completely different signal into the side chain allows that signal to "punch through." One use might be in a band, where a lead singer's audio could take priority over audio from instruments.

FIGURE 10.26

Compressor used for ducking.

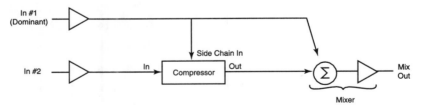

Limiters

A limiter is similar to a compressor in basic operation. The main difference is that the threshold level of a limiter is normally very high, and the compression level is fixed at infinity. A limiter is a brick wall (or rather a stone ceiling) that peaks cannot penetrate. A limiter can be used in front of a recorder to prevent overloading.

Although a compressor could be used as a limiter, purpose-designed limiters often produce a more pleasing sound. Limiters are used to prevent overloads and also to protect speakers and headphones from large peaks.

Noise Gates/Expanders

Another device often included in the same box as a compressor is the *noise gate*, or *gate*. Gates control gain, but unlike compressors, they function during the quiet periods. When the amplitude drops below an adjustable threshold level, noise gates automatically reduce the gain.

A ratio adjustment controls how much the gain is reduced. At a high ratio, the noise gate acts like a switch, shutting off the audio and achieving total silence. At a low ratio, the effect is less dramatic.

So why reduce the gain when it's already quiet? The answer is noise control. The effect can be dramatic, especially during voice recording. When a narrator is talking, the voice itself masks out low-level environmental and electrical noises. During pauses, however, breath noises and other low-level sounds can be clearly heard. With a noise gate in the circuit, voice comes through normally, but the pauses are silenced.

When it is properly used, a noise gate creates a cleaner, more professional recording. Like the compressor, gates must be adjusted to achieve the desired effect for a particular type of sound. One adjustment is the threshold level below which the gate attenuates the signal. The other common adjustment is the ratio setting, which controls how much the signal is attenuated. Experimentation is the best way to determine proper settings.

By happy coincidence, a noise gate can also be used as an expander, which is the opposite of a compressor. This function isn't immediately obvious—it seems an expander should leave low-level signals alone and boost the high levels. Expansion can also be achieved by leaving the high levels alone and attenuating the lows, which is exactly what a noise gate does. When used as an expander, the threshold control on a gate is set high, and the ratio knob controls the expansion level.

Effects Boxes

An effects box is a special audio signal processor designed for creating sound effects. Most effects boxes work by creating simulated echoes and reverberations electronically. Most of the newer units use a fully digital design. Analog inputs are immediately converted to digital form, processed, then converted back to analog form.

Figure 10.27 shows an example, the Alesis NanoVerb digital effects processor. Although it is physically much smaller than most competing units (requiring only 1/3 of a single rack space), it provides a full selection of mono and stereo effects.

The NanoVerb can simulate the acoustics of a range of large concert halls and smaller recording studios. Rotating speakers, and plate reverbs (mechanical reverb systems first used in the 1970s) can also be simulated. Other effects include delayed echoes, flanging (the manual describes it as a "jet airline sound"), chorusing, and nonlinear distortion.

Many reverb effects are stereo effects. Many reverb boxes, including the NanoVerb, create stereo outputs even for a mono input.

Voice Processors

Human speech starts in the larynx, or "voice box." Air from the lungs causes vocal folds (cords) in the larynx to vibrate. The larynx acts as a resonator, amplifying the sounds and changing their pitch to a limited extent. These basic sounds are turned into speech as they pass over and through the throat, mouth, and sinuses.

Formant frequencies represent the resonant frequencies of the larynx. These frequencies are where a relatively large part of the energy of the voice is located. They give each person's voice its unique qualities, despite changes in pitch.

Special digital voice processors are currently available that enable these formant frequencies and other voice properties to be modified in real time to create interesting and useful effects.

By raising the formant frequencies, a man can be made to sound like a woman, a child, or a chipmunk. Lowering the formant frequencies can make a woman sound like a man or a 500-pound gorilla. Much more subtle effects, such as a slight deepening of the voice, are also possible with less modification of the formant frequencies.

Hearing oneself speak in a totally different voice is a startling effect at first. It is also fun to explore. Serious applications of voice processors are just being defined. Creating extra voices in radio plays without adding extra cast members is one use. Science fiction and horror dramatizations, as well as comedies, can certainly benefit from the unearthly voices created by these processors. Dejays can use them to liven up their shows with comic effects.

An example of a voice processor is shown in figure 10.28. This unit is made by Roland and is marketed under the BOSS brand name as a VT-1 Voice Transformer. Faders give you control of format frequencies, pitch, the wet/dry mix, and reverberation. A button labeled "Robotic" turns ordinary speech into a mechanical, monotone drone. Eight predefined settings can be called up at the push of a button. Four are user definable. The other four cannot be altered, but five different sets of settings can be used. A bypass button passes the input directly to the output without being processed.

FIGURE 10.28

BOSS (Roland) VT-1 voice transformer. (Courtesy Roland USA. Copyright 1996)

Guitar and Other Instrument Signal Processors

Special-purpose audio signal processors are available for guitars and other musical instruments. In addition to some of the compression and noise gate functions already described, these processors might contain features such as the following:

◆ Vacuum tube or solid-state preamps

◆ Controlled distortion for effects

◆ Specialized effects

◆ Equalization

◆ Instrument tuner

◆ MIDI support

◆ Foot pedal control

Recorders

A recorder is an essential part of any audio system. Even in the case of a live Internet broadcast, it is usually desirable to record for future replay or for posterity. Recorders come in many performance and cost ranges, including the following:

◆ Consumer and professional analog cassette decks

◆ Professional open-reel analog tape recorders

◆ Digital tape recorders

◆ Direct-to-disk recorders

◆ Computers with sound capabilities

◆ Multitrack Recording Units

Recorders are often the most expensive component of an audio system. Selecting the best recorder for the job helps to maximize capabilities while controlling costs.

Tracks

Ideally, each vocalist and instrument should be recorded on a separate track. This gives the maximum flexibility during editing and mixing. For cost reasons, this is not always practical.

Analog Versus Digital Recorders

The signal on an analog audio tape slowly degrades with time and wear. Humidity, fungus, and chemical vapors can greatly accelerate this deterioration.

Digital audio tapes are prone to the same deterioration because they are made of the same basic materials as analog tapes. However, the signals are stored in digital form, fully saturated in one polarity or the other. The tape must undergo much more deterioration before the recorder fails to recognize a bit as a zero or a one.

Analog tapes also have an inherent hiss that adds about 3 DB of noise to the signals recorded on them. Each generation of copying adds another 3 DB. Analog tapes also have a limited dynamic range.

Digital tape recorders do not have these noise problems. Their main limitation is that they are more expensive than analog tape recorders.

Tape Speed

For analog audio tapes, the higher the tape speed, the better the frequency response and the lower the noise. Some studio-grade analog tape drives run at speeds up to 30 inches per second. This high speed has become popular in the waning years of audio tape technology because it offers maximum quality. Other common speeds are 15 and 7.5 ips.

Analog Cassette Decks

Consumer-grade stereo cassette decks are appealing only for their very low cost. They have no real editing or synchronization capability, and they can't be precisely controlled.

In a pinch though, they are adequate for simple recording. Dolby noise reduction is essential for achieving a usable signal to noise ratio (SNR). Metal tapes achieve the best results, assuming the deck is designed to handle their high bias settings. A dual-drive deck is the most versatile because it makes tape copying simple.

Professional cassette decks are also available, but at a much higher cost. Their performance far exceeds the consumer grade units in terms of sound quality and controllability.

Open-Reel Analog Tape Recorders

High-quality analog tape recorders with two to forty-eight tracks have been available for many years. These are open-reel units, using two separate tape reels instead of a tape cassette. They use tape formats as narrow as 1/4 inch and as wide as 2 inches, depending on the number of tracks. They are still in production, although digital tape drives are rapidly eroding their market.

For home or small business use, these recorders are less desirable than digital tape recorders or direct-to-disk recorders. They are large, harder to use than the digital units, require more maintenance, and are generally much noisier. You are better off with a digital unit unless you already have an open-reel tape recorder or have found a good used one at a low price.

Digital Tape Recorders

Digital tape recorders using an open-reel format are commercially available for professional use. Of greater interest to most readers are the digital tape recorders that use a cartridge tape. These fit into two categories: the two-track DAT (Digital Audio Tape) recorders and the digital eight-track recorders.

The cartridge-tape units use a rotating head design that greatly reduces the necessary tape speed. This head technology is similar to what is used in analog VCRs. It provides a long record time (up to two hours for eight-track, longer on two-track) on a single cassette.

Almost all digital tape recorders provide 16-bit sound quality. Common sampling rates are 48 KHz and 44.1 KHz. The excellent audio coming from these machines is equivalent to that of a CD.

DAT recorders are available in both studio- and battery-operated portable versions. The portable units are small enough to fit in a briefcase or a large pocket and are very handy for on-location recording as well as studio work.

An example is the TASCAM DA-P1 Portable DAT Recorder. This unit is slightly larger (at 11 7/8" × 7 11/16" × 2 3/16") than some of its tiny competitors, but it uses that extra size to provide professional features not found on the smaller units. These features include both XLR and RCA input jacks, line and mic level inputs, phantom power for microphones, line level output, an S/PDIF digital I/O port, and a 1/4" stereo headphone jack.

Digital eight-track (multitrack) tape recorders have gained popularity in recent years. In operation, they are similar to DAT recorders, except they have eight tracks instead of two.

Alesis Corporation builds and markets the popular ADAT® series of multi-track digital recorders. These record eight tracks of digital audio on S-VHS cassette video tapes. Alesis released their next-generation ADAT-XT (see fig. 10.29) recorder in 1995. This builds on the strengths of the ADAT by adding advanced features such as a vacuum-fluorescent front-panel display and a faster tape transport.

Teac offers competing products under their TASCAM brand name. Their recorders use a Hi-8mm tape cartridge instead of the much larger S-VHS format.

Direct-to-Disk Recorders

A direct-to-disk recorder uses a hard drive instead of a tape drive as the recording media. This approach provides numerous advantages, such as random access. Any part of a session can be accessed in milliseconds, rather than seconds or even minutes as is required with tape. Data can be easily moved, copied, and deleted, making such a system ideal for editing.

A disadvantage of direct-to-disk units is limited recording time. After the disk is full, its contents must be deleted or transferred offline. One way around this is to use fast removable-media hard drives, such as the I/OMega JIF drive. JIF cartridges are available in 500 and 1,000 megabyte sizes. Some direct-to-disk systems support SCSI interfaces for adding more disk drives or communicating with a tape drive.

Computer-Based Recording

A direct-to-disk recorder is nothing more than a specialized computer with one or more hard drives and an analog interface. Why not just add a little extra hardware to a Macintosh, PC, or other computer and do the same thing?

Manufacturers provide hardware and software add-ons that do exactly that. Two things are needed to turn your computer into a direct-to-disk recorder. The first is audio capability (a sound card or built-in audio hardware). The second is recording software that can write digitized audio to the disk in real time. This software is fairly sophisticated because it must operate in real time without glitches or dropouts.

As far as the audio hardware goes, most PC owners are familiar with the 8- and 16-bit computer sound cards, such as the SoundBlaster series from

Creative Labs. All Power Macs and some other Macintosh computers have built-in 16-bit stereo inputs and outputs.

These entry-level approaches lack some of the features of professional systems, such as balanced microphone inputs and multitrack (anything more than two track) recording. However, they are very economical and all but the low-end models are capable of delivering two tracks of near-CD-quality audio.

Technical specifications for the Sound Blaster® 16 Series, for example, include an 80 DB SNR (amp out). This SNR is quite acceptable for most Internet-related audio work, although it is not as good as what can be obtained using high-end sound cards specifically designed for pro-audio use. Most of the consumer-grade audio cards also support FM synthesis that can be used for playing MIDI sound files with the proper software (see Chapter 8 for a discussion of MIDI hardware and software).

More complex audio cards and subsystems are also available, allowing multitrack sound recording with 2, 4, 8 or more tracks. Digidesign is probably the best-known player in this arena.

Digidesign's offerings include the Session 8 digital audio system. This combination of hardware and software turns a Windows-based PC (plus an extra, external SCSI hard drive) into an 8-track direct to disk recorder with full mixing and editing capabilities.

Digidesign offers even more for Macintosh computers. Mac-based products start with Session®, a software-only editing tool that uses the Power Mac's built-in audio hardware to create a direct-to-disk recording system with editing.

A step up from Session is the Audiomedia II® card with Sound Designer II software. This adds features such as an S/PDIF digital I/O connection and better specification than the Power Mac's built-in audio hardware (88 DB SNR and 19 KHz frequency bandwidth for the Audiomedia II card, versus 78 DB and 12 KHz for the Power Mac). The Audiomedia III® card is a PCI-bus upgrade of the Audiomedia II with improved specifications.

The top end of the Digidesign product line is the Pro Tools III® system. This offers 8 to 64 tracks of audio I/O, 16 to 48 tracks of record and playback, and integrated digital mixing. The Pro Tools software for this system is extremely powerful, offering not only full editing and signal processing capability, but also plug-in modules from Digidesign and other companies that allow new features to be added.

Audio recording and editing software tools are discussed in more detail in Chapter 11.

Multitrack Recording Units (Portable Studios)

The term *multitrack recording unit* is something of a misnomer because these units are much more than just recorders. They are complete (or nearly so) mixing and recording consoles in a single box. They are also called *portable studios*. They contain four to eight input channels, mic preamps, equalizers, mixers, and a multitrack tape or disk recording unit. Some units even have effects processors and other advanced features.

Multitrack units are cost-effective options for many home and small-business recording applications. Their price is often much less than the equivalent collection of audio components. Another attractive feature of these units is their compact size, which makes them very useful for on-location recording. Portable studios range in size from roughly the dimensions of a notebook computer to about three times that size.

Four-track versions are ideal for voice recordings such as news reports, radio plays, and dramatic readings. They are also useful for small bands and for creating song demos. Six- and eight-track units are better suited for music recording.

Almost all multitrack units provide some sort of basic editing capability. This ranges from simple bouncing or *ping-ponging* (mixing two or more tracks down to a single track) to fairly sophisticated random editing in the case of the direct-to-disk recorders.

The recording mechanisms used in the first multitrack units produced in the early 1980s were analog cassette tape drives with four to eight channels. Such units are still produced. They are an economical solution when digital sound quality is not required and budget is a prime consideration. With Dolby or DBX noise reduction, these units produce reasonable sound quality (about 70–80 DB SNR) on first-generation tapes. As with all analog units, the SNR degrades with tape wear and as tracks are bounced.

The latest multitrack units avoid tape noise and other sound-quality problems with digital recording mechanisms. For example, the Yamaha MD4 Multitrack MD Recorder, as shown in figure 10.30, is a four-track unit. It records on MD DATA discs, which are rewritable optical media that look much like 3.5" floppy disks, except they are considerably smaller (about 2.5" on a side). The MD DATA disc is a recordable version of the audio MiniDisk media. Thanks to an efficient ATRAC compression algorithm implemented in the MD4, one disc can hold 37, 74, or 148 minutes of digital audio (for 4-, 2- or 1-track recording respectively).

FIGURE **10.30**

Yamaha MD-4 Multi-track MD Recorder. (Courtesy Yamaha Corp. of America. Copyright 1996)

A more powerful digital multitrack unit is the Roland VS-880 (see fig. 10.31). It offers eight tracks instead of four, fully digital mixing, and an optional effects board. These increased capabilities are not free. The VS-880 costs approximately twice as much as the MD4 (as of September, 1996).

Each of VS-800's eight tracks can have eight "virtual tracks," thus raising the total number of tracks (for editing) to 64! Only eight can be recorded at once, however. Unlike the MD-4, the VS-880 uses either an internal hard drive or a built-in JAZ drive instead of MD DATA disks (JAZ is a removable-media hard drive with 1-gigabyte cartridges). A SCSI port allows external hard drives or JAZ drives to be added.

FIGURE 10.31

Roland VS-880 digital multitrack recorder/ mixer. (Courtesy Roland USA. Copyright 1996)

Digital multitrack recording units such as the Roland and Yamaha products are often an excellent choice for use in the home or small-business studio, on the road, or as a backup unit in a project or professional studio. Other companies are expected to release their own digital multitrack units in the near future.

Multitrack units are attractive for their all-in-one approach and small size, but they also have weaknesses. Most, including many of the high-end digital units, do not have balanced microphone inputs; therefore, in-line impedance matching transformers or a separate preamp or mixer with balanced inputs is required.

Multitrack units can also restrict the flexibility of the audio system. Their architecture is fixed—the configuration of the internal components cannot be changed, as could a system made up of a separate mixer, recorder and so forth. This makes multitrack units seem an all-or-nothing proposition. However, external equipment, such as mixers or effects boxes, can be added to expand capability.

MIDI Hardware

MIDI, or Musical Instrument Digital Interface, is a serial data bus designed specifically for linking digital musical instruments to each other and to computers. A MIDI bus does not pass audio even in digital form. Instead, it passes commands and timing information to devices that can generate music.

MIDI-compatible keyboards, synthesizers, samplers, and other hardware can be connected to create elaborate music generation systems. MIDI and related hardware are discussed in more detail in Chapter 8.

Equipment Racks

For all but the smallest installations, equipment racks are used to mount audio equipment. Racks simplify construction, protect the equipment, make transportation easier, and create a more professional appearance.

Rack-mountable equipment is securely fastened into racks via screws on the front panel. Heavier equipment requires internal guides or side braces to help support the weight.

Rack-mounted shelves allow equipment that is not designed for rack use to be mounted. These shelves are available in plain and predrilled versions. Shelves can either be fixed or roll out like a drawer. Drawers are also available for storing supplies.

Large studio racks are readily available. Special desks with built-in racks enable one to create a customized audio workstation. Well-designed desks have provisions for computers as well as audio equipment.

Low cost, open-frame racks for desktop use are also available. These minimalist racks are skeletons made from steel or aluminum tubes (with square cross sections) welded together to create a basic mounting frame. They provide support, but no protection for the equipment. One advantage is ready access to the rear panels of equipment mounted in them.

Racks come in one standard width (19 inches), but heights vary. This height is often specified as a number of slots. A single-height (one-slot) device is approximately two inches tall (an eight-slot rack holds eight such devices).

Portable Racks

An alternative to the studio rack is the portable rack. Built into rugged carrying cases, portable racks are excellent choices for home or small business installations in which equipment must be stored between recording sessions, or in applications in which on-location recording is expected.

These case-mounted racks come with removable front and rear covers that allow the unit to be sealed tight against contact, dust, and weather. This is a valuable feature when transporting equipment or when recording outdoors. Look for cases with tight-fitting latches and rubber-sealing gaskets.

A wide variety of case-mounted racks are available, with as few as two slots or as many as twelve or more. When selecting cases, make certain they have feet on the bottom and matching indentations on the top so that several cases can be safely stacked to create larger portable setups.

If rough handling is expected, case-mounted racks are available with internal suspension systems that provide some degree of shock isolation. Although larger and more expensive than plain cases of the same capacity, case-mounted racks provide better protection for the even-more-expensive audio equipment inside them.

Cooling a Rack

Special care must be taken to ensure proper cooling of rack-mounted equipment. All audio equipment generates heat during operation. Large power amplifiers generate the most heat, but even signal processors and battery-operated equipment generate heat. This heat must be constantly removed or the temperature rises to dangerous levels. This rise in temperature drastically shortens equipment life and could even become a fire hazard.

Always test a new rack configuration by "burning it in" for a few hours under close scrutiny. Frequently check the case temperatures of every piece of equipment during this test. If anything feels abnormally warm or if you smell an odor, immediately remove power and rearrange the setup to improve cooling.

Don't operate equipment in portable racks unless the covers are removed. Also, don't block cooling holes or vents. Large studio racks often have rear or side doors that can be opened during operation. Unused bays in racks can be left open or covered with perforated panels that allow air flow.

Power Modules

Power modules are rack-mounted power outlets. One switch on the front panel controls power to numerous 120 volt AC power sockets on the back side. An outlet may also be mounted on the front panel. Power modules are often built in thick steel cases to provide some degree of magnetic shielding. This shielding prevents stray magnetic fields generated inside the power modules from escaping and inducing hum in sensitive audio equipment that is nearby.

Surge protection features prevent high-voltage spikes on the power line from damaging expensive audio equipment. Most units also have an EMI/RFI filter that stops high-frequency noise coming in or going out from the power line.

Power-and-light modules represent an improvement on the basic power module. In addition to having all the features of a power module, a power-and-light module also has small lights mounted in retractable metal tubes. These light tubes are useful in places such as darkened clubs or nighttime concerts. A light switch separate from the main power switch and a light-dimmer knob are usually provided.

Consumer Tips for Buying Pro-Audio Equipment

Choosing the right equipment is not a simple task. Computer enthusiasts who feel at home in a computer superstore or consumer electronics outlet are often bewildered in a music store's pro-audio department.

What looks good in a magazine ad or direct-mail flyer may or may not work as expected in the studio. Salespersons give conflicting views. Different manufacturers produce models that look similar, but only one may be "right" for a certain application. How does one make the decision of what to buy and where to buy it?

The following tips should help:

◆ Plan before you buy. Consider the entire system, not just a piece at a time. See Chapter 11 for a discussion on audio system design and integration.

◆ When buying a piece of equipment, create a checklist of features you want. Classify each feature as either essential or nonessential and rank its priority. Refine this list as you do your research. Be careful not to rank frills ahead of basic needs. (Don't buy a microphone that has a fancy gold-plated case and a built-in vacuum-tube amp, but also has a frequency response curve that looks like a roller coaster.)

◆ Look beyond immediate needs. A more expensive unit with more features may be a better buy than a simple unit you may outgrow in six months. Don't go overboard, however, because you could end up paying for features you may never use.

◆ Do your research. The World Wide Web has a wealth of data on audio hardware. Use caution—plenty of hype and misinformation also exist amidst the data. Newsgroups such as rec.audio.pro or rec.audio.tech are useful resources for gathering opinions and obtaining views of experienced users. Be specific, check for recent discussions before posting queries, and stay within the charter of the group if you expect good answers. Magazine reviews, such as those found in *Mix* or *Electronic Musician,* are also good sources of information. Some of these are online as well as in-print. Books are excellent sources of information, but unfortunately they cannot be published fast enough to keep up with specific models. The references at the end of this chapter are recommended.

◆ Get a demo before you buy. Within reason, reputable stores are glad to do one for you. Use your checklist to compare features.

◆ Build a professional relationship with the sales staff and store management who seem the most knowledgeable and treat you fairly on a consistent basis. They are a valuable resource.

Despite the best efforts of the buyer, quirks and qualities of the audio gear are often not revealed until the equipment is used in the intended application.

For this reason, buy from stores and mail-order outfits that have money-back guarantees. Such guarantees should be standard store policy and should come without restocking fees or other strings (sometimes the buyer must pay return shipping for mail orders, however). The return period should be valid for at least a few days, although thirty is preferred. Save all receipts and packing materials at least until the end of this return period. To be fair, don't abuse this privilege to try equipment you know you won't keep. If you abuse this privilege you will lose it.

Summary

This chapter has presented a brief survey of pro-audio equipment and how it is used. This survey was intended to get the reader started and to cover everything needed to set up a basic home or small-business recording studio.

The survey was not meant to be exhaustive; that would require at least several volumes the size of this book. Literally hundreds of types of audio gear have not been mentioned. For those interested in this equipment, a visit to a large, well-stocked music store that handles pro-audio gear will be very enlightening. Alternately, a web surfing session can provide similar information. Start with a web search using keywords such as audio, MIDI, sound recording, or microphone.

Knowledge of audio equipment is only a start. The right components must be pulled together into a complete system and properly used to achieve quality results. The next chapter, "Digital Audio Recording and Editing," covers audio system integration and other topics, discussing how to build and effectively use a sound recording system.

Further Reading

For in-depth discussions of the topics discussed in this chapter, consult the following references:

[BARTLETT]: "Practical Recording Techniques" by Bruce and Jenny Bartlett. Sams, 1992. ISBN 0-672-30265-9. Paperback, 511 Pages.
Less technical than [HUBER1] or [NARDAN], but still a solid treatment of equipment and recording techniques.

[HUBER1]: "Modern Recording Techniques" 4th ed. by David M. Huber and Robert E. Runstein. Sams Publishing, 1995. ISBN 0-672-30639-5. Paperback, 496 pages.
An excellent, moderately technical treatment of audio equipment with plenty of practical examples. It also covers basic studio acoustics and recording techniques.

[HUBER2]: "Hard Disk Recording for Musicians" by David Miles Huber. AMSCO Publications, 1995. ISBN 0-8256-1433-3. (In the UK, ISBN 0-7119-4353-2.) Paperback (large format) 192 pages.
A specialized text focusing primarily on computer-based sound, music, and multimedia production. Despite the title, the majority of the book is also of interest to nonmusicians who use direct-to-disk recording. Huber takes a more practical, less technical approach in this book than in [HUBER1].

[MCIAN]: "Using Your Portable Studio," by Peter McIan. AMSCO Publications, 1996. ISBN 0-8256-1437-6. (In the UK, ISBN 0-7119-4357-5.) Paperback (large format), 301 pages.
Despite a frequently flippant narrative, this book is an excellent reference for owners of portable studios. It covers all aspects of basic recording in a practical, highly readable manner.

[NARDAN]: "Sound Studio Production Techniques" by Dennis N. Nardantonio. TAB Books, 1990. ISBN 0-8306-3250-6. Paperback, 293 pages.
Not as thick a book as [HUBER1], but nonetheless a good, moderately technical survey of acoustics, audio equipment, and recording techniques.

C H A P T E R

11

DIGITAL AUDIO RECORDING AND EDITING

You might be a musician, poet, comic, playwright or author who wants to offer his audio creations to the world. You might be a candidate for city council with something to say to the voters. Perhaps you're a researcher or teacher who wants to use the Internet to distribute your collection of bird calls. Or maybe you belong to an amateur theater group and want to have a home page, complete with audio, featuring your latest production. Or maybe all you really want to do is spruce up your personal website with a few sound clips.

For the first time ever, there is a media that enables you or anyone else with persistence, basic computer skills, and relatively little money to be quite literally heard around the world. This media, Internet audio, is the next best thing to owning your own international radio network.

In this chapter, we show you how to record and edit your own audio in a form suitable for posting on a website. In simplest form, recording is nothing more than plugging a microphone into your PC's sound card or your Mac's sound port, then loading the audio software that came bundled with your system. Recording can also be a more elaborate affair, using several microphones, a multitrack recorder, signal processors and other equipment. (See Chapter 10, "Audio Equipment Basics," for a discussion of essential audio equipment.)

Recording and editing audio was once entirely in the realm of the professional. This has changed. It is now driven by the availability of low-cost computers, powerful audio editing software, and innovative audio equipment. A person, group, or small business with a few hundred to a few thousand dollars to invest can soon be recording songs, advertisements, talk shows or anything else.

A good recording session is a wonderful, creative experience for performers and audio engineers alike. Stage fright or recording jitters vanish as the singer raises her voice to the heavens, or the poet delivers his sonnets in beautiful baritone. The engineer (amateur or professionl) contributes heavily too, working like a master chef, blending raw ingredients to create a product that is greater than the sum of its parts.

Professionals lend their talent and long experience to the craft of sound, but amateurs have their own magic, offering a freshness that cannot be duplicated. It's truly amazing what some people will do in front of a microphone—compensated only by personal satisfaction and perhaps the promise of hot pizza and cold beer.

This is not to say it doesn't take practice, patience, and the right equipment to produce quality results. Don't be discouraged if your first efforts at recording or editing aren't what you expected. Even if they sound terrible, remember that you will improve rapidly as you keep practicing and learning.

As you develop your skills and collect the right equipment, you'll find youself capable of producing more audio of better quality in less time.

This chapter covers the essentials of setting up a recording session and editing the results into a workable form suitable for posting on a website. The approach concentrates on getting your equipment ready for the session, setting up an improvised studio, conducting the session properly, and editing the audio.

More specifically, the following subjects are examined:

◆ How to integrate various pieces of audio gear into a working audio system that will meet your recording needs

◆ How to improvise a recording studio in the home, school, or small business

◆ How to conduct a recording session for maximum effect

◆ What audio editing software is available to finish the job

◆ Basic audio editing tips

A Small Percentage

My friend and coauthor Patrick Seaman took a job with a startup company called AudioNet early in 1995. About six months later, he called me with an unusual idea. He had convinced his management to start an audio "Book Nook" on AudioNet's website and wanted to give me the opportunity to post dramatic readings from my science fiction novel, *A Small Percentage*. These readings would be done in episodes, giving them a flavor reminiscent of the radio serials of the 1930s and 40s.

I accepted the offer, although I didn't really know what to think of it at first. Patrick made it quite clear that it was experimental. The bulk of AudioNet's content at that time consisted of sporting events and live feeds from radio stations, so this was something very different. As far as we knew, this had never been done before. I had a solid technical background in computers and engineering, but knew nothing about recording or sound editing.

Fortunately, I found help from Donny Barton, a friend from work. Donny had paid his way through college as a radio dejay. It had been years since he had done any

continues

recording, but he was willing to give it a try. We were soon joined by another friend, Sami Mikhail, a fellow writer and computer enthusiast.

Figuring out how to record and edit sound on a computer turned out to be a lot easier than I expected. I wrote the script and served as producer, engineer, and director. Donny served as our reader and technical advisor. Sami did voices and kept us honest as our resident drama critic.

Our first episode was posted on AudioNet a few weeks later. I was a little nervous about it. It was obviously an amateur production, and I worried if anyone would take it seriously.

The most amazing thing happened a few days later. We received our first fan mail! At that point I realized we were on to something. Audio on the Internet was a whole new media.

Integrating an Audio System

The journey into recording begins by putting together the right equipment. Just as a carpenter must have the right tools to frame a house, an audio engineer, whether professional or amateur, must have the right audio gear to make a recording. Exactly what is needed and how it is connected depends on the type of recording being made.

Almost any imaginable audio system can be created using the wide variety of off-the-shelf components available. (See Chapter 10, "Audio Equipment Basics"for a few examples of these components.) Unfortunately, this same variety also represents a nearly infinite set of choices. Putting together a reasonable solution to your audio needs can seem a daunting task.

Too little effort in the planning stage often results in an expensive hodge-podge of equipment that can't get the job done. Even if a working system is eventually produced, there will also be a closet full of mistakes. However, too much planning results in "analysis paralysis," an infinite planning loop in which nothing ever gets built.

The best way to avoid both traps is a top-down, five-step design process. This process is described in the following sections.

Step 1: Define Your Goals

Define what you want to do with the audio system. This definition need not be elaborate, but it does need to be done. A problem can't be solved until it's defined!

Don't define your goals in terms of equipment:

> "I want a mixer and a power amp and ten microphones and—"
> (WRONG!)

This statement is wrong because it isn't a list of goals. It's a list of assumptions—many of which are probably wrong. Instead, focus on the intended uses:

> "I want to record a six-piece band, a lead singer, and two backup singers. The band's instruments consist of drums, bass guitar, two guitars, sax, and piano." (CORRECT!)

Or perhaps:

> "I want to record a series of dramatic readings from various books. These readings will be done by a narrator and several voice actors (usually no more than three, but there could be more on rare occasions). Some of these books are science fiction, so I anticipate a need for special effects to create alien voices, machinery sounds, and so forth." (CORRECT!)

Goals can, of course, include several different purposes, such as recording both the gospel singing and the preaching from a church service.

Don't forget to think a few years out. You may want to record only the essentials at first and add more elaborate recording capabilities later. Recognizing this up front helps in later stages of planning. Don't go too far out though. It's virtually impossible to accurately plan more than a few years out. Even if you can, one audio system won't be able to span the entire time.

Step 2: Derive Requirements

After your goals are established, use them to derive a set of requirements. This still isn't an equipment list, so fight the urge to begin specifying things you don't yet know you need. Instead, try to define requirements by answering these questions:

◆ What will be the maximum number of unique sound sources? What type will they be? Singers? Musical instruments? A single news reader?

◆ How might the sound sources be grouped together?

◆ What are the basic characteristics of each sound source or each group of sources? Are they vocals? Percussion? Acoustic instruments? MIDI synthesizers or samplers? Do they have internal audio pickups, or will external microphones be needed?

◆ Will special effects be needed? If so, will they be recorded at a studio or on location?

◆ Does the system need to be portable? Mounted in a van? Shipped across the country? Small enough to fit in a backpack?

◆ How good does the sound need to be? CD quality? AM-radio quality? Phone line quality? Will the final product be used only on the Internet, or will there also be CDs or audio tapes?

◆ Where will the sound be recorded? In a studio? At home? At a concert? On a sidewalk at a busy intersection?

◆ What's the budget? Is it a one-time expense or spread out over a period of time?

◆ How much room for growth is needed? Will the system need to expand over time, or will it simply be replaced at some point?

One of the traps at this stage is to go back to the prior step and begin adding more goals. A little of this is to be expected and will result in a more versatile design. Too much results in analysis paralysis or an overdone, over-budget system.

Also, infinite detail isn't needed. A general understanding of the requirements is usually sufficient. Too much detail is rarely productive, and it wastes time.

Step 3: Generate a Generic Equipment List

Using the list of requirements, begin defining the equipment that will be needed. Keep it generic at this point. Check off each requirement as it's met.

An excerpt from the generic equipment list might look something like the following:

> Microphones, vocal, cardioid: 2
>
> Microphones, vocal, omnidirectional: 1
>
> Microphones, instrument, hypercardioid: 4
>
> Microphone stands and booms: 6
>
> Mixer, with (list of features)
>
> Direct-to-disk recorder with (list of features)
>
> Studio rack
>
> Power and light module

Refining the list requires some iteration. Begin looking at product reviews at this point for ideas, but avoid specific equipment as much as possible. If you need help—and most people do—the following sources of information might be of assistance:

◆ The references listed at the end of Chapter 10, "Audio Equipment Basics."

◆ An Internet search on the topic in question.

◆ Usenet newsgroups such as rec.audio.pro or rec.audio.technical.

◆ Sales staff at pro audio and music (not consumer audio) stores. Be warned that many will try to steer you toward specific products before you are ready to select.

◆ Magazines with pro audio coverage, such as *Mix* or *Electronic Musician*.

Step 4: Select Equipment

Real products are selected using the generic equipment list as a guide. This is probably the most complicated step. It's also the step in which the most assistance is required. A trusted salesperson (no, that isn't an oxymoron) is an invaluable resource at this point. If you live in a larger city, you might be fortunate enough to have a number of good choices from which to buy audio gear.

Some iteration is to be expected. Changes are made based on budget and new equipment discovered during the search. Avoid impulse buying.

Step 5: Integrate and Test the System

If Steps 1 through 4 of this process have been followed with care, Step 5 is a relatively simple matter of mounting everything in a rack and plugging it together. A few minor problems can be expected, though, no matter how careful your planning.

Testing is needed to find and solve these problems and to learn how to best use the system. Common problems include figuring out how to fit everything into a rack, or how to eliminate ground loops. (See the section on Ground Loops, later in this chapter). More serious problems are sometimes encountered, such as the wrong equipment selection or damaged products.

Comments on the Process

The five-step process works if you stick to it. This doesn't mean you won't have a few problems. There are always mistakes, but the effects will be minimized if you work carefully.

One of the worst traps is to buy equipment on impulse. You might be offered a "great deal" and buy an expensive piece of gear before you know what you really need. Usually this doesn't work out as expected. Even worse, there is a temptation to force it to work, which can cause even more problems.

In summary, follow the process and work carefully. The effort required to do the planning pays off in a system that meets your audio recording needs in an economical manner.

Hardware Versus Software Processing

A question often encountered during audio system design is the hardware/software tradeoff. With the wide variety of signal processors and effects boxes available today, it's a simple matter to fill a large rack full of them. Such an installation of hardware is powerful and flexible, but it's also expensive and hard to automate. With recent advances in audio-editing software, most of the same functions can now be done off-line, on the computer, at a much lower cost. More functionality is available with every new release of software.

Does this mean specialized audio hardware is obsolete? It depends.

If you're planning live Internet broadcasts, the audio must be processed in real time. Hardware is the only choice. If the broadcasts are prerecorded, however, processing can be done off line, and hardware processors become redundant.

But this isn't always the case. High performance audio software puts a heavy load on a computer in terms of memory, CPU speed, and disk space. Not all machines have the processing power to support this. A $300 effects box might be an attractive alternative to a $3,000 computer upgrade. Whether you use hardware or software processors depends on your needs and budget.

Hardware can also save you time during the editing process. If reverberations and other effects are inserted during recording, they don't have to be added later during editing. The danger here is that after these effects are inserted, they can't be removed. A mistake might require another recording session to fix the problem. In such cases, it makes sense to record unprocessed audio on a spare track as a backup.

Follow the five-step process before buying anything. Define your audio plans and needs in steps 1, 2, and 3. Then, during step 4, determine what requires hardware and what can be done in software. Such planning not only saves money—it results in a more optimized system.

Audio Quality

Another design decision you must make is the level of audio quality you need for your website application. Audio professionals strive to capture and maintain the most accurate, lowest-noise signals during recording. This is fine for creating a hit record, but how much of this is needed for the Internet? What is the right sampling rate? Is an 8-bit format okay, or is the added quality of 16-bit audio needed? This decision is important because the higher the quality, the higher the need for Internet bandwidth to support it.

The best solution is to use only as much audio quality (and bandwidth) as you need to get your message across. CD-quality stereo audio adds nothing to the reading of a stock report. Even on something more demanding, such as a radio play, high fidelity is nice, but not essential. As has been discussed in the discussions on static and streaming audio formats (see Chapter 2, "Static (Downloadable) File Formats" and Chapter 4, "RealAudio"), overkill is a waste of precious Internet bandwidth. Often, 8-bit audio at a low sampling rate is adequate.

This selection of the lowest bandwidth solution raises another question. Suppose you don't need top quality audio for your site. Should you bother to make the original recording at a higher quality?

Yes, you should bother for two reasons. First, even if nothing more than 8-bit, low-bandwidth sound is ever needed, you don't want to degrade the quality further by using a bad master recording.

Second, a higher resolution version of your audio work might be needed at a later date. For example, suppose that a song, dramatic reading, or play first posted on the Internet becomes popular. It might become commercially viable to sell copies on CDs or cassette tapes. Or perhaps you just want to pass out a few high-quality copies to your friends, classmates, or business associates.

High-quality masters are needed to produce high-quality copies. Also, Internet bandwidth will not always be as low as it is today. Someday, we will all have our own high-bandwidth Internet connections, and sending high-quality, high-bandwidth audio will not be a problem.

An Example Audio System

Following is a design example that follows the five-step, top-down process. It's described in compressed form for the sake of brevity. Numbers correspond to steps in the process:

1. The goal was to build a small audio system designed for recording dramatic readings and "radio" plays for Internet broadcast. The system would usually reside in a home studio, but limited field use was also anticipated. Even at home, some portability would be needed because

the "studio" was actually a den that had to be returned to its original purpose after each session.

2. While defining requirements for this system, it was determined that recording would be kept relatively simple. Effects and other sophisticated functions would be done off-line using Macintosh sound-editing software. Even so, some limited effects and signal-processing functions were needed during recording. Isolating the voices of actors who would be standing fairly close together during recording was essential. Effects processing would be required for doing alien voices during science fiction readings. Music, if used, would either be canned or recorded from acoustic instruments.

3. The generic equipment list included a four-channel, digital tape recorder. This would meet the requirement to accommodate four cast members or three cast members and a backup channel. Digital sound quality was highly desirable. Portability drove the need for a case-mounted rack. Hypercardioid microphones and noise gates would help isolate actors' voices and reduce background noise. Compressors and noise gates in each channel would handle the wide dynamic range encountered during some of the more spirited readings and also reduce noise.

4. Product selection was fairly straightforward for most components, with a few exceptions. The recorder posed the greatest problem. A four-track, digital tape recorder was not to be found. Eight-track units were plentiful, but all exceeded the budget for this project. The solution came in the form of the new Yamaha MD-4 Multitrack MD Recorder, supposedly the first one sold in the Dallas/Fort Worth area.

5. The most difficult part of system integration was drilling and cutting sheet metal to accommodate several components that were not originally meant for rack mounting. A minor ground loop problem (see the section on Group Loops later in this chapter) was encountered that took longer than expected to fix.

A large wooden kitchen cart was commandeered for service as an audio "crash cart." It proved an excellent portable platform to hold the rack and most other audio equipment needed for a small recording session. In use, it's wheeled from the recording studio (the owner's den) to the editing room (the owner's home office) as required. When not needed, it is stored out of the way in a back room or a large closet. Figure 11.1 shows the completed system.

FIGURE 11.1

Audio system for recording dramatic readings.

To summarize, the end result is a small but capable audio system that's well optimized for its intended purpose. It's not a high-end system, but that's not the goal. A good solution is one that meets the user's needs in an economical manner—not some monster recording machine that can do anything.

Systems much like this one are within the budget of an individual, band, small business, or school. Combine it with a computer for sound editing, and you have a practical means of creating audio destined for the Internet.

Ground Loops

If you work with audio equipment for any length of time, there is a very good chance you will encounter a noise problem known as a *ground loop*. Figure 11.2 illustrates this problem. Ground loops, in one form or another, will happen sooner or later in almost all audio systems.

In this example, a mixer output is connected to the input of a power amp through an unbalanced, but well-shielded, cable. The mixer has a low-impedence (see Chapter 9, "Sound Basics and Audio Theory") driver with plenty of reserve power to drive the line. The amp has a low-noise input circuit. All equipment is properly connected and is known to be in good condition. No significant electric or magnetic fields are in the area, and the AC power is clean.

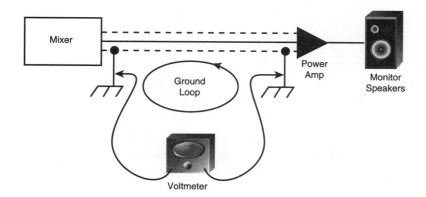

FIGURE 11.2

Ground loop in an audio system.

Almost no noise should be introduced in this arrangement, yet a loud hum is heard on the studio monitors. What's wrong?

After some experimenting, the audio engineer discovers the mixer and power amp are plugged into different AC power sockets. When both mixer and amp are plugged into the same socket, the problem disappears. On further examination, a potential difference of a few hundred millivolts AC is measured between the safety grounds of the two sockets.

Although small, this voltage difference causes a large 60 Hz current to flow in the low-impedance ground sheath of the audio cable. As a result, it stops behaving as a shield and couples 60 Hz of AC hum into the audio signal.

Ground loops such as this are common in large audio systems or in systems that are distributed over a wide area. Less severe problems can happen even in small systems.

Ideally, the ground potential on all safety grounds in a building should be the same. No current should flow in these ground wires, except in the case of a *fault* (a short circuit). In practice, this is rarely true. Unless a serious problem exists, these differences are at worst a few volts and don't represent a safety hazard. This is of little comfort to the audio engineer attempting to send clean audio signals between different pieces of audio gear that operate on different AC power circuits.

Warning If the voltage difference between safety grounds is more than a volt or two, this can indicate a dangerous wiring problem or a short circuit in a motor, appliance, or lighting fixture. Consult a qualified electrician immediately.

Another type of ground loop can be created in very long cables—even if no safety ground problems exist (for example, in a microphone tied to a distant preamp). In such cables, the resistance of the shield becomes significant. An ideal shield would have zero resistance and would therefore have the same voltage (referenced to earth ground) at any point on it. Short cables with heavy ground sheathing come close to this ideal. Long cables, particularly the cheaper variety, are not so good.

When fields from nearby AC wiring or radio transmitters encounter a weak ground sheath, currents are created that reduce the effectiveness of the sheath's shielding and induce hum and other noises in the signal lines.

"Long" and "short" are subjective assessments. It's difficult, if not impossible, to assign hard values to them because the severity of ground loops of this type also depends upon the strength of the offending fields and the design of the cables.

To summarize, ground loops are currents flowing in ground sheaths of cables. They reduce the sheath's ability to function as a shield and also introduce hum or other noise. They're caused by a difference in ground potential between the ends of the cable or an external field that induces a current in a long, resistive sheath.

Fixing Ground Loops

Ground loop problems are corrected by the following methods:

◆ Eliminating the voltage difference causing the ground loop

◆ Breaking the ground loop

◆ Using balanced inputs, outputs and cables to reduce the impact of the ground loop

In the example of the mixer and power amp, plugging both pieces of equipment into the same AC wall socket solves the problem. This is often an effective solution in small, localized audio systems in which a single AC circuit can safely provide enough power to operate the entire system.

In larger systems, this isn't an option. Group loops are sometimes prevented by isolating each piece of equipment from rack ground using nylon mounting screws and electrical tape to prevent metal surfaces from contacting each other. The isolated components are then tied to a safety ground at a single point, using heavy ground wires or braid. This is called a *single-point ground* or a *star ground*. Voltage differences are eliminated because all component grounds are connected to the same point.

Warning

Although it might be tempting to remove the safety ground on a piece of audio gear, *don't do it*. This practice is dangerous and unnecessary. Other methods, such as those described in this section, can prevent ground loops.

Most low-powered audio gear use small plug-in power transformers. If they have two-prong unpolarized plugs, reversing the way they're plugged in to the AC power can sometimes reduce hum. This should be done one transformer at a time, checking to see whether the hum is reduced before going on to the next one.

Also, these transformers produce strong magnetic fields. What appears to be a ground loop could actually be *inductive pickup* (see Chapter 9) from a transformer. Dynamic microphones and high-gain amplifiers are particularly sensitive.

Another way to break the ground loop is to disconnect the shield at one end of an audio cable, thus breaking the ground loop. The end of the cable with the ground connection should be connected to the audio source. The unground end should be connected to the destination. Disconnecting the shield is usually done by modifying a cable, but there is also a special adapter—a *direct box* with a *ground-lift* switch that disconnects the ground shield. (Direct boxes are adapters for connecting circuits of different impedance.)

Systems with balanced inputs and outputs—connected with balanced cables—also help. Although they don't prevent the ground loop, they do greatly reduce its impact. Differential amplifiers with balanced inputs are sensitive to the voltage difference between the two balanced input signals— not their absolute voltage. Hum from a ground loop usually appears as the same voltage on both balanced conductors. As a result, the hum is canceled.

Safety Checklist

Working with audio equipment is generally a safe activity; however, a chance for injury exists if common sense safety rules aren't obeyed. Failing to take adequate safety precautions endangers not only the equipment operator, but performers and bystanders as well. The following list is not exhaustive, but it does cover many of the common hazards:

Follow Instructions: Read and follow the instructions and warnings provided with your equipment.

Damaged Equipment: Don't use equipment that's known to be defective, has been damaged, runs excessively hot, has been wet, has caused a shock, or creates an odor.

Cooling: Never block cooling holes or otherwise impede air flow. Don't stack equipment in such a manner that it traps heat. This includes, but isn't limited to, rack-mounted equipment.

Stacks, Racks, and Lifting: Don't stack equipment in an unstable manner, or so high that it could cause injury if it falls. Racks are usually front heavy and can tip forward with unexpected ease. Use caution when moving or lifting them. Two people are needed to lift them. Lift with your legs, not your back.

Bystanders: Always be watchful of children, pets, and overly curious visitors.

Water: Water and high voltage don't mix. Most audio gear isn't designed to operate in the rain, near swimming pools, or in bath tubs. Water can ruin equipment, create a shock hazard, or even start a fire if something shorts out.

Cords and Cables: Worn or damaged power cords should be replaced immediately. Never disconnect a safety ground. Cords and cables should never be placed on the floor in high traffic areas. Even in a studio setting, route cables carefully to minimize the chance of someone tripping over them. Power cords require extra care since they could also cause a shock or start a fire if damaged. It may be necessary to tape down cables, or use special plastic or aluminum bridges that lie flat on the floor and cover cables to protect them.

If a hazard can't be eliminated, warn performers and visitors about it. Post warning signs if necessary.

AC Wiring: Always be cautious when setting up in an unfamiliar building or outdoors. It's all too common to have miswired power outlets that can create a dangerous hot-chassis situation. It's a good idea to bring a voltmeter or at least an AC circuit tester. Low-cost circuit testers can be found at any hardware store that will identify incorrect grounding and other problems. Be particularly careful when dealing with multiple AC circuits that are on different sides of the 240-volt main. Consult a qualified, licensed electrician if any problems are found.

GFIs: Ground fault interrupters (GFIs) are special circuit breakers that disconnect AC power very quickly when a current is detected in the safety ground wire. They can prevent shocks in certain situations and are required by most local electric codes when using electrical equipment outdoors or near water. If you are having trouble with a GFI tripping too frequently, fight the urge to bypass it. It is tripping for a reason, and that reason could be a dangerous short-circuit in a cord or inside equipment.

Repair: Always unplug equipment before you work on it. Don't attempt to repair or modify equipment unless you're qualified.

Hearing Damage: Prolonged exposure to loud music or other sounds, or even short-term exposure to very loud sounds, can cause permanent hearing damage, tinnitus, and other health problems. Such damage is insidious, often going unnoticed until the problem is severe. Keep the volume down, wear hearing protection, or—better yet—avoid exposure. Don't forget about headphones. Like speakers, they too can generate high sound pressure levels.

Safety Codes: If you're setting up in a public place or in a business, you might be subject to electrical codes and OSHA or other safety rules. Even home installations are subject to local electrical codes if they are permanently installed. Always check with management or appropriate authorities when in doubt.

Think: Most importantly, think before you do! Most accidents are the result of negligence, ignorance, haste, or fatigue.

Improvising a Recording Studio

After completing the audio system, the next step is finding a place to record. If you have the money or the connections to have ready access to a professional recording studio, you're far ahead of the crowd. Few readers will have this option though.

A large, well-equipped, well-staffed recording studio can cost hundreds of dollars an hour in rental fees. Studio owners can defend these prices because of their heavy investments in equipment and facilities and the salaries of skilled technicians. Smaller studios with lesser capabilities are more reasonably priced, but even they're too expensive for many potential users.

The solution is often the home (or small business, school, and so on) studio. Turning a spare bedroom or storage area into an improvised rehearsal hall and recording studio can eliminate, or at least reduce, the need for professional facilities.

If you need something larger, you might be able to borrow space in a school, community center, or local theater. Arrangements could even be made to trade audio/Internet expertise for use of the space.

Studio Acoustics

A critical factor in the selection of a room for a studio is the acoustics. Some rooms are said to be *live*, or *hot*. Ceramic floor tiles, paneled walls, and an absence of furniture make a room lively, turning it into an echo chamber. Environmental noises also seem louder because there is little to dampen them. In some cases, such as for a rock band, a live room may be an advantage because it provides a natural reverb effect. For other cases, such as a news report or a dramatic reading, the echoes in an overly live room can be a major problem.

Sound leaves its source and strikes a surface. Part of the energy is absorbed, part is transmitted through the object, and part is reflected back toward the source and other surfaces. Sound can reverberate many times before it's finally dissipated as heat.

The time required for all the reverberations to die down to inaudible levels is called the *reverberation time*. (A more technical definition calls for a 60 Db reduction in sound levels.) The reverberation time is almost always frequency dependent, usually longer at low frequencies than at high ones. Times may be as long as a second in a very large and particularly lively room.

Reverberation times on the order of .40 seconds are preferable for popular music recording. Longer times tend to produce deterioration in the quality of music and vocals. Far shorter times—approaching zero—are often preferable for speech recordings, such as news reports.

Live rooms can be deadened somewhat with carpets and wall hangings, but the results are often unacceptable. Low (bass) frequencies are not easily absorbed by mere surface coverings. They pass right through them to reflect off hard surfaces underneath. High frequencies, however, are easily absorbed. For example, data in [EVEREST] indicates that a heavy carpet on a concrete floor absorbs 65 percent of the incident sound at 4 KHz, but only 2 percent at 125 Hz. Too many surfaces like this in a studio result in a muddy, unnatural sound that lacks clarity and sparkle.

Special acoustic insulation is available that does a better job of absorbing a broader range of frequencies. There are several types of this material, including dense foam and rigid fiberglass. The fiberglass material requires a cloth covering to prevent contact with irritating glass fibers. Consult a building contractor or the manufacturer if you are not familiar with safe handling and use of fiberglass. This insultation is available through pro-audio outlets and some building supply companies

A room also has *resonances*. The shape of the room tends to reinforce certain frequencies much more than others. This is similar to what happens when a tuning fork is struck. The result can be an unpleasant, booming effect, usually at low frequencies. Small square rooms tend to be the worst. Large rooms that are rectangular or irregular in shape are much less affected.

A room can be also too "dead" for its intended use. A small, heavily insulated room with plush carpets, thick underflooring, lots of upholstered furniture, a drop ceiling, and heavy draperies may be very dull acoustically. Environmental noises are reduced, but musical instruments seem to lack volume and ambiance due to a lack of reflecting surfaces. Recording outdoors can produce a similar effect.

What's ideal as a studio depends on the application. Music tends to work better in a live room; speech recording doesn't.

As a compromise, it may be desirable to have a room somewhere between the extremes. There are enough reflecting surfaces to create a natural sound ambiance, yet the reverberation time isn't so long that echoes are overwhelming.

A large, open room with a carpeted floor and plasterboard walls and ceiling may be the best choice in a house. The den or living room usually works fairly well for many purposes.

Electronic Compensation for Bad Acoustics

Modern audio technology can compensate for some acoustic problems. The acoustics themselves aren't modified. It's the audio that's processed to simulate the effects of more desirable acoustics.

Low-gain, unidirectional microphones can be placed as close as possible to sound sources to receive mostly direct sounds and reject reverberations. This isolates the sources from the room acoustics. Effects units or equivalent software can then be used to process the audio to simulate the more desirable acoustics of a large hall or recording studio. Some effects units even feature modes that emulate a range of idealized concert halls and recording studios.

The end result is a recording that's more pleasing, but also very different from the live sound. Note that this is a one-way process. It's always possible to add reverb, but almost impossible to remove it.

Soundproofing

Another acoustic quality of a good studio is how well it's isolated from outside sounds. Low-frequency sounds are particularly difficult to stop. An example of this penetrating capability of low-frequency sound is a blaring stereo in a neighbor's house or apartment. A thin, uninsulated wall, or even a pane of glass, is enough to stop most of the high frequencies—yet a much thicker wall hardly touches the thump of the bass.

A stopgap approach to sound isolation is to locate a studio at the center of a house or building. Surrounding rooms provide some degree of isolation, assuming the source of the noise isn't located in one of the surrounding rooms.

More thorough soundproofing can be accomplished with special acoustic panels, thick insulation, double walls, and special bass traps. They greatly increase the effectiveness of bass absorption, and indeed the absorption of sound across all frequencies. This also helps reduce reverberation time and resonances. These techniques are discussed in a number of references including [EVEREST], [HUBER1] and [BARTLETT]. These references are listed at the end of Chapter 9.

Sheer mass is another way to increase soundproofing. A brick or concrete wall stops more sound than a window. The quietest room in a house is often the basement because it's underground. Dense, amorphous matter such as sand and dirt are also good absorbers of sound. Dry sand is often used as a low-cost, sound absorbing insulation even in professional studios.

Other sound isolation techniques include the following:

◆ Placing weatherproofing around doors and windows

◆ Caulking or otherwise sealing all cracks to the outside

◆ Using solid doors instead of the hollow-core variety

◆ Using several layers of padding and plywood under carpets

Purpose-Built Studios

Discussion so far has centered on finding an existing room in a house or building with suitable acoustics and soundproofing. Rather than depending on what's already available, rooms can, of course, be modified to isolate them from external noises, and to give them a more acceptable acoustic "signature." A detailed discussion on this involved subject is beyond the scope of this book, but can be found in [EVEREST] (see the references listed at the end of Chapter 9).

Most major cities have building contractors specializing in the construction of sound studios, auditoriums, and other acoustic-critical structures. Even if it's a do-it-yourself project, consulting with such a professional during the planning phase helps you achieve better results and prevents expensive mistakes.

Conducting a Recording Session

Once you have your audio system assembled and have selected a suitable studio, you are ready to call your band, cast, or crew together and begin recording. In this section, the practical, technical, and legal aspects of conducting a recording session are examined. Much of this is also applicable if you are making a live Internet broadcast.

Preparations

Recording is rarely a one-person operation. Lining up the schedules of everyone in a band or cast of a play is no simple matter. Recording and rehearsal time is precious and shouldn't be wasted due to lack of preparation. The following tips should help you get the most out of a session.

◆ Scripts, sheet music, and other printed materials needed for the session should be ready to go before the start of the session. They should be marked up as needed to show each performer's part. Keep a set of different colored highlighters handy for this purpose. Set up enough easels to hold the printed materials.

◆ Stands for musical instruments, audio gear and monitors will need to be set up and adjusted.

◆ Determining optimum microphone placement takes time and experimentation. Although final adjustments probably require help from the performers, much can be done before they arrive.

◆ Microphone distance and angle from sound sources have a profound effect. Room acoustic must be taken into account. Flat surfaces act as sound reflectors, causing unwanted echoes that can combine in strange ways. Walls, ceilings, and floors all reflect sounds, but so do easels and other movable objects. Room corners tend to reflect sounds back in the direction of the source and, as such, might require special treatment.

The reader is encouraged to consult a reference such as [HUBER1] or [BARTLETT] for a more detailed discussion of microphone techniques. Also, most microphone manufacturers publish detailed application notes describing proper use of their microphones in a variety of applications.

◆ Microphone stands and booms must be properly adjusted, making sure all adjustment knobs and setscrews are tight. Microphone wind screens and pop screens must all be in place. To prevent tip overs, booms must be balanced and stands stabilized.

◆ Signal processors, mixers, effects boxes, and other equipment require proper adjustment. This takes experimentation. Gain controls must be set so that nothing overloads and causes distortion. Compressors, limiters, and noise gates take a particularly long time to adjust properly.

◆ Level controls should be set as high as possible, short of saturation. This will maximize the all-important SNR.

◆ Any time a new setup is made, it must be tested to verify that any hum and other noises are minimized. New ground loops and noise sources might be encountered.

◆ Audible noise sources must also be tracked down and eliminated. Equipment with fans (including computers) and blowers must be shut down or moved to another room. An improvised studio often has air conditioners, forced-air heaters, refrigerators, and other appliances that must be shut down. A ringing telephone also interrupts a session.

◆ Some noises will be obvious, whereas others won't. The human brain is a remarkable filter. It's very easy to become insensitive to a noise that has been present for a period of time—the rush of air through a vent, for example. Leaving the studio for a few minutes and then returning helps you to rediscover those hidden noises. Sometimes, the same effect is achieved by putting on headphones, turning up the volume a little, or otherwise changing the listening environment.

◆ Recorders should be loaded with a fresh tape or disk. Extra tapes or disks should be readily available. Batteries in portable equipment must be fresh or recently recharged. Don't forget about the batteries in some condenser microphones.

◆ Operators should be well trained and familiar with their equipment. Even so, it's a good idea to keep a set of manuals handy.

◆ Log sheets will be needed to record what's on each take and track, plus other session data. Keep a notepad ready, too.

◆ Cables for headphones, microphones and other equipment must be laid out carefully to minimize clutter and the chance for someone tripping over them. It's a good idea to perform a basic safety inspection on the setup. See the section, "Safety Checklist," presented earlier in this chapter.

◆ When everything seems ready, perform a preliminary sound check to make sure nothing was overlooked, all equipment is functioning, and all is ready for recording.

◆ Keep a small toolkit handy. This should include a selection of screwdrivers that span the range from tiny ones (that fit connector shells on cables) to giant ones (for mic stand set screws). A set of large pliers is also handy for dealing with mic stands and other heavy supports. A soldering iron, solder, insulation stripper, cutters, and needlenose pliers are essential for repairing cables. No self-respecting engineer would be caught dead without electrical tape and a supply of cable ties of various sizes.

◆ Keep a stock of beverages and snacks nearby. Recording is surprisingly hard work. Singing or doing voices is especially taxing on the throat.

With all that done, it's time to bring in the performers, make a final sound check, and perform last-minute adjustments.

Recording Mixes

Some amateurs try to capture a final product during a recording. If they want effects, they insert effects boxes in the main audio chain. If they think EQ (equalization) is needed, they do it as the recording is being made—sometimes changing settings in real time. Then they mix everything down to just a few tracks.

This is an extremely dangerous way to record. One mistake and the whole session can be ruined. After two or more sound sources are mixed, it's almost impossible to separate them. Some effects, particularly reverb, can't be removed. What sounds like barely enough reverb during recording may sound like far too much during editing.

Perceptions are different during recording than they are later because the brain acts as a filter. A recording session is a busy event also, and it's easy to overlook a mistake. For these reasons, it's much safer to make a straight recording of each sound source on a separate track and then do the final mixing, equalization, and effects during editing.

This doesn't mean effects shouldn't be put into the monitor mix for the performers to hear. This keeps everyone in synch and gives them a rough approximation of the final results after editing. Some musicians like to monitor a special mix that emphasizes their instrument because it gives them better control of their performance. Control sections of larger, more sophisticated consoles allow several mixes and submixes to be created for such purposes. Extra mixes can also be created using a second console. Figure 11.3 shows an example of such a setup in schematic form.

FIGURE 11.3

Using a second console to create extra mixes.

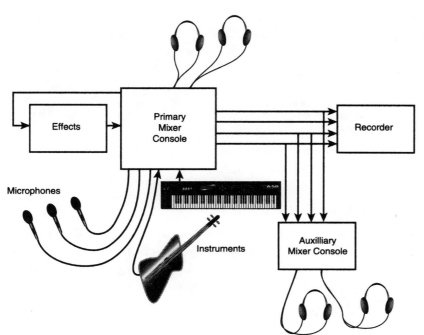

Managing a Recording Session

A recording session is a lot of work, but it should also be fun. Try to keep the session focused (and on time) by defining clear goals and fostering a sense of teamwork—yet, don't run it like a slave labor camp. Gentle persuasion and genuine leadership almost always work better than taskmaster discipline.

Actors and musicians (engineers, too) do better if they know what's expected of them. They also need a relaxed, low-stress environment in which they can concentrate on the creative aspect of their duties. This is particularly important in unpaid amateur productions where the only reward is the work itself.

Tip

Keep a Log Book!

Even a modest audio system seems to have more switches, knobs, and displays than the cockpit of a jet fighter. Remembering optimal settings, connections, and microphone locations for a particular type of recording is virtually impossible.

The solution is to keep a good log book, even when only experimenting. Record the purpose and nature of the session, the equipment used, the settings for knobs and switches, the type, and location of microphones, and so forth. A sketch of the block diagram of the audio chain is also useful.

Making and using a good log book saves time, prevents repeated errors, and helps you figure out what happened in the event of a problem.

Finally, always maintain a sense of humor. Someday, you might even sell those foulups as a blooper reel. Or maybe not…

Sound Effects Libraries

If you need sound effects, it isn't always necessary to personally record every one you'll ever need. Libraries of sound effects are available on tapes and CDs. Use of these libraries can save a lot of time and effort, assuming one can be found containing the desired effects.

The most famous of these is available from the BBC. This is a large package intended for commercial use. The cost is prohibitive to most individuals. Much smaller libraries from various suppliers are advertised in the back of many music and audio magazines. They tend to be focused on a single subject, but are much lower in price.

A word of caution: Always check and obey the licensing agreement included with these libraries. The sale price may (or may not) include licensing fees, which brings up the next topic.

Legal Issues

This section might seem a bit out of place in a technical book, but it's important to have a basic understanding of publishing law before beginning any Internet recording or broadcasting project. This understanding is particularly important because all too many people hold the false impression that copyright and other laws don't apply to the Internet. This is an absurd and thoroughly dangerous attitude. You are legally responsible for your website. Period.

Please note that the authors of this book aren't legal experts, and this section is not meant to be taken as sound legal advice (no pun intended). Our purpose is simply to raise the reader's awareness. Consult a qualified attorney for legal advice.

Copyrights

A copyright is the legal right to create, sell, and distribute copies of a creative work such as a song, play, or book. Copyrights are one form of intellectual property. Intellectual property can be bought and sold much like real property, such as a car or a house. Just as it is illegal to steal another person's real property, it is illegal to violate the copyright owner's legal rights to a protected work.

Copyrighted items can include software, sound clips, pictures, and other items commonly found on websites. A recording is considered a creative work and is protected under U.S. and international copyright law. There is usually also a separate copyright on the subject matter (the script, song, book). Permission must be obtained from both copyright owners to use, sell, or distribute the recording, even if no money is involved. Not to do so is to invite a costly lawsuit or even criminal charges.

Even unintentional copyright infringement can result in legal action. Suppose that Alice, a law-abiding webmaster, finds a nice sound clip on Usenet and incorrectly assumes it's in the public domain. She downloads and uses it on her own website, not realizing it actually is copyrighted material that has been illegally posted. Alice has committed a copyright infringement—albeit an innocent one. In our all-too litigious society, there's no guarantee that she won't be sued or that the copyright owner won't demand an inflated payment for her use of the material.

Licensing is another consideration. Copyright owners put restrictions on how their work may be used. For example, suppose you buy a Rolling Stones CD. You own the CD itself (the media), but you're licensed only for private, personal use of the music it contains. This means you can play the CD as often as you like in your own home. You can also give the CD away, sell it to a friend, or even burn it if you so decide. But you can't legally broadcast it over the Internet, in whole or in part, without a more extensive license from the publisher.

These examples show how easy it is to violate copyright law if care isn't taken. If rights to both the subject matter and the recording aren't clear, it's wise to either contact the copyright owners, forget about the posting, or consult an attorney specializing in intellectual property rights before proceeding.

Defamation and Invasion of Privacy

Slander is making false or misleading statements that injure a person's reputation. Put it in print and it becomes libel. Collectively, these acts are called *defamation*. Victims of defamation can bring suit against those persons responsible and recover damages.

Posting text, pictures, or audio on your website that unjustly injures a person's reputation could be considered defamation. Companies and organization can also be defamed if false or misleading statements damage their public image or cause them to lose business.

The intimate, personal details of a person's private life are his own business. This belief is reinforced by laws that provide protection against invasion of privacy. Using your website to reveal someone's sexual habits, medical problems, financial status, or other personal information without his permission could be an invasion of privacy that can result in a law suit. The fact that the information is true is not a defense.

Public figures have less protection under the privacy laws. A website featuring an unauthorized biography of a rock star would be far less risky than a similar unauthorized site dedicated to an unknown office worker, but even the rock star has some rights to privacy.

Consult a qualified attorney before beginning any project that could potentially cross the line from journalism or entertainment into invasion of privacy or defamation.

Digital Sound Editing

After the recording session is completed, it's time to edit the raw tracks to create a final product. In the "good old days," this involved a lot more work than it does today. Banks of analog tape recorders would play back the raw tracks through a control console. Engineers would manually change the gain and EQ in real time and add effects. All the tracks were bounced (mixed) down to create two stereo master tracks that were recorded on another tape recorder. The master still wasn't finished until the master tape was edited to remove errors. This involved cutting and splicing analog audio tape using a razor blade and special adhesive-backed tape.

Fortunately, the days of tape splicing are long gone. Engineers still work in front of control consoles, but these consoles are usually highly automated and controlled by computer. In fact, the entire editing process can be done on a computer. This method is the main focus of this section.

Macintosh or PC-based sound-editing software costing a few hundred to a few thousand dollars provides capabilities that would have cost tens or even hundreds of thousands of dollars only a decade ago.

By the way, the Macintosh is by far the dominant platform in professional, computer-based sound recording and editing. This might come as a surprise to many who come to sound recording from other areas. This doesn't mean you need to rush right out to buy a Mac, though; there are plenty of good tools for the PC.

The Basic Sound Editing Process

The first step in digital "sound" (it's really audio) editing is getting audio onto the computer. Some sound-editing software packages support direct-to-disk recording (see Chapter 10, "Audio Equipment Basics"), making this a relatively simple matter. The computer serves as a recorder and editing tool, so it's already there.

In other cases, the audio has been recorded on a separate tape or disk recorder. It must be transferred into the computer, either two tracks at a time or many tracks at a time, depending upon available computer hardware. It can also be in analog form or transferred digitally using a digital audio interface.

Digital Audio Interfaces

The two most common digital audio interfaces are AES/EBU and S/PDIF (also known as IEC-958). Although these serial buses use different connectors (XLR balanced and RCA-phono unbalanced respectively), they're similar in format. AES/EBU was originally developed for professional equipment, and S/PDIF for consumer gear. Today, this distinction has blurred, however, because many professional-audio manufacturers put S/PDIF interfaces on their products.

Both of these formats support only two channels of digital audio. For larger applications, the MADI (Multichannel Audio Digital Interface) was developed. It supports up to 56 channels.

Other digital audio formats are also in use, including those using fiber-optic links. These are proprietary, but often use the same communications protocols as their electrical cousins.

Editing the Audio

After audio is in the computer, editing can begin. The actual editing process is reminiscent of text or graphics editing in some ways, and very different in others. Depending on the tool, audio tracks are displayed as long rectangular blocks or oscilloscope traces (*waveforms*).

Pieces of these blocks or waveforms can be selected, moved, or cut away, much like graphics can be moved around in a graphical editor. The main difference between sound and other types of editing is that you can't tell what you're working with simply by looking at it. It has to be played. Often. This is true even if the sound is shown as waveforms, although some clues can be gathered from its shape. This is really not a problem, but it does take a while for the newcomer to adjust.

Waveform editing is usually prefereable to editing blocks. Waveforms enable the user to easily spot peaks, overloads, and signal levels. In some editing packages, it allows extremely fine control, down to a single sample.

Basic functions of almost all sound editing tools include cut, copy, paste, and move. Features unique to sound include fades, synch, level adjust, pan adjust, equalization, and pitch shifting.

◆ Fades are a way to gradually turn on or turn off audio. A linear or log fader window is applied to the beginning or ending of a piece of audio to bring its level up (or down) slowly. This prevents loud clicks that would be heard if the audio were turned on or off abruptly.

◆ Synch (synchronization) is a way of synchronizing audio tracks from different sources. For example, a 16-track recording session may be done using two 8-track recorders. Getting these tracks onto the computer can be done two or four at a time. There must be a way or resynchronizing the tracks on the computer.

◆ SMPTE (Society of Motion Picture and Television Engineers) time codes can be placed on tapes or with digital audio during a recording session to allow precise synchronization when the tapes are played back. A SMPTE time code identifies hours, minutes, seconds, and frames. Some audio editing tools support SMPTE time codes, allowing tracks to be re-synchronized, even if they're loaded into the computer one at a time.

SMPTE codes can also be translated into MIDI commands via MTC (MIDI Time Codes), an extension to the MIDI 1.0 standard.

◆ Pitch shifting is used to make audio higher or lower in frequency without changing the sampling rate. This rather neat trick can be used to correct speed problems with analog audio tapes and to create special effects. Pitch shifting is also used to restore the original pitch of a piece that has been time compressed or expanded. (Haven't you always wanted to talk at 400 words per minute without sounding like Alvin the Chipmunk?)

Bouncing

After basic editing is complete, the audio can be *bounced* down to a small number of tracks. *Bouncing* is simply mixing two or more tracks to obtain a new track. For most audio, the final product is mono (one track) or stereo (two tracks).

Bouncing can also be used to produce intermediate results. For example, suppose that more tracks must be edited than what can be supported by the software or hardware. Several tracks can be edited, then bounced down to a single track. The original tracks are then removed, making room for new tracks.

Many other aspects of audio editing abound, most of which are beyond the scope of this book. Becoming proficient at it is a matter of practice, experimentation, and determination. It's not rocket science, but it does take time to learn.

The Learning Curve

Digital sound editing has a steep learning curve. This is good news. As the sound editor becomes more skilled, the time required to produce the same or better results drops rapidly.

The tool itself (Digidesign's Session™, running on a Power Mac 7100) was straightforward and highly intuitive. What took time to develop were the learning and creation of editing techniques. This included learning when to take shortcuts, when not to, how to avoid time-wasting mistakes, and how to save time by different approaches to editing.

The first 15-minute episode of *A Small Percentage* required about twenty hours of actual editing time, and the results were something less than spectacular. (It was so unspectacular that it was eventually redone.)

The second episode (all are approximately 15 minutes long) required about 8–10 hours of editing and was noticeably better than the first. The editing time continued to drop until, by about the eighth episode, it had leveled off at roughly three hours. All during this time, the quality continued to improve.

Please note that these times are only for editing and do not include preparation, recording, or dubbing time—nor the time to translate to the final format (RealAudio). Unfortunately, these times didn't drop as quickly or as much.

Also, the reader should be aware that three hours of editing for fifteen minutes of audio isn't a universal rule of thumb for all types of audio. Editing a three-minute song to perfection, starting with 48 raw tracks, could take days. The editing time on a live Internet broadcast, no matter how long, is, by definition, zero.

Actual editing time depends upon many factors, including the following:

◆ **The number of tracks in the raw audio:** The fewer the tracks, the quicker the editing. This is usually a tradeoff between time and quality. Fewer tracks also means fewer options to choose from during editing.

◆ **The number of tracks in the master:** Each track on the master is its own mix with sources, levels, and so forth to worry about. Stereo doesn't take twice as long as mono, but it does take longer.

◆ **Complexity and variety of effects:** Heavily processed audio takes longer to create because it involves many steps.

◆ **Quality of the raw audio:** Good, clean, raw audio with few mistakes is a pleasure to use. The stuff where bits and pieces from fifteen different takes have to be merged together to get one decent passage is another story.

◆ **Quality of the final mix:** Filmmakers call it production values. The effort, detail, and budget that go into a two-hour movie is far greater than what goes into two hours of a TV series. The same is true for audio projects. A song requires a lot of time to make it sound just right. Creating a weekly, or even worse, a daily episode of a radio play requires taking a few short cuts. These shortcuts aren't necessarily bad; they're just not an all-out quest for perfection at any cost.

◆ **Quirks and limitations of the sound editing tool:** All software tools have them. Some are mere nuisances. Others restrict the user to a specific way of doing something that might not be the most efficient. Bugs don't help, either. It's better to use a stable tool with fewer features than it is a more powerful tool that crashes all the time.

◆ **The degree of automation in the audio system:** A system in which effects, equalization, and mixing can be controlled with the click of a mouse button is much faster than one that requires cables, changes, and manually operated equipment.

◆ **Speed, memory, and disk space on the host computer:** If your machine crashes, runs out of room, or can't keep up with real-time audio, you're in trouble. You lose time and possibly data.

Freeware and Shareware Sound Tools

The sound-editing tools that come bundled with most sound cards (except for the professional variety) are usually very limited. These tools are often little more than demos. Although they do have some basic editing capability, they cannot write audio to the disk in real time as the recording is being made. This lack of direct-to-disk recording capability is a severe restriction because it limits all recording to the amount of digitized audio that will fit in your computer's RAM memory. This is generally no more than a few seconds to a few minutes worth of audio.

Another severe restriction is that most of these tools perform *destructive editing*. This means that changes to the audio are permanent. If you change your mind, you have to reload the original audio from its source and start over—or, at least patch part of it into the edited version. Audio editing is a highly iterative task, often requiring trial-and-error tests to determine what sounds best. Destructive editing makes this inconvenient and slow. Nondestructive editing, a feature of more powerful tools, is generally preferred.

Few, if any, of the low-end tools support more than two tracks. Few support hardware interfaces other than common sound cards such as SoundBlaster or the audio hardware built into a Power Mac. Most support only a few audio formats.

Even with all their limitations, these low-end packages have their niche. Some are more than adequate for creating and editing short, simple sound clips. Some even show a surprising level of sophistication in applying various effects. Special-purpose sound tools can create sound effects, convert between different audio formats, or turn your computer into an oscilloscope or frequency meter.

The low-end freeware or shareware packages can't be beat in terms of cost, and there's little risk in downloading and trying them. As of early October 1996, the sound section of the University of Texas Mac Archive (`http://wwwhost.ots.utexas.edu/mac/main.html`) contained eleven sound tools, including a sound effects editor, sound file players and format converters, an oscilloscope program, and a frequency measurement/musical-instrument tuning program.

A quick survey of the much larger Info-Mac Archive (use a mirror, such as `ftp://mirror.apple.com/mirrors/Info-Mac.Archive/`) produced a three-screen-long listing of MIDI tools and an eight-screen long listing of sound tools.

On the PC side, the multimedia section of the top software selections on c/net (`http://www.cnet.com/Resources/Software/`) produced 15 sound tools, including sound-file players, a MIDI editor, and a sample editor. A search of their SHAREWARE.COM download service using the keyword "audio" produced a long listing of players and other sound tools, along with the usual chaff encountered on such a general search.

Professional Sound Editing Software

This section examines a sampling of the commercial software commonly used for professional sound editing. This is not meant to be exhaustive, nor is it meant to be an endorsement for any of the products listed. Other manufacturers produce equivalent products that may be just as good or even better for your application.

For the purposes of this book, "professional sound editing software" means that an editing package has the following minimum features:

◆ Direct-to disk recording capability

◆ Nondestructive editing

◆ Support for at least eight tracks of audio (given enough CPU speed)

◆ Basic level, pan, and equalization controls

It's worth noting that even some commercial packages do not meet all these requirements. This may be because the application is old or because it's for a more specialized purpose than general audio editing. Specialized applications include sample editors designed specifically for editing short audio files used in digital sampler hardware. (A *sampler* may be thought of as a musical instrument in which stored samples of sounds are played as musical notes. This definition is oversimplified, but basically accurate.)

Syntrillium

CoolEdit is Syntrillium's PC-based audio editing tool. Don't be fooled by the fact that it is a low-cost shareware package. It is every bit as sophisticated as many of the commercial packages, which is why it is listed in this section.

CoolEdit is available is 16- and 32-bit versions for Windows and Windows 95. There is no Mac version. CoolEdit supports direct-to-disk recording and can edit very large mono or stereo audio files up to a gigabyte long. Many PCM (pulse code modulation—a form of encoding) files formats are supporting, including WAVE, VOC, AU and AIFF (PCM mode) (see Chapter 2, "Static (Downloadable) File Formats" for a discussion of these formats). CoolEdit can be used to convert between formats.

Signal processing functions such as filters, amplification, compression and noise reduction are supported. Effects are also supported, including reverb, delay, echo, flanging, distortion, and envelope functions.

CoolEdit can be downloaded from Syntrillium's CoolEdit page at: http://www.syntrillium.com/cool.htm. You can "audition" all of CoolEdit's features, but not all at once. That requires registration and the payment of a small registration fee ($25 to $100 as of late 1996, depending upon what you want).

All things considered, CoolEdit is an excellent entry-level audio tool with a long list of features.

Digidesign

An excellent example of a package exceeding the minimum requirements for professional sound editing software is Digidesign's Session™. Available in Mac and Windows versions, it caused a stir on its introduction in 1995 because of its advanced features and low cost. The Mac version supports Power Mac audio hardware in addition to Digidesign's Audiomedia sound cards. It can support up to 16 tracks during editing, depending on computer speed. The Windows version is bundled with an Audiomedia III PCI-bus sound card.

Session 8™, another Digidesign product, is a hardware/software system that turns a Windows-based PC into an 8-track direct-to-disk recorder and editing system.

Sound Designer II™ is an older package from Digidesign that uses destructive editing. Its age and lack of nondestructive editing make it less desirable than Session or Pro Tools (described next). However, it still has a strong following, and many sound-editing programs will read and write Sound Designer II format files.

Digidesign also produces Pro Tools III, the industry benchmark for Mac-based hard-disk recording and editing. The Pro Tools III system includes rack-mounted hardware, computer interface cards, and extensive software. A high-end Pro Tools III system can support up to 48 tracks of simultaneous audio record/playback. Needless to say, this is not a cheap system.

Part of the power of Pro Tools system is the capability to use *plug-ins*. These are add-on software packages produced by Digidesign and third-party manufacturers. Plug-ins use an interface that Digidesign calls its TDM Bus, which enables full access to system inputs and outputs, effects, and other features.

A recent Product Guide pamphlet published by Digidesign lists plug-ins and other products. Some plug-ins are relatively simple, whereas others are sophisticated. Some are software only, whereas others require extra hardware that can be added to a Digidesign audio system. A few examples from this list include the following: a declicker from Steinburg (removes clicks from old vinyl LPs); a compressor/gate from Waves; and a real-time sound effects processor from Arboretum Systems.

Steinberg (Steinberg North America)

Steinberg produces the Cubase series of sound and MIDI recording, editing and processing tools for the Mac and PC.

For the Mac, the entry-level product is Cubase 3.0 for Macintosh, which incorporates their Virtual Studio Technology (VST) for Power Mac (a non-VST version is available, but it does not include sound recording). The sound source is the Mac's built-in audio hardware. It also accepts commands from a MIDI instrument. This package has many powerful features, such as up to 32 tracks, up to 128 EQs, and a virtual effects rack (see fig. 11.4). It has strong support for MIDI, including sequencing, editing, and scoring. Indeed, the Cubase series is MIDI-oriented, although it can record and edit nonmusical audio also.

Steinberg's intermediate product for the Mac is Cubase Score 3.0, which has all the features of Cubase, plus advanced musical score layout and printing.

Steinberg's top-of-the-line Mac product is Cubase Audio 3.0 XT for Macintosh. This does everything Score can, plus adds support for Digidesign audio hardware and TDM. Steinberg is a manufacturer of TDM plug-ins for Digidesign's Pro Tools products.

For the PC, Steinberg's products include Cubase Audio 3.0 XT for Windows. It supports Windows sound cards, Yamaha CBX-D3 and CBX-D5 hardware, and some Digidesign hardware (AudioMedia III and Session 8). Up to eight stereo audio channels can be recorded at once (depending on hardware). During editing, the number of audio and MIDI tracks is limited only by CPU speed and memory. Other features include time expansion; pitch shifting; and editors for audio, MIDI, key, list, musical scores, and other functions.

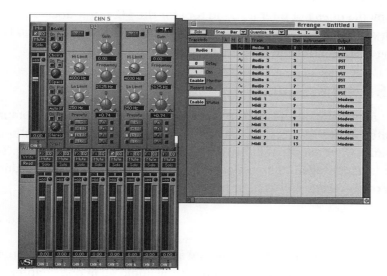

FIGURE 11.4

Steinberg Cubase audio editing software. (Courtesy Steinburg North America. Copyright 1996)

Macromedia

Macromedia takes a different approach from the other manufacturers mentioned so far. Macromedia is known as a multimedia software company, rather than a sound software company. This may be seen as a strength by many readers because Macromedia can provide a complete multimedia production package in the form of its Director Multimedia Studio bundle.

Macromedia offers two sound editing tools for the Mac: Sound Edit 16 and Deck II. They can use a Power Mac's built-in audio hardware, plus other hardware in the case of Deck II.

Deck II and Sound Edit 16 are available individually or as a bundle. At first look, these packages seem to be redundant. Although some overlap of features does exist, closer inspection reveals they are quite different and complementary. Deck II is a general-purpose audio editing tool. Sound Edit 16 is a multimedia sound tool. Deck II's strength is as a multitrack editor and mixer. Sound Edit 16 shines as a finishing tool to add compression, perform detailed spectral analysis, change format, change sampling rate, insert audio into QuickTime files, change word length, and so forth.

Macromedia does not offer a sound tool for the PC, but it does bundle Sonic Foundry's Sound Forge with the Director Multimedia Studio. Sound Forge was the first tool to legitimize the PC as a sound editing platform.

Other Sound Products

As was mentioned at the start of this section, the products and companies presented in this section were meant to be only a sample. Many other companies offer excellent hardware and software for sound editing. The reader is encouraged to investigate these further by reading magazines such as *Mix* or *Electronic Musician* or by surfing the Internet.

Summary

Learning about the basics of designing an audio system, finding a studio, conducting a recording session, and editing audio all in one chapter is reminiscent of drinking out of a fire hose. It may seem like a lot to digest—and it is—but it is all well within the capabilities of any reasonably intelligent individual with the persistence to make it happen.

Further Reading

See the list of references at the end of Chapter 9.

12

What Makes Good Net Sound (Content/Programming)

"Image is everything," some people say. In broadcasting, however,
content *is everything. Most content—even the evening news on*
television—is a form of entertainment. (Those Human Resources
department videos that talk about insurance matters are actually an
alien plot, so we won't count those as entertainment.)

As a broadcaster, you want your audience to appreciate your programming and come back for more. This is true whether you're involved in a comedy show, a concert, or even a corporate shareholder meeting. In any case, your business partners, advertisers, investors, or boss needs to be convinced the effort is worthwhile (after all, someone has to pay the bills).

So, on which area should you concentrate first: technology or content? Both are important, but people forgive you if the programming is compelling enough. Why else would anyone stand in long lines for movies, concerts, or sporting events? If the show is really good, and seating is limited, people come early. In sports, season ticket holders reserve their seats months (or even years) in advance. By concentrating on content and keeping your delivery at least competent, you can build a regular and loyal audience.

Clearly, the acquisition and development of quality content is a top organizational priority for any web broadcaster. Even if you're setting up an Intranet for internal broadcast of Human Resources materials and other company information, attention to quality is crucial to employee and management acceptance. If they don't come back, your job might not come back either.

Bottom line: No matter what kind of broadcasting you're doing or planning, quality programming can overcome shortcomings in many other areas. Your listeners (or viewers) will forgive technical flaws, limited bandwidth, and other problems if they want to listen badly enough.

Enhancing Your Content

What can you do to enhance your content and keep your audience coming back? This is the same problem faced by traditional media broadcasters who spend millions of dollars every year on programming that never succeeds, in the hope of hitting a home run every now and then. What can you do to avoid the same money pit? There are certainly no guarantees, but the first place to start is to count your advantages over traditional media. You might not have television-quality video yet, but you can do many of the same things it does, and a few it can't:

◆ **Personal touch:** If the audience has an opportunity to interact with the performers, they'll feel more connected and take a personal interest in the show or program. On the web, this can be as simple as adding an e-mail link so people can send correspondence to the personalities.

> Putting an e-mail link to the performer(s) on a show's web page brings a sense of connection, interaction, and even intimacy between audience and players. Because of this, you should consider making the e-mail link a "forwarding" address. For example, let's say your website is www.celebsRus.com, and you have a well-known personality on your show. You want to set up an e-mail link to that person's private e-mail address which is Iamfamous@bigname.com. Don't make the link go directly to his private address. Instead, set up a new e-mail address at Iamfamous@celebsRus.com that will automatically forward to the private address. Your listeners won't know the difference, and it adds at least one layer of privacy for Iamfamous.

◆ **Accept and respond to e-mail messages during the program:** This usually works best if you have an assistant standing by with a fast e-mail checking refresh who screens the incoming questions and comments and passes along the most appropriate ones to the appropriate participant in the show or program.

◆ **Live telephone call-ins:** This adds the same sense of immediacy that it does to radio and television. See the later section, "Talk-Radio," for further discussion.

◆ **IRC style chat:** Invite your viewer/listeners to converse via keyboard with your personalities (or assistants) during the program. Depending on the circumstances, you'll probably want to set up the chat room as a moderated room so that "undesirables" can be dealt with appropriately. It's a sad but true reality that some really bizarre and, frankly, scary people seize upon chat lines and radio-show call-in lines as their opportunity to prey upon your guests. At the very least, you'll be perceived as not being in control and it will detract from your program.

In one case, a celebrity whose spouse had been brutally murdered some years before was asked by someone in an unmoderated chat room why the celebrity had killed his loved one. Fortunately, the celebrity was distracted by other goings-on, and the web show operator was able to discreetly remove the comment and kick the offender out of the chat room. The celebrity left the show without ever knowing about the potentially nasty incident.

Don't let this scare you away from the concept of doing the chat room for your show; just beware of the weirdos out there and make sure the room is well monitored.

◆ **Downloads:** These are links to high-resolution, downloadable images, or *posters*. For example, suppose that you're planning to broadcast the premiere party for the insanely expensive remake of Buck Rogers. To promote the movie, broadcast, and website, you work with the producers to release exclusive bitmaps of exciting scenes from the movie. You might even have online interviews with the movie's actors and producers, and release each bitmap as it's discussed by your guests. Grab your listener's attention with promises of high-resolution bitmaps of the new Wilma or Buck. This kind of buildup and carrot dangling, by releasing the bitmaps throughout the program, will attract and keep your listeners throughout the duration of the event.

◆ **Links to bio, fan, organizational, or other background information:** Make sure any links are to pages on your own site. That way you have an oppor-tunity to sell ad space on those pages as well as the event page(s). There's almost no limit to the amount of information you can provide visitors to your site, including archives of previous recordings, speeches, interviews, and so on.

◆ **Trinkets (bribes):** Keep your audience interested by giving away items at random points during the program. The items don't have to be expensive, just desirable. If you're interviewing someone on a book tour, give away a couple of copies of the book at some point during the show. Make sure the last copy is close to the end of the show! Radio show hosts are pros at this technique. You should make an effort to scan the radio dial and study how professionally produced radio programs hook you and keep your interest.

◆ **Teasers:** Radio and television regularly provide "coming next" blurbs. These are intended to coax listeners and viewers to stay tuned to their channel a little longer. A good example is the "40 minute tease" in which at forty minutes past the hour, radio stations often play a quick list of breaking news items or other items intended to make you want to keep listening so you can get more information.

◆ **Direct, online merchandising:** Set up a secure merchant-server to accept credit card orders online during your programming. Merchant servers can manage inventories, reorders, and so on. Examples of merchandising items include the following:

    ◆ Collectibles signed by visiting guests or program personalities for direct, personalized sale.

    ◆ Copies of a performer or guest's book, video, CDs, and so on.

    ◆ Performer autographed or personalized concert T-shirts.

    ◆ Program- or show-related calendars or T-shirts.

    ◆ Tapes of the show itself (if you've got all the necessary rights).

    ◆ Program sponsor or advertiser products and services.

◆ **Audio-to-Text Transcription:** Closed-caption-style transcription for vision-impaired listeners. This can be an expensive option and might be one to save for higher-paying, special broadcasts and events.

Quality Assurance

So your website is up, and your program's on the air. Or is it? In any broadcast are many points of failure. Consider a simple speech. Every piece of equipment, every microphone, cable, connector, mixer, or hybrid, everything between the mouth of the speaker and the ears of your listeners is a potential point of failure or problem area. After you've acquired the audio source, encoded, and transmitted it, your streams have to traverse the treacherous Internet waters before reaching your audience.

How do you deal with these problems? Certainly, a professional audio engineer can help you avoid common point-of-origin pitfalls. However, even a professional audio engineer might not catch the problem before it "pipes out" to your listeners. The same is true with your network engineer, whose status monitors may show no errors.

The only way to ensure that your broadcast is truly OK is to have someone monitoring it full time. But what do they monitor? Here's a checklist:

A. Listen to the pre-encoded audio

B. Listen to post-encoded audio, prior to transmission

C. Listen via a workstation on your local area network

D. Listen via a machine on a dial-up PPP account

E. Listen via multiple dial-up PPP accounts with different paths to the Net

F. None of the above

G. All of the above

The answer? You guessed it: G. Like a production line, your audio product should be sampled at each stage of manufacture. That way, when problems are spotted, they can be more quickly isolated and fixed.

If you only listen to the finished product, you might not be able to quickly determine where a problem is occurring. If you had been monitoring each stage, you might have noticed that it sounded OK on the pre-encoded source, but not in the post-encoded version. That narrows your search for the problem, which could be as simple as a loose connector.

Note

To effectively monitor the quality of your Internet broadcasts, make every effort to experience them as your listeners do—over a dial-up modem connection. It doesn't stop there, however. To really keep an eye on the broadcast, you should set up several quality control machines with dial-up accounts on several different ISPs each with a different path to the Internet. Why? Let's say you set up quality control machines on ISPs that use MCI, Sprint, and UUNET to connect to the Internet. Further suppose that your Sprint machine has problems, and you do a trace route that shows that a Sprint router is down. How does this help? When your listeners call in or e-mail service complaints, you'll be able to reply that you've determined that a router is down on an Internet provider between you and the listener and that you've already reported the problem to the offending ISP. Bottom line: You've turned the problem around and demonstrated that you are proactively on top of the situation, improving your image with your listeners.

Be careful not to create a situation in which quality control becomes a drudge job relegated to a fixed set of low-wage, low-motivation employees. Try rotating your production crew through the quality control area. If treated correctly, it can be viewed as a less stressful reward and a desirable opportunity. You might also want to consider establishing various incentives, such as for identifying and resolving a problem before it leaves your shop. Don't get carried away with this idea, however, or it might create friction between your production crew and incentive-seeking, quality control team members.

Talk Radio

This section covers the Net broadcast of existing radio or television talk shows, as well as custom, Internet-only talk shows. Promoters of existing programs might be exploring Net broadcasting for business, promotional, or exploratory reasons. They might also see it as a way to provide more issue-related information to their listeners, such as political dirty laundry on the opposition, consumer product warnings, or other, often emotionally charged topics.

Developers of Internet-only programs might view the Net as their true and intended audience, or they might see it as an opportunity to explore a concept they hope to export to traditional radio. Many of these pioneers are radio and television industry veterans who have seized Net broadcasting as the infancy of a new medium that will rival the industries they grew up in. They hope.

Whether your format is political, sports, self-help/advice, consumer rights, fitness, or any number of other areas, all share a few common needs and capabilities. First is the capability to archive your shows for subsequent, on-demand playback. If your web page is well designed, your listeners will be able to catch that important interview they missed with their favorite actor, sports star, or politician. An important feature of archived shows is that they let people whose schedule doesn't allow them to hear it live to listen to the shows.

Listenership isn't limited to areas where the program isn't available on the radio. Even in the same city where a program airs on traditional radio, a listener can catch the archive at a more convenient time if he misses the show. In fact, Net listenership is often *higher* in cities where the program is available on radio, due to increased awareness of the program's existence.

Some radio station owners worry that Net broadcasting might somehow diminish on-air listenership or dilute their advertising reach. In fact, Net broadcasting extends *local* radio station coverage by bringing it to the desktop where radios are increasingly rare and don't work well inside modern office buildings anyway. With the ability of office workers to listen to their favorite daytime or nighttime shows, radio stations can significantly increase local listenership and potentially, as the technology improves and the numbers grow, increase ad rates and revenues.

Note   A side benefit of maintaining archived shows and their descriptions is that the keywords in those descriptions improve the chance that people using the search engines will find the page.

Talk Radio Stations on the Net

The first live, continuous, commercial radio broadcast on the Internet began on September 9th, 1995. The radio station was Talk-Radio KLIF (http://www.audionet.com/radio/talk/klif/) in Dallas, Texas, and the simulcast Net broadcaster was AudioNet (http://www.AudioNet.com). Ever the innovator, KLIF also broadcast the first triplecast program, a computer talk show that aired on radio, AudioNet, and a local television station.

Another early entrant to Net broadcasting was talk radio station WOR, New York at http://www.audionet.com/radio/talk/wor/. Like KLIF and other radio stations, a complete schedule of the station's programming is included on the web page, and archives of past shows are also available.

CFRA, a News Talk radio station in Ottawa, Canada, uses Xing Streamworks, rather than RealAudio (like KLIF and WOR) to deliver a Canadian perspective to the Net.

Equipment Sources for Call-In Shows

To produce a talk show program, you'll probably need to be able to receive, screen, queue, and play live telephone call-ins (to take questions and comments from your listeners). This can range from something as simple as a dual-line conference phone connected to a telephone hybrid, to multiline systems managed by a separate operator. The larger systems often include a dual computer system in which the operator types a description of each caller on her computer. The description is displayed on the personality's computer screen. The personality can then review and act on the information provided by the operator, selecting calls with foreknowledge of what the caller wants to talk about.

Sounds great, you say, but how do I find out what kind of equipment is needed? Except for the rudimentary end of the spectrum, this kind of telephone equipment isn't something you can find at the shopping mall electronics store. In fact, used in broadcasting and corporate help desks, an entire industry has grown up around this area. This section discusses some of the basic equipment and where it can be obtained.

Telephone Hybrids and Couplers

With a telephone coupler, you can connect an ordinary phone line with audio input and outputs so you can send or receive audio. A simple telephone handset connects via the standard, telephone-industry RJ-11C jack and operates as a normal telephone when the coupler isn't being used. Some units are intended for portable use and are battery-powered or *passive*, whereas others are rack-mounted.

These low-end units are one of the cheapest routes to get calls on-air; however, the broadcast industry doesn't recommend them as primary equipment. Higher-end equipment includes many features to handle the various line problems and audio artifacts that aren't handled well by the cheaper versions. The cheaper equipment is recommended for radio station listen-lines, receiving stock, news, weather, or traffic reports. For those on a budget and who are willing to accept some of its shortcomings, inexpensive telephone couplers and hybrids might be just the ticket. Price range: $200–$800.

Digital Hybrids

Digital hybrids use sophisticated signal processing technology to improve audio quality—eliminating feedback, line noise, and high frequency switching noise. Some models include automatic nulling, adapting to changing line conditions throughout the call. Like couplers and analog hybrids, digital hybrids attach to standard telephone lines. They also separate the microphone and caller audio. Price range: $1000+.

On-Air, Multiline Telephone Systems

When you're ready to bring your talk show format into the big leagues, you're probably ready for a more flexible way to handle your calls. These broadcast-quality systems are the same systems used by radio and television stations around the world. They provide on-air features such as multiline conference calls, on hold, computer-based call screening, and off-air connections to show producers or others. Prices range from the low thousands and up, depending on which features and options are selected.

Used Equipment and Systems

With all the radio and television station acquisitions, mergers, and buyouts taking place lately, many stations are moving to new facilities, shutting down, or being revamped by new owners. As a result, if you make friends with the station engineer, you might be able to purchase some old equipment at a steep discount. Naturally, you'll need the skills of a professional audio engineer to take this pile of treasure (junk) and turn it into something you can use, but if you're lucky, you can save a bundle.

Another source for surplus audio equipment is the U.S. Government. Auctions of seized and surplus equipment are routine, and lists of the items to be disposed of are available from the respective agencies.

Many large corporations have departments responsible for intra-company broadcasts and communications. It probably won't be easy to navigate their bureaucracy, but if you can reach the right person, you may be able to arrange a purchase of unused equipment.

New Equipment Suppliers

A great resource for telephone audio transmission products and radio station studio equipment is Gentner at `http://www.gentner.com/`. A nice feature of the Gentner site is that they include images of most or all of their products to give you a better idea of what they are talking about, where the plugs go, and so on.

Another terrific resource you should be aware of is Telos at `http://www.zephyr.com/`. Telos manufactures products for sending high-quality audio over the dial-up telephone network such as the Telos Zephyr, which can transmit near-CD quality audio over a single ISDN line. Telos also makes telephone interfaces for radio and television talk shows, phone patches for recording studios, and intercom connections. Like Gentner, Telos includes images of its products on its web pages, which helps show you the connectors required.

Another broadcast resource is Harris Allied at `http://www.broadcast.harris.com`, which supplies an enormous line of radio and television equipment in more than one hundred and fifty countries. Harris sells everything from connectors to television broadcast vans.

Background Ambiance

During the 1996 Olympics, NBC's website played a familiar fanfare, helping set the mood for visits to the site. The clip was brief, but it illustrates how organizations can enhance the experience of visiting their websites by adding background music, helping to create a certain ambiance. Large organizations with easily recognizable jingles can incorporate these sounds into their auto-loading HTML, playing on-entry to the site. It seems likely that these organizations already own the necessary rights to play the clips over the Net, so copyright issues are less likely to be a factor for these types of clips.

Of course, after the clip is over, what do you play next? The same problem is faced by other organizations who don't have the benefit of these popular or well-known tunes. What if you decide to play copyrighted music, such as from Enya or Miles Davis, to set the mood for your site? First, you need to ensure that your site is covered with the necessary releases or licensing, such as with the American Society of Composers, Authors, and Publishers (ASCAP) at `http://www.ascap.com/` or BMI at `http://www.bmi.com/`.

Next, you need to decide whether you want to play the background music continuously or create a half-hour or hour-long clip, which would cover the duration of most website visits. Be careful, however, if you go this route. It could be construed as providing an on-demand version of copyrighted material, which will bring the record labels and others down on you legally unless you've already gone to the labels or artists and received the appropriate permissions.

It might be easier to work with a local performance artist or group to produce original background music, with which you would retain the copyright or permissions to broadcast it. Many of these artists might be willing to provide the material in exchange for the exposure it would bring them, provided you give them appropriate credit on your web page(s).

The thing to remember about this is that you want to include *background* music that enhances the quality of a visit to your site—and doesn't detract from the actual content of your site that you're trying to promote. If it's presented in a way that creates an error message for visitors who don't have the player installed or enough bandwidth to play the music, you've probably done more harm than good. If, however, it's presented in a way that works for those who have the necessary software and bandwidth and is transparent to those who don't, you're on your way to creating the desired effect.

Space on your web page mentioning the background music should be minimal and unobtrusive, maintaining the strategy of emphasizing the rest of the site, instead of what some might consider to be elevator music. Information on the music might be as simple as a hyperlink at the bottom of the web page and copyright information on the player, as shown in figure 12.1.

FIGURE 12.1

Background music player copyright configuration.

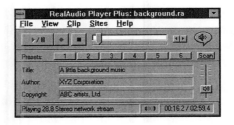

If you have the resources, you should consider placing promotional spots within your background music for your organization, events, or products. These will probably work best if they're kept short—in the fifteen to thirty second range. Text might sound something like the following:

> "Thank you for visiting XYZ's website! Don't miss our special, Internet-only, widget prices this week. Just click the word SPECIAL on any page at our site to order yours today."

Depending on how the above spot was produced, it would run in the 10–15 second range. If you're using streaming audio, such as RealAudio, you might find that some people keep the music playing *after* they leave your site. Including the brief promotional spots embedded within your background music provides a gentle reminder of your organization and its products or services. Keeping the spots low-key reduces the chance of someone becoming irritated and leaving your site.

As long as you keep website ambiance sound in perspective, don't let it overshadow the *real* purpose for the website, and don't let it get you into copyright hot water, you should do OK. Bottom line: Keep the experience low-key and low-hype.

Sound Bytes

Like using background music to create an ambiance for your site, sound bytes are used to do the following:

◆ Enhance recognition of your organization, products, or services by playing a brief clip of music or other audio that's commonly associated with your organization. Microsoft has its trademark opening sound that plays when you open Windows 95. Microsoft might add appropriate tags to its HTML to cause that sound byte to play whenever you visit the company's website.

◆ Provide a sample of products or services available from your organization, such as clips from music CDs, audio novels, and so on.

◆ Reinforce hot political issues. Slogans and famous lines might be used on politically oriented websites. For example, political talk shows might include audio clips that quote their opposition and help illustrate their position.

As always, be aware of copyright issues. Even if you're a hobbyist with a small website, it's illegal to use copyrighted material without necessary permission. Just because you happen to like the Little Caesar's "pizza pizza" sound byte doesn't mean you can legally copy it and use it on your site— even if you're not using it for commercial or objectionable purposes.

Music Programming

Probably the fastest way to have the music industry's legal hounds on your back is to digitize and broadcast your favorite recording artist's CD. The record labels and other organizations such as the American Society of Composers, Authors, and Publishers (http://www.ascap.com/) and BMI (http://www.bmi.com/) routinely scour the Net for offenders.

Assuming you've satisfied any necessary legal requirements to broadcast music on your site, where do you start, and what are the options?

Why Are You Putting Music on Your Website?

Is the music content the primary purpose of the site? If so, is the content original, as in created by you or persons employed by your organization? Record labels and recording artists create sound-enabled sites to promote their material. NetRecord labels create these sites to promote their lineup. Labels also create artist sites to further promote their titles and increase sales. Artist-created sites are often intended as an interactive billboard, placed on the Net in the hope that a record label will see and hear—and sign—the artist. Music retailers create sound-enabled sites to provide a means of promotion and direct merchandising.

Those for whom music isn't the primary intent of their site might include new-age bookstores promoting the rest of their product line along with the latest chant CD or any other organization in which music plays an important, but minor, part of the business.

Another important role for website music is to set the mood, as with background music. This can be in the form of a small MIDI file loaded in the background on your home page to play your company jingle or to set the mood for your content. An online book store might have different mood music for each subject area, such as ominous chords in the Mystery/Thriller section. Sites related to movie releases might play the movie theme song. Similarly, online music stores might play clips from featured titles. Regardless of the subject matter of your site, adding background music can make a striking difference in how your site is perceived.

What's Your Focus?

Is there a particular type of music you want to emphasize on your site? Suppose that you have a chain of jazz clubs and you want to create a site to promote your establishment and the artists who play there. You'll need to create an atmosphere on your site that resembles that of your clubs. This will start with the appearance of your web page, which will need artwork and colors that set the tone for a visitor's experience at your site.

The following music-related websites cover a range of relative sizes and areas of interest.

On the small end of the spectrum, "The Bone" (`http://www.thebone.com/`) is a blues club in Dallas that broadcasts a weekly live blues jam and archives past performances. The Bone's focus is to promote itself and the artists who perform there.

If you represent a record label, you might create a site that looks like Sony's (`http://www.sony.com/Music/`) where you can listen to selected titles, get information on featured artists, search by keyword for items of interest, and so forth. This is a good-sized site from a very large company with a lot of resources for creating a specific look-and-feel. Sony's focus is to promote its product line and featured artists.

Rockweb's small but growing site is located at `http://www.rockweb.com/` and features album cover type information and showcases a growing list of bands with brief audio clips in .AU and RealAudio formats.

AudioNet's music site is located at `http://www.audionet.com/music/`, and its huge jukebox of full-length music CDs (approaching 1,000 at the time of this writing) is at `http://ww2.audionet.com/jukebox/`. AudioNet's focus is to provide a broad range of concerts, CDs, and music radio stations that cover every major category of studio and live music.

Whether you plan to provide brief clips designed to promote and sell music CDs, broadcast live performances, or establish a collection of playable-on-demand, full-length CDs, the quality of your recordings is paramount. Refer to Chapters 9, "Sound Basics and Audio Theory" and 11, "Digital Audio Recording and Editing" for tips and techniques. Every music recording you make available on the Net should be carefully played and checked prior to release.

Visitors to your site who listen to a baseball game will usually forgive minor sound defects—especially because the original sound feed is often of AM-quality, anyway. Audiophiles will notice *any* audio defect and cringe. The higher their expectations, the harder they will be to please. Although you might not be able to control some of the Internet problems that can intrude on the quality of your broadcasts, you can do everything possible to ensure the sound being encoded is of the highest possible quality. This truism applies to traditional media broadcasts, as well as to the emerging new media types discussed in the next section.

New Media, VR

For quite some time, multiplayer video games have been available for play over a LAN. Increasingly, new video games are being released that allow

users to interact via the Internet. For example, Microsoft's *Hellbender* (http:/
/www.microsoft.com/games/hellbender/) released in late 1996 included features to interconnect users via the Internet.

What do video games have to do with website sound? Plenty, if they're an
indication of the future, in which virtual reality environments enable people to
interact verbally (as well as in relation to mouse movements). Multicast
streaming audio seems like the natural way to distribute each player's verbal
reactions to other players, making each user a defacto Internet audio broadcaster. Indeed, streaming audio might help bridge the gap between today's
rudimentary VRML efforts and the promise of more sophisticated engines to
come. Consider a hypothetical browser plug-in that has ten or twenty predefined character representations, a browser-compatible interactive landscape, and the capability to send one and receive several very-low-bit rate
audio streams. Presto: You've got an Internet-based VR environment.

VR-enabled websites, such as VRML (Virtual Reality Markup Language),
can be used to create a virtual-mall environment in which visitors can
dynamically interact with sales or information representatives from represented companies, organizations, or governmental agencies. Using streaming
audio, participants can interact with other individuals present in the virtual
landscape. This scenario would allow for the use of pre-programmed visual
representations of the people you meet. Participants might use
preprogrammed visuals or upload their own customized version to a central
VR-image database.

Discussion of this kind of futurescape is included in this book to provide a
glimpse of where today's two-dimensional websites are going. Indeed,
traditional cinema—used to produce movies that we sit down in front of and

watch—will be challenged by interactive VR dramas. Imagine a virtual cityscape where thousands of Internet-connected players live out exotic adventures, or a science fiction epic where players struggle to colonize Mars. Instead of playing against a computer, you'll interact with many, perhaps thousands, of players. Imagine a corporate sales office, where clients from around the world are moments away from meeting with your top sales or technical staff, seeing demonstrations of your products and getting to know your employees, face-to-face, with live point-to-point audio streams.

If all this sounds too far-fetched for your tastes, you should be aware that the technology to do most of these things already exists—especially for one-on-one interactions. How likely is this in the near future? To some extent, you might even be able to hold your breath.

How to Keep Them Coming Back

How do you keep your listeners coming back? Audiences are fickle, and those who stay have high expectations. If your content grows stale and is not kept fresh, interest will wane. You should always let your audience know what you have planned for them tomorrow so that they will have an incentive to return. Tease them.

Keep it fresh. If you can easily picture your home page in your mind, it is probably too old and could use an update. This doesn't mean that you have to frequently and dramatically change your pages. Instead, you should make frequent small changes and save the dramatic changes for major growth spurts when you've outgrown the old design.

Attention to detail and dedication to quality will result in a site that reflects your efforts and can weather technical difficulties more easily. Your commitment to quality programming will result in a core following of dedicated listeners that you can build on and listeners who are more likely to forgive your growing pains and broadcast glitches.

C H A P T E R

13

BANDWIDTH AND COST CONSIDERATIONS

To broadcast a radio station, you must purchase an FCC license, assemble a staff, buy or lease equipment and a transmitter, and, of course, obtain the content you plan to broadcast. You go through a similar process for television and an even more complicated process to start a cable TV network. The steps to become a Net broadcaster are also similar except for the current lack of governmental regulation and a startup cost that, for many, is vanishingly small compared to traditional media.

Some liken small web broadcasting sites to a small press that distributes to a small subscriber list. These small broadcasters can be heard from Kenya to Kentucky and from Sydney to San Francisco. On the other hand, many of these small sites can also be compared to retail shops in poorly located strip malls with no traffic and no effective way for customers to find them. But what about the search engines, you ask? The vast expansion of websites on the Net has resulted in search result-sets that go on and on. If hundreds of sites exist on a particular topic, how likely is it that someone will find the one listed on search page 47? Bottom line: Even with lots of bandwidth, it's still up to you to get noticed!

Speaking of bandwidth, Net broadcasters of all sizes must obtain content, retain staff, purchase or lease equipment, and perhaps, most important, get access to the Net's equivalent of a transmitter: bandwidth. Whether you are multicasting or unicasting, running Xing or RealAudio, you cannot escape the need for more bandwidth.

How to Find a Service Provider

The sections that follow deal with what to look for in an Internet service provider (ISP), as well as how to spot a service provider that you should avoid. But where do you find a service provider? Word of mouth is certainly important, and so are the recommendations and past experiences that come with these references. Other resources include printed guidebooks available in many bookstores and, of course, guides on the Net.

An excellent resource that combines online and print materials is provided by *Boardwatch Magazine* (http://www.boardwatch.com), which publishes an insightful monthly magazine and maintains a website counterpart to the printed magazine, as shown in figure 13.1.

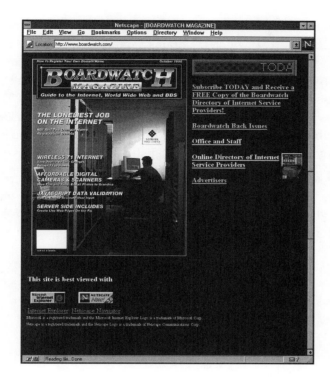

FIGURE 13.1

Boardwatch Magazine, a resource for locating ISPs.

Boardwatch also publishes a detailed directory of Internet service providers, which, at last count, had more than 7,200 Internet service provider listings.

Another Internet resource for locating service providers is TheList at `http://www.thelist.iworld.com`, which maintains a database of service providers. TheList (see fig. 13.2) used to include a section of user comments (mostly complaint*s*), but because of the fear of liability and the inability to verify the source of the complaints, the comments section was dropped. The database that remains is a terrific resource for obtaining information on ISPs by region, graphic map, area code, and so on. To use the map, you simply point and click anywhere on the map to get a listing.

After you research the ISPs available in your area, you need to research which offers the best service. The following sections describe what your network might look like, what to look for in an ISP, and what problems to watch out for.

FIGURE 13.2

TheList, a resource for locating ISPs.

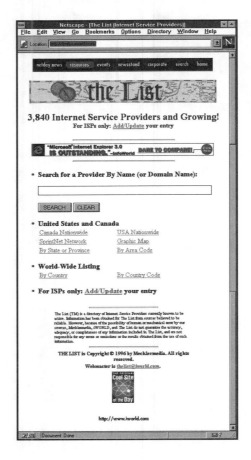

Quality Bandwidth

Unfortunately, not all bandwidth is created equally, and the cost-effective acquisition of quality bandwidth is something of an art. At every tier, service providers are hesitant to divulge significant levels of detail about the inner workings of their networks; therefore, the search for bandwidth becomes something like a detective story.

Suppose that you are starting up a Net broadcasting operation and you want to bring T-1 service to your location. To explain the steps involved, the following list describes, in general terms, the operation of a completed T-1 connection to the Internet. The connection types and options included are for one out of many possible configurations. Please refer to Appendix A, "Glossary of Internet Terms," for definitions of networking and Internet terms.

1. Data (packets) travel from your computer, across a hub, to a router, and then to a CSU/DSU that connects to the actual T-1 circuit. The circuit is usually provided by an RBOC (Regional Bell Operating Company) or an RBOC competitor.

2. The T-1 circuit is connected to a local RBOC's or competitor's facility via CSU/DSU or other telephone or data switching equipment. The packets are then routed or switched to an outbound circuit, such as a T-1 or larger capacity line.

3. The outbound circuit terminates at the Internet service provider and connects to a CSU/DSU or equivalent that is connected to a router. From here, the ISP routes your packets to another router that connects to a CSU/DSU or possibly an ATM or other high-speed interface with the ISP's outside bandwidth. This outside bandwidth is usually a collection of T-1s or a larger circuit, such as an Ethernet 10 MB or DS3 45 MB service.

4. The ISP's outside bandwidth circuit is usually provided by an RBOC or an RBOC competitor such as MFS (Metropolitan Fiber Service). This circuit usually provides connectivity between the ISP and a long-distance data circuit service such as MCI or UUNet. Once again, the data service connects via a CSU/DSU or (higher speed) equivalent.

5. The long-distance circuit routes your packets to one of the main Internet Service Access Points, such as MAE-East, MAE-Dallas, or MAE-East. After the packets are connected at the MAE, companies such as MCI and UUNet

interconnect their networks on the basis of private "peering" agreements. Participation in these agreements is usually by invitation only.

6. From this point, your packets travel the Internet backbone and are routed via a series of routers to the router that services the destination Internet address. This portion of the journey is usually to the destination address.

As you can see from these steps, your data traffic passes through many lines and networks before even reaching the Internet. Indeed, this network traffic flow means that you are sharing the local loop provider's capacity with its other customers. What happens if the provider overbooks its network? The same thing that happens when an airline overbooks a flight: Someone is going to get bumped! How do you address this problem? Press the local loop provider to explain, in writing, how it plans to prevent this kind of problem from happening and to provide statistics to prove the solution.

After you get through the local loop provider to your service provider, you run into the same issues all over again. To get to the Net, the service provider must contract with another company. This company peers to the NAP (Network Access Point) at MAE-East or MAE-West, for example, or it contracts with an intermediate company that, in turn, has a peering arrangement. Your network traffic finally gets to the Internet backbone through this peering arrangement.

This process involves routing your network traffic through more intermediate networks. To accomplish this routing, your service provider must first set up a long-distance line to get the traffic to the local loop at the far end. This local loop may be a first-tier provider, such as MCI, UUNET, or Sprint, or a second-tier company that buys and resells lines from the first tier.

You may very well contract for T-1 service with a company that, in reality, has only T-1 service itself. How can companies get away with this service? Simple. Like the airlines, they are betting on how much actual traffic their clients will use. For most companies, network bandwidth consumption is a daily roller coaster of high and low consumption.

For example, if the service provider's first customer is a business that opens between 8:00 a.m. and 5:00 p.m., then, in theory, its use of the T-1 capacity will be only during those hours. The pipe will be empty for the remaining hours of the day. The service provider is taking a gamble that it can juggle all its clients. The company is also hoping that no one will notice or understand what is happening if, occasionally, the lines have too much congestion.

Users have started to catch on to this trick, however, and some providers are now advertising that they maintain a fixed percentage of unused bandwidth on their networks as a buffer to prevent overcrowding. If the companies go over that percentage—65 percent, for example— they promise to buy more bandwidth. This promise is only as good as the policies of the company that provides bandwidth to your provider, however. If the bandwidth company doesn't have the same policy, the pipe can easily fill up downstream from yours.

For another example, suppose that you would like to have two or more separate T-1 lines. In addition, you don't want to depend on a single local provider in case it goes down during a critical moment (which it eventually will). What happens if your competing service providers both use MCI's services? Then you are really buying the same bandwidth twice. This situation can be an advantage if one of the providers goes down because you will still have service on the other provider. But if the Net problem is with MCI or somewhere downstream, you will go down in either case. Your service provider should be willing to tell you who they are buying bandwidth from and, in turn, who the other providers are upstream from them. You should also ensure that your service agreement requires the ISP to inform you of any changes they make in who provides them with bandwidth. Otherwise, your careful research might be wasted if ISP #2 decides to switch to the same provider as ISP#1.

For example, major metropolitan areas are often interconnected via a 45 Mbps T-3/DS3 connection, which limits the total combined simultaneous traffic to 45 Mbps. This figure is a total theoretical capacity of about 29 T-1s, although the actual number will be lower, depending on the overhead required to operate the circuit. The aggregate capacity out of the city is limited by the size of the outgoing pipe.

What is the bottom line? When you buy bandwidth, you are building a multisection pipeline with each section owned and operated by a different company. Each of these companies is selling capacity on its own section of pipe. The secret of getting the best deal for your money is to understand what you are really buying. Does this mean doom and gloom? Not at all. You are just acquiring ammunition so that you can make the best buying decisions possible.

Leave Yourself an Out

Today's pace of technological change is self-evident and extends to bandwidth and Net infrastructure. Service providers often offer discounts for multiyear contracts that lock you into today's technology and prices. In the Internet business, every week is a month, and every month is a year. Three years is almost infinity. Think hard before handcuffing yourself to a multiyear contract.

What happens if your service provider fails to perform to your expectations? Although the language in your contract may address some of these issues, the service company can easily claim to be meeting the terms of the contract. If you want to dispute the contract, you may end up in a legal battle. Make sure that your contract has a 30-day out clause, for example. Even if you still have to pay a small penalty, paying the penalty is better than going to court.

One of the best strategies for dealing with an ISP that does not perform well is to keep highly detailed logs of all service problems and outages. For example, packet loss can be traced back to individual routers. Every time you have a report of packet loss and can verify that it is coming from your ISP's router(s), log the occurrence and file the trace route printout. Also, if you experience service outages, you should be refunded for the service not provided. Again, keep detailed logs and file printouts of trace routes proving the outage. If your provider promises a certain percentage of uptime, these records can provide the leverage you need to get the problem fixed or to terminate the relationship without having to pay a penalty.

When tracking down and documenting a network problem using a trace route or similar tool, make sure that you trace in both directions. That is, if you experience packet loss or an outage, run your trace route outbound from your network and then inbound toward your network. The two traces should collaborate your story and document the outage or packet loss. To trace inbound to your network, use a separate dial-up Internet access account or have the individual or organization reporting the outage or packet loss run the trace from their network and e-mail you with the results.

Features and Services Your ISP Should Offer

Assuming that you have already dragged your provider through the issues of to whom they connect and the downstream architecture of the pipe segments between you and the backbone, you should also ask the provider about other important services. First and foremost is the availability of customer and technical support in the event of a connectivity problem. The service provider should be able to provide hotline support during *your* hours of operation.

If you broadcast from a local jazz club every Saturday night, for example, be sure that you have the name and number of a person you can call at the service provider in the event of a problem. Don't take this suggestion for granted. Many local service providers do not keep staff on duty outside of normal business hours. Be sure to ask for references concerning this issue, and check them!

Per Megabyte Charges

Some providers charge you a rate based on the number of megabytes of data that you use on their network. For a Net broadcaster who sends out continuous streams of data, this charge can be a quick ticket to bankruptcy. Unless you really know what you are doing, run—don't walk—away from these providers. Comparison shop and try to stick with a contract that specifies a fixed amount of bandwidth to which you have guaranteed access during your hours of operation.

Reliability

You should also check out the service provider's facility and inspect its operation. A disturbing number of service providers are run out of someone's spare bedroom. This situation is probably fine for undemanding dial-up clients looking for a bargain, but not for a serious Net broadcaster.

You should also look for the following signs of reliability in service providers:

◆ Are the routers and servers running on uninterruptable power supplies that can run for many hours in the event of a power outage?

◆ Do they have a backup generator?

◆ Is the wiring plant well managed? Are the racks neatly organized, or are the wires dangling everywhere?

◆ Is the equipment and infrastructure up to date?

◆ Are they located in a flood plain or other hazardous location?

◆ Do they have a disaster recovery plan? Can they prove the existence of the plan?

◆ Do they have enough technical expertise to keep the operation running if a key employee leaves or suffers some unpleasant fate?

◆ Is the facility reasonably secure from intruders, hackers, theft, and so on?

◆ How long have they been in business, and how long have they provided the current level of service?

Multicasting

Multicasting is the process of delivering one stream to a network, in which the network itself multiplies the stream to clients who request it. At the time of this writing, multicasting—such as with the MBONE—is not widely implemented on the Internet. Such carriers as MCI and UUNET are rightfully concerned about the impact that turning on RSVP (ReSerVation Protocol), for example, will have on their network. The expectation is that large multicasting-enabled sections of the Net will be enabled by late 1997. The technology and protocols already exist; however, the organizations involved must decide how to cope with the changes that multicasting brings.

If and when multicasting capability becomes widespread, it will change the dynamic of Net broadcasting. With unicasting, a single stream is sent by a server to each client. This technology requires broadcasters to make large investments in bandwidth. Multicasting, on the other hand, promises to reduce dramatically the number of streams sent out by a server. In a multicasting environment, as the stream passes through multicasting-enabled segments of the Net, the stream is multiplied, or replicated, by the routers in that portion of the Net on request by clients supported by those routers.

For example, you can send out one stream to a particular multicast-enabled portion of the Internet. The router on that multicast island listens for requests for a copy of the stream from the clients attached to it. Each client's software then sends a request to the router, which, in turn, duplicates the stream and sends a copy to the client. One stream delivered to the island results in the generation of large numbers of multicast streams.

Reductions in point-of-broadcast bandwidth requirements, if they happen, will probably not result in a reduction in bandwidth expense, however. Multicasting ISPs will want to allocate multicasting streams within their network and then charge back to the broadcasters. To make this charge, ISPs may allocate and sell ports or ranges within their network to individual Net broadcasters.

Should you hold off your expansion plans in anticipation of the implementation of multicasting on broad portions of the Internet? Probably not. To date, no large-scale tests of multicasting protocols, such as RSVP (ReSerVation Protocol), have taken place. Even if no significant technical problems arise, large numbers of service providers will have to be convinced to spend the time and money to enable the service on their networks. ISPs will need new billing procedures, and software vendors will need new strategies for pricing software because per-stream prices fall apart in a multicasting environment. Unless the service providers receive heavy market demand, multicasting will probably not happen quickly.

Router manufacturers have been adding multicasting capability to their routers for the last few years. In many cases, multicasting can be turned on via software updates and memory upgrades. Net broadcasters should be able to convert their servers to multicasting with a software upgrade (if available) from their streaming software manufacturer. Similarly, clients should be able to receive multicasting simply by upgrading their player software.

Makers of Net broadcasting software may also be trying to figure out how to charge for streams in a multicasting environment. The number of streams delivered to clients may be much greater than the number transmitted by the Net broadcaster. In addition, because unicasting allows for extremely detailed tracking of client listenership statistics, going to a multicasting scenario may well scrap the reporting capabilities that customers and advertisers value so greatly.

In short, multicasting is a technology that is well ahead of the capability of most network and content providers to adopt, control, and exploit without the potential for serious damage to current operations, pricing plans, and billing practices.

A few multicasting protocols are as follows:

◆ **DVMRP:** Distance Vector Multicast Routing Protocol

◆ **MOSPF:** Multicast Open Shortest Path First

◆ **PIM:** Protocol-Independent Multicast

◆ **RSVP:** ReSerVation Protocol (resource)

Lately, RSVP is the most discussed multicasting protocol. Major hardware vendors tout its flexibility and scalability, as compared to conventional reservation protocols. It is designed to support both unicast and multicast routing protocols and to operate under heavy multicast loads. RSVP was designed as part of a broader effort to improve Internet infrastructure.

Lead Times to Install Fiber Optic Cable

When mapping out your bandwidth expense plans, be sure to consider the availability and lead time on the installation of the necessary infrastructure to deliver the bandwidth capacity. Whether you are installing a T-1 or a T-3, lines have to be run, and, depending on your location, the lead time may be weeks or even months. In the case of fiber runs (T-3+), the costs may be prohibitively high. You may even discover that it is cheaper to move your location closer to an existing fiber loop than to dig up streets to run the fiber to your location.

If your facility is not located near an existing fiber loop, you may be forced to move to a location that is. Because competing fiber companies are often located in major metropolitan areas, the move might be an opportunity to connect to a bigger or better ISP. Another strategy is to move to the same building as your service provider. This scenario can save money if you can cheaply run cables between the two offices.

If your ISP can't help you with getting fiber installed, you will probably have to contact local fiber providers—such as an RBOC, GTE, MFS, TCG, and so on—for a fiber loop map. Be warned that they may not want to give out very much information due to concerns about competition. After you have an idea where each loop is located, you can look for suitable space at locations that are already wired.

In any event, installing fiber at your location gets you only to a local loop, which is something like having a local telephone number with no long distance service. You will still need to contract with other entities, as described previously, to obtain service to the Net.

Have You Outgrown Your Service Provider?

How much total bandwidth does your network provider have today? If your bandwidth comprises most of the provider's capacity, you may have outgrown the provider. Suppose that you are ready to purchase your first T-1, and your service provider has only one or two T-1s itself. The provider will need to upgrade its back-end bandwidth to support you. On the other hand, if your provider has several T-3s and maintains a 65 percent capacity rule and can prove it, your T-1 probably won't significantly have an impact on the provider's overall bandwidth capacity.

Similarly, if you plan to upgrade to a T-3 and your network provider has only a few T-1s, then it is probably time to buy the ISP, look for a larger, more experienced partner, or build your own network. Providing and supporting this level of bandwidth requires broader expertise and experience, as well as a much greater investment in equipment and materials.

Whose Packet Is It, Anyway?

Ultimately, your fastest connection to the Internet is limited by the size, capacity, and throughput of the smallest and most congested pipe between you and the Internet backbone(s). After you get to one of the backbones, you are limited also by its available throughput. The same is true, in reverse, after your traffic leaves the backbone. Your network packets are ultimately delivered to your listeners by Netcom, PSINet, or any number of the thousands of large and small network providers in the United States and abroad.

For example, the listener in Kansas City who sends you an e-mail complaining of lost packets could be correct in his assumption that his difficulties are a result of a problem at your end. Like most listeners, however, he probably doesn't realize that the difficulty may also be a result of one or more problems at any of a dozen or more points between your transmission point and his computer. The bottom line is that for all practical purposes, after the stream leaves your network for transmission via the Internet, you have no control over what happens next. The sections that follow discuss strategies for regaining control over the delivery of your packets.

Private Networks and Other Strategies

The lack of control does not leave you without options, depending on the depth of your pockets. One approach to expanding your reach is to purchase several routes to the Net with, for example, one connecting to MAE-West and the other to MAE-East. You can then put some of your content on one and some on the other, and you can even list each connection on your pages. In this way, if one route is down or heavily congested, some or all of your content will still be accessible.

Another admittedly expensive approach is to build a private network that connects to the public Internet at various highly distributed locations. On this private network, you can route packets to an Internet entry point closest to the client with, hopefully, a minimized number of router hops. With the traditional Internet backbone becoming increasingly overloaded, more and more companies are exploring this approach to minimize their use of the public Internet backbone(s).

Ongoing discussions among many of the smaller service providers about establishing their own local and regional minibackbones are also taking place. For example, ISPs in south Florida may band together and set up interconnections among themselves so that packets originating locally and pointing at local Net resources would never leave the local or regional Net. These regional backbones make a lot of sense as opposed to the backbones that go out to MAE-East, across to Santa Cruz, up to San Francisco, over to Dallas, up to Chicago, and back to Florida to travel three miles, as the crow flies. So far, this idea has mostly stayed in the talk stage, although some ISPs are starting to peer with each other at existing local NAPS (Network Access Points) using BGP (Border Gateway Protocol).

The Nitty-Gritty of Bandwidth Upgrades

When strategizing your Internet bandwidth growth curve, make sure that you plan your equipment purchases appropriately. If you plan to be at T-3 level, 45 Mbps within six months, you need to make sure that your web, audio, and other servers have a 100 Mbps or faster NIC (network interface card). Then, of course, your network hubs and switches also need to support the faster speeds.

If you are transitioning from ISDN to T-1 service, you may want to stick with 10BaseT (10 Mbps) NICs, hubs, and so on. The price difference between 10BaseT and 100BaseT NICs is pretty small, so you may want to consider buying the 100BaseT cards as insurance against your own success. 100BaseT network switches and hubs are much more expensive than 10BaseT equipment, so you may want to wait for this kind of equipment until you really need it. You can run your 100BaseT NICs at 10BaseT speeds.

For T-1 service, the cost for the CSU (Channel Service Unit)/DSU (Data Service Unit) and router is in the low thousands. Some service providers include this equipment in their rates, but in many cases, you are required to purchase or lease this equipment separately. When you are working out the agreement with the service provider, make sure that the information about who will install, configure, and maintain the router and other equipment is clearly spelled out in the contract.

The next step up in service is a 10 Mbps Ethernet connection to your service provider. Due to overhead requirements, your actual bandwidth on this type of service ranges from 4 Mbps to 7 Mbps, with an emphasis on the lower end of the scale. It may, in fact, be more cost effective to purchase two or more T-1s. Equipment requirements are much the same as for T-1 service, where you need a router that includes an appropriate port configuration, such as with the Cisco 25xx series.

T-3 service provides up to 45 Mbps of bandwidth. To operate at these speeds, you need much more expensive equipment with high-speed interfaces. For example, you need an ATM switch for ATM configured circuits, or an HSSI (High-Speed Serial Interface) card ($8,000 to $12,000) for clear-channel circuits. You also need a high-speed, high-capacity router with lots of memory. This kind of router puts you in the Cisco 7000 and 7500 series, which has prices starting in the mid-$30,000 range, with a rapidly escalating price tag as options are added. You can easily configure such a router in the $60,000 to $80,000 range. You also need an IDSU, another multithousand dollar item.

Which is the better network topology for your network: ATM or clear channel? The answer depends on whom you ask. Not surprisingly, those who have invested in ATM favor it over clear channel, and vice versa. ATM appears to be the implementation of the future; however, some major networks have actually removed ATM switches from their network because they didn't use some of the features that were consuming bandwidth. For example, if you are not pushing voice on your network, why sacrifice a chunk of your bandwidth for something you aren't using? A common counterargument from the ATM camp is that you probably weren't using that bandwidth anyway, so why be forced to re-install or buy new equipment later? With major router manufacturers such as CISCO pushing the ATM standard, it appears that it will win out in the long run.

As mentioned in the earlier section, "Lead Times to Install Fiber Optic Cable," T-3 service requires a fiber run to your facility with appropriate fiber interface equipment at your site. You may want to consider asking your local loop provider to install a higher-capacity connection at your site for future growth. Such a connection may be an OC-3 (Optical Carrier level 3) capable circuit, which is the second fastest optical rate, at 155.52 Mbps, in the Sonet standard.

When you add the installation and monthly cost of your local fiber-loop connection to the monthly charges for your bandwidth connections, the price total ranges from $20,000 to $50,000 or more per month. If you include leasing your router and other equipment, the rates will be correspondingly higher. The lower rate corresponds to the smaller, hungrier first tier providers, whereas the upper end can go through the roof.

As with the rest of technology, new versions and competing equipment hit the market frequently, so these examples may well be obsolete by the time this book goes to press. The area that seems less likely to change dramatically is the price tag.

In addition, rates are often based on whether you are being guaranteed burstable or fixed bandwidth capacities. Burstable rates are usually significantly lower than fixed rates, and they operate on the premise that you only occasionally need the full amount of bandwidth purchased. In other words, you can negotiate for 30 Mbps sustained traffic, burstable to 45 Mbps for a certain percentage of time. This option can save you a lot of money, especially if your content varies in popularity from hour to hour with certain peak times.

The best option may be to select a burstable configuration with a no-penalty upgrade policy. Then if your site grows faster than you expected, and your site's bandwidth demands tax your burstable configuration, you can upgrade to a faster connection. If not, then you won't have committed to the higher-priced fixed bandwidth capacity that you're not using.

Outsourcing

Outsourcing, despite the fear it strikes in the hearts of MIS managers everywhere, finds a particularly attractive niche in website sound. If you are in the content business—that is, you create programming that others broadcast—you may discover that you would rather not become embroiled in the volatile world of technology, the Internet, and its uncertainties. Outsourcing provides a way for you to be hip by getting you on the Net without the danger of anyone seeing you wearing a pocket protector. Or, more simply, outsourcing enables you to concentrate on what you do best rather than divert your energies to other areas.

Piggybacking on someone else's network allows you the luxury of not having to invest large sums of money in new technology, employees, and resources. Outsourcing can be compared to putting your content in a high-traffic shopping mall rather than in some deserted strip mall where you are forced to attract customers by yourself.

The terms under which Net broadcasters carry your programming depend on many factors, but you can count on one truth: The higher the visibility of your programming and the more popular and recognizable your content is, the better the deal you can strike. Net broadcasters are looking for two things: visibility and revenue. The more visible they already are, the more they will lean toward revenue. If you are willing to take a risk with a smaller Net broadcaster, you are likely to get better terms.

How do you find an appropriate outsourcing company? Do some web surfing and see who is broadcasting similar or comparable material. Also look at the size and experience of the operation and then keep track of several to see how well they perform. Keep in mind that some problems you observe may be due to a Net problem or configuration problem at your end. And remember, don't count out a candidate because you haven't done your homework!

By far the largest outsourcing broadcaster is AudioNet (`http://www.audionet.com`), which describes itself as a content aggregator and Internet broadcaster. At the time of this writing, AudioNet had signed 127 radio stations, TV stations, and networks and offers the following programming: sports from more than 100 colleges, universities, and professional teams (more than 500 college football games broadcast in the fall of 1996); more than 700 full-length CDs in its Jukebox; a constant stream of live concerts; more than 10,000 hours of on-demand programming; an ongoing series of high-profile corporate live events, such as Keynotes and product splashes with Silicon Graphics, Microsoft, and Asymetrix; a long series of Intel product announcements and conferences; Audio Intranet projects; corporate annual shareholder meetings, such as Bell & Howell's; and many other conventions, seminars, political conventions, Internet-only radio shows, and so on.

Interest in AudioNet's content lineup has drawn minority investments by companies such as Motorola and Premier Radio Networks, and strategic partners such as Host Communications, one of the largest sports-event marketing firms in the United States.

Steve Lehman, president and chief executive officer of Premiere Radio Networks is quoted as saying, "We see AudioNet as one of the leaders of the next generation of broadcasting over the Internet. We believe this alliance will provide increased programming penetration and global distribution and will add a new dimension to the radio industry. AudioNet has successfully demonstrated the ability to deliver live and on-demand Internet broadcast programming on a large scale, which we see as the ultimate evolution of the Internet."

Why is all this information important to you? No matter whom you partner with to broadcast your content over the Net, the relationships and investments described in this chapter demonstrate the seriousness with which Internet broadcasting should be taken. You may need these examples at your next board meeting when someone asks how important the Net really is, with respect to broadcasting in general. The experts in the web broadcasting business like to remember the days when people asked why they should pay for cable TV when they could get it for free with rabbit ears?

Today, you have many small Net broadcasters on one end of the spectrum, and then you have AudioNet, the "WalMart of web broadcasting," at the high end. No doubt, over time, the rest of the spectrum will fill in with more competition and innovation.

Conclusion

Whether you decide to outsource the broadcast of your content or build your own network, the amount of money involved is likely to be very important to your bottom line. It is unfortunate but true that in the fast-paced and much-hyped Internet market are a lot of fast-talking salespeople and unreliable "experts" who, intentionally or otherwise, lead the uninformed astray. The bottom line is that you need to ensure that you understand, to your own satisfaction, what services are being offered to you, and that you have a way out if the service provider does not live up to your expectations. Before you decide on a provider, ask for and check their references.

When you decide with whom you will be working, keep detailed notes, logs, and documentation on any service outages or problems. Many problems are likely to be downstream from your provider and out of their control; however, careful record keeping on your part can be crucial for resolving disputes in your favor.

CHAPTER 14

FUTURE OF AUDIO ON THE WEB

*Mainstream audio on the web is streaming audio, which begins
playing almost immediately after the user requests it. People expect a
quick response to their actions on the web, just as they expect a
quick response from turning on a television or radio. You turn on a
radio, and it plays. As long as these expectations are met and enough
bandwidth is available on the Net to satisfy consumer demand, it
appears that the demand for Internet multimedia—and web sound in
particular—will continue to grow.*

The future of audio on the web is bright. Improved broadcast quality and interest in Internet broadcasting by all of the traditional media and entertainment channels illustrate web audio's growing influence. With the September 1996 release of RealAudio 3.0—with decent stereo on a 28.8 (25 Kbps) connection and near-CD quality on a 100 Kbps ISDN-type stream—you can see that the future will indeed include streaming audio with better sound. Transport protocols are being tweaked to provide better error correction and stream reliability. And, significantly, a more mature generation (which means that it has gone through several versions) of both the server and the client software is now available.

The growing maturity of Internet multimedia servers and clients demonstrates that the public has room to grow in the traditional dial-up modem Internet market. Despite the higher version numbers, the public is still in a mode in which new Internet multimedia products are able to leap over the competition because of all the features and performance that they offer. Much market share competition is still ahead for the technology companies that are involved. Like the early days of the spreadsheet wars, no clear winner has surfaced yet; however, like spreadsheets, Internet multimedia seems destined to become a part of our everyday lives.

Over time, Internet multimedia will seep into more and more consumer products, the most obvious being television. In the near future, many stores will be selling Net-capable televisions. Proponents of these new TVs hope that few people will ever again want to consider buying a PC that isn't also a TV and vice versa. The trend will cross over to other consumer items, too. Don't be surprised if a manufacturer comes out with a Net-connected toaster oven that plays streaming audio recipes to hapless cooks and wannabe chefs. Or how about a PC in your car that connects to an RF LAN/WAN and lets your back seat passengers surf the web while you listen to a live, streaming audio radio station from New Zealand?

The future of audio products and their integration on the web is rich and varied. As the quality of streaming audio improves on low bandwidth dial-up connections, the meshing of audio and multiframes-per-second video will take on new life. Better sound at the same bandwidth, combined with improved compression and streaming techniques for video, will gradually add video to the mainstream.

What about the technology companies competing for market share? The competitors with deep pockets—such as Microsoft, IBM, Intel, and so on—are just now entering into the fray. Will they be nimble enough to keep up with the smaller companies, such as Streamworks and Progressive Networks, that really created the market? Will their marketing juggernauts and buyout departments annihilate or assimilate the smaller players?

You can count on several events taking place. For example, latecomers will try to buy their way into the market while they look for decent technology and startup principals ready to cash out. Some of the smaller players will consume each other in an attempt to grab market share while they can. And the big players will spend a lot of money to make sure that they don't miss out on this new medium.

Where Is the Net Going?

A taste of the future was described previously in the discussion of the infiltration of Internet multimedia technology into consumer products. Indeed, above your talking toaster oven may be a touch screen with a link to your front-door cam/ID verification link. When the cable guy arrives to install your cable modem, his picture and ID badge code are automatically sent via secure public key encryption packets to the cable company. The company then validates the code, image, time, and place as correct and sends a live audio/video stream of a smiling customer service representative who verbally confirms the installer's credentials.

Will the Net survive? Doomsayers foresee the imminent collapse of the Net into a tangle of smoldering fiber, counting every Internet "brownout" as proof of their concerns. Proponents point to the frantic pace of backbone upgrades, router and software improvements, and new standards initiatives designed to transform the Net from its original design into a more robust and efficient network. The original design of the Internet was as a military command and control network that was capable of surviving a nuclear attack. Perhaps the long-term answer lies in the evolution of the Net into a more highly distributed, multilevel, and multilayer conglomeration of public and private Nets. This new combination would interlink a broad spectrum of consumer, business, and governmental resources into a more dynamic and responsive network.

What do all the conflicting opinions mean? The future of the Net is not really an issue of bigger backbones, faster consumer bandwidth, or who wins the browser wars. The future of the Net depends on how seamlessly and effectively it evolves into an intelligent, reliable, and responsive infrastructure for enriching our everyday lives. Its success depends on the degree to which it becomes invisible and indispensable.

Bandwidth: Cable Modems and ISDN

Cable modems, ISDN, ADSL, and other attempts to provide more bandwidth to end users should help improve the listening experience. However, these improvements won't necessarily help web broadcasters with their own bandwidth problems; in fact, the improvements will likely have the effect of requiring them to acquire even more bandwidth.

How is this dilemma possible? Remember what happened to the size and corresponding download time of the average Internet web page when the transition began from 14.4 to 28.8 modems? Content size quickly expanded to fill the void. Streaming audio software manufacturers already support up to dual-channel ISDN for CD/broadcast quality audio. As more users have faster connections, the demand to deliver your streams at the higher rates will rapidly consume your bandwidth. Multicasting will help when it is widely supported and implemented, but a lengthy transition period seems likely (see Chapter 13, "Bandwidth and Cost Considerations").

Cable companies have made many bold statements and announcements about new technologies that speed up consumer access to the Net; however, this posturing seems to be aimed more at pacifying stockholders asking "What are we doing about the Net?" than any serious threat to existing technologies.

The most obvious solution to providing faster user access is running fiber directly to the users, which is actually happening today. However, the expense of going back and digging new trenches and replacing the copper on a significant scale is horrendous. Certainly, the companies would be wise to stop running any new lines with copper, but this process is destined to take a *very* long time.

Cable Modems

You have all heard the term *cable modem* used about as much as the now painful *Information Superhighway*. What is the reality behind the hype? Unfortunately, the reality is pretty dismal. The technology and infrastructure of cable modems will take years to mature.

First, think about the industry that is supposed to be driving this effort. Remember its last real innovation of pay per view and scrambling premium channels? How long ago were these items introduced? This is not a promising innovation rate for an industry trying to leverage itself into the global data Net. Where are the 500 channels that the public was promised back in the 1980s?

The cable industry is promising connections to the Internet at speeds between 10 Mbps and 30 Mbps. Reality indicates that you won't see these products or services until after the turn of the century, if then. Why not? This cable technology is comparable to ethane technology, which requires your PC to have a network card, some sort of router, and a hub if you have more than one computer. Would you want a cable installer opening up your PC to install a network card?

The cable industry itself doesn't have the technical support staff, experience, or infrastructure to build and support a massive high-speed data network. Currently no cable modem standards exist; the situation is reminiscent of the days of proprietary 9.6 modems that couldn't talk to each other. Also, the cable system is mostly one-way technology, which limits most systems to inbound-only connections. This situation won't change until the existing cables are replaced with broadband bidirectional fiber.

Early cable modem trials used POTS (dial-up telephone or *p*lain *o*ld *te*lephone) lines to provide the outbound connection. Don't throw away your modem—you'll still need it to send e-mail or files, select the web resources you want to use, and, of course, stream audio or video. As long as the existing copper coax networks are in place, the coax will be a one-way pipe, delivering data to the end user and requiring outbound bandwidth to be delivered via traditional telephone lines and modems. Many new cable installations use a fiber optic network that permits communications in both directions.

Even if these problems are solved, the much touted 10 Mbps to 30 Mbps speeds are theoretical limits for a single-user configuration. When hundreds or thousands of homes and apartments are connected, the throughput drops every time someone logs in.

What can be done to salvage the situation? A well-managed implementation will project future use and analyze current bandwidth consumption. Prudent network architecture improvements, such as segmenting the network, adding additional external bandwidth, and proactive customer support should be enough to keep most networks successful.

If you work for a large company with employee access to the Internet, you see what happens to the performance as more and more people discover the Internet. Throughput slows to a crawl, and memos begin to fly about conserving precious company network resources. In many cases, MIS departments severely curtail employee Net access or cut it off entirely. Many similarities exist between the proposed cable networks of hundreds or thousands of homes and large corporate offices with hundreds or thousands of employees. The solution lies in the implementation and management of these systems. Those that are managed well can probably avoid the many pitfalls that await less savvy operators.

Wireless Networks

Similar to the cable modem networks, new asymmetric wireless networks are emerging as an alternative. These networks promise an overall inbound throughput of 10 Mbps per 6 MHz RF (radio frequency) channel. Because this network is a one-way connection, all outbound traffic is carried over conventional dial-up modems, ISDN, T-1, and so on.

The channels are distributed in a cellular model with each cell servicing approximately 200–300 customers, depending on the overall network load. Each customer's computer needs an Ethernet 10BaseT card if one isn't built into the computer, and, of course, an RF antenna.

The biggest advantage of these wireless networks is the capability to deliver bandwidth without wiring. Aside from obvious applications in rural areas, the implications for delivering bandwidth using existing cellular towers to mobile users is intriguing. The impact on Internet broadcasters would seem to be on how end users receive broadcasts, rather than as a bandwidth solution for broadcasters.

ISDN

Integrated Services Digital Network (ISDN) dates back to 1978. It is usually configured with two 64 Kbps bearer, or B, channels and one 16 Kbps data, or D, channel over existing copper. This combination (2 B channels + 1 D channel) is called a *BRI*, or Basic Rate Interface. When first implemented, the B channels were intended for voice and the D channel for data. Times have changed. By inverse multiplexing 2 B channels, you can have 128 Kbps of available bandwidth. Taking this one step further, you can use 23 B channels and a D channel to create the equivalent of a T-1 at 1.54 Mbps, which is called a *PRI*.

As mentioned previously, ISDN has been around since 1978. Why have you heard about it only in the last few years? The telcos blew it. For many years the standard languished as an obscure service that eventually caught the eye of the broadcast industry for the transmission of very high-quality audio. When the need for widespread, high-speed connectivity began to emerge in conjunction with the explosion of the World Wide Web, a few manufacturers saw the potential of ISDN and brought relatively low-cost ISDN bridge/routers—such as Gandalf (`http://www.gandalf.ca/`)—on the market. Many in the computer industry quickly jumped on the ISDN bandwagon. Unfortunately, the telcos and their regulating bodies never really comprehended the demand and opportunity.

Where available, ISDN prices range from $20 to $80 per month, with unlimited connect time in some areas and per minute charges in others. Even as the telcos scramble to add appropriate switching equipment and bring ISDN online, they are requesting a doubling of the rates in some areas and cutting them in others. This confusion is a result of widely varying tariff structures and decentralized decision making on the part of regulatory and corporate bodies.

What is the future of ISDN? As you will see in the later section entitled "Will ADSL Kill ISDN?," the telcos have blown the opportunity to promote and exploit ISDN, and today's efforts are too disjointed and chaotic to be effective. The field is ripe for new initiatives and new technologies to step in and reap the harvest of users hungry for more bandwidth.

ADSL

Asymmetric Digital Subscriber Line (ADSL) uses existing telephone lines (twisted pair) to provide access to high-speed data lines. ADSL service is asymmetric because the incoming data rate is different from the outgoing data rate.

An ADSL circuit has three channels: a 1.5 Mbps to 6.2 Mbps incoming channel, a 64 Kbps to 640 Kbps outgoing channel, and a POTS line. The POTS line is split off from the digital channels to guarantee that the POTS line is always available, even if the high-speed channels die. Each digital channel can be submultiplexed into lower-speed channels. Improved—that is, next generation—ADSL equipment should be available in late 1996 to provide an incoming rate of 9 Mbps and an outgoing rate remaining at 640 Kbps.

The outgoing data rate ranges from 64 Kbps to 640 Kbps, depending on line configuration, the type of equipment you have, and the distance from the telephone company switch office. The incoming rate ranges from 1.5 Mbps to 6.2 Mbps, again depending on the line configuration, the type of equipment you have, and the distance from the telephone company switch office.

The 640 Kbps outbound and 6.2 Mbps inbound speeds can be achieved only if you are within two miles of the phone company and have a top-of-the-line ADSL modem. The 64 Kbps outbound and 1.5 Mbps inbound speeds are similarly available if you are within three miles of the phone company office. If you are more than three miles out, you are probably out of luck and will have to install a traditional bandwidth solution, such as a T-1.

Detailed ADSL specifications, modem vendors, and market information can be found on the ADSL Forum's website (`http://www.adsl.com/`).

If you are an Internet broadcaster and you are close enough to an area offering ADSL service, it presents a compelling alternative to ISDN and Fractional T-1 service. However, because ADSL is optimized for an individual or organization with more incoming than outgoing Net traffic, it may not be well suited for many Internet companies.

As with any bandwidth purchase, be certain to find out how much bandwidth the provider has upstream from you. For example, if you purchase T-1 service, and your provider has only a T-1 itself, you can bet that your actual throughput is substantially less than a full T-1. This situation happens quite often.

The bottom line for ADSL is that it will probably have a bigger impact as a service provided to end users than as a bandwidth solution for broadcasters. Were ADSL to become wildly popular, it would improve the ability of the end user to receive higher bandwidth broadcasts, such as those including higher frame rate video.

Will ADSL Kill ISDN?

The Regional Bell Operating Companies (RBOCs) and their regulatory bodies have completely missed the boat in pricing (too high), marketing (none), and delivering (hard to get) ISDN service. They have, in effect, erased an enormous time lead of several years over competing standards and equipment. The demand for this service was never fully comprehended by the regulatory bodies; therefore, they established installation and monthly rates that were clearly out of the reach of the consumer market. For example, the Texas Public Utility Commission only recently issued a new tariff for Southwestern Bell (SBC) that reduced the installation charge from $485 to $250. This reduction comes after a reduction earlier in 1996 from $578.20. Monthly rates have also slowly dropped and now vary widely from as low as $25 per month for unlimited service to as much as $39 per month with a $.03 per minute surcharge. If you are a light user—for example, one hour per day, three days per week, for four weeks—you would pay $60.60. Those of us who live on the Net would receive a very painful monthly statement.

ADSL has a very good chance of killing the unstable consumer ISDN market if it can deal with the following issues: distance from the phone company office, availability, and cost competitiveness. Right now, supporters claim that the vast bulk of users are within the effective radius. On the other hand, ISDN is widely used in the radio and television field, and it provides a medium to transmit high-quality digital audio and, when multiplexed, video. With its installed base of hardware and customers, ISDN will linger, as switched 56 has, but it will have to drop in price significantly to stay competitive.

Better Client Hardware

In case you haven't noticed, while the Net has blossomed and everyone is screaming for more bandwidth, faster connections, better browsers, and better multimedia, the performance of your computer systems has also increased dramatically. From mid-1995 to mid-1996, the computer industry has gone from the 100 MHz Pentium PC to the 200 MHz Pentium Pro PC that makes the 100s look anemic. Motherboards are more tightly integrated, and more functions are being added to the primary CPUs all the time. You can hardly buy a PC these days that is not capable of handling multimedia. Major chip manufacturers—such as Intel with their MMX (multimedia extension) plans—promise to more tightly integrate multimedia functionality—including native image and audio capabilities—into their CPUs. In fact, Intel has described their planned MMX upgrade to the Pentium Pro line as being the biggest architectural change to their line of products since the introduction of the 80386.

These increases in performance and features don't appear to be slowing down, and they promise to have a profound impact on Internet multimedia that may well precede any significant changes in consumer bandwidth availability. Simply put, these dramatic improvements in processing horsepower will make it easier for you to decode audio and video on the fly. More data can be compressed and crammed into the same bandwidth, and the viewing and listening experience will be substantially improved.

What These Implications Mean

Improvements in client software and hardware will accompany spotty increases in available consumer bandwidth. These improvements will allow more frames per second to be combined with better audio codecs for improved audio and video. When website sound first appeared, the quality was low, as were user expectations. Gradually the software and technology improved, leading to tremendously improved audio quality for the end user. This process feeds on itself, creating a challenge to telcos and content providers; when the listening (and soon viewing) experience improves, consumers demand ever better service.

Data compression and transmission technology is a hot research and development area. The telcos are striving to squeeze more and more bandwidth out of their existing fiber. At the same time, the telcos are laying new fiber as fast as the backhoes can dig, and they are stringing fiber bundles through defunct oil pipelines even faster. At the same time the Internet is facing a bandwidth crunch, there are fantastic financial incentives for providers to enhance and expand bandwidth infrastructure.

Initially a novelty, computers and televisions are merging. We already have computers built into our coffee machines and microwave ovens. The chip makers and software manufacturers are struggling to drag us into a future in which computers that recognize our voices are built into every aspect of the average American home. This glimpse of the future paints a seductive portrait of what our technology-studded lives will be.

What does all this future speculation have to do with website sound? This thinking illustrates the direction that the chip makers and software manufactures are barreling you toward: consumer-grade, high-quality integrated audio and video at a rate that will leave many spinning in its wake. The posturing and content grabbing going on today are attempts to line up your surfboards to catch the tsunami. Don't miss the excitement!

Appendix A

Glossary of Internet Terms

10BaseT A 10 Mbps (10,000,000 bits per second) version of Ethernet, in which computers are networked with twisted pair cable (usually category 3 or better). See also *100BaseT*.

100BaseT A 100 Mbps (100,000,000 bits per second) version of Ethernet, in which computers are networked with category 5 twisted pair cable. See also *10BaseT*.

56 Kbps Line A digital phone-line connection (leased line) capable of carrying 56,000 bits per second. At this speed, a megabyte takes about three minutes to transfer. This is four times as fast as a 14,400 bps modem.

Anonymous FTP Enables a user to retrieve documents, files, programs, and other archived files from anywhere in the Internet without having to establish a user ID and password. By using the anonymous ID, the network user bypasses local security checks and has access to publicly accessible files on the remote system. If the system being accessed does not permit anonymous users, access is usually denied.

ANSI American National Standards Institute: the U.S. standardization body. ANSI is a member of the International Organization for Standardization (ISO).

API Application Programming Interface: a road map for how to call the services of one program from another, usually unrelated, program. For example, Netscape API defines how to write an external program in C++ or Visual Basic so that the external program can reach inside Netscape and perform an operation, such as clicking a button, changing a screen, and so on.

Arpanet   The Advanced Research Projects Agency Network: network developed in the 1960s and 1970s for government and university use. It is the grandfather of today's Internet. Arpanet was decommissioned in June 1990.

ASCII   American Standard Code for Information Interchange: a widely used standard within the computer industry. In ASCII, numbers are assigned to represent certain alphanumeric characters and symbols. For example, a simple text file, such as one created by the Windows Notepad, contains only ASCII characters.

ATM   Asynchronous Transfer Mode: a packet (a collection of bits and addressing information)-based network protocol (one that transmits data in small, usually fixed sizes) that is optimized for voice, data, image, and video. ATM reserves a portion of available bandwidth for the overhead necessary to manage each of these formats, regardless of whether a format is in use.

Backbone   The means by which different parts of your network connect to each other. Because of expense, a backbone may be the slowest part of the network. For example, if you have two facilities running 10BaseT that are connected via a T-1, the T-1 becomes the bottleneck because it is running at 1.54 Mbps, whereas the 10BaseT network inside the buildings is running at 10 Mbps.

Bandwidth   The number of packets you can send through a connection. Bandwidth is usually measured in bits per second. For example, a T-1's bandwidth is 1.54 Mbps.

BBS   Bulletin Board System: a computer and associated software that provide e-mail, file archives, and any other services or activities of interest to the bulletin board system's operator. Although BBSs have traditionally been the domain of hobbyists, an increasing number of BBSs are connected directly to the Internet, and many BBSs are currently operated by government, educational, and research institutions. Many current Internet service providers were, originally, BBS operators.

BIND   Berkeley Internet Name Domain: an implementation of a DNS server that was originally developed and distributed by U. C. Berkeley. Many Internet hosts run BIND, which is the ancestor of many commercial DNS programs.

Bit   Binary digIT: a single-digit number in base-2. A bit is either a one or a zero. Note: Bandwidth is usually measured in bits per second.

Bps   Bits per second: a measurement of the speed that data is moved from one place to another. A 28.8 bps modem can move at 28,800 bits per second.

BRI   See *ISDN*.

Bridge   A device that connects two or more physical networks and forwards packets between them. Based on input criteria, Bridges can filter, or screen, certain packets.

Broadband   A term that describes networks that multiplex multiple independent network carriers onto a single cable. Often using frequency division multiplexing, this technique keeps traffic on separate networks from interfering with each other.

Broadcast   A packet delivery system in which a copy of a given packet is given to all hosts attached to the network. The term is also loosely used to describe any Internet uni- or multicasting operation.

Brouter   Concatenation of *bridge* and *router* that refers to equipment that acts as both a router and a bridge.

Browser   Describes a client program for the World Wide Web. Popular browers include Microsoft Corporation's Internet Explorer, NCSA (National Center for Supercomputing Applications) Mosaic, and Netscape Communications Corporation's Navigator.

Byte   A set of bits that represent a single character. You can have from 8 to 64 or more bits in a byte, depending on how the measurement is made and what kind of hardware and operating system is used.

Caching   The process of storing frequently used or accessed computer files. When a file is requested again, the copy—usually stored in RAM—is used, rather than the original. The caching process takes nanoseconds rather than milliseconds to accomplish the retrieval. Caching has good and bad points. On the plus side, it can dramatically speed up network and computer operations. On the negative side, if the original information has changed since the copy was made, no benefit is achieved from caching, and in some cases, incorrect or out-of-date information is sent back to the requesting program or user. Also, keep in mind that the computer or network has only a primitive basis on which to decide which information is cached. The computer or network can frequently guess incorrectly.

CCITT Consultative Committee for Telegraphy and Telephony: a unit of the International Telecommunications Union (ITU) of the United Nations. CCITT recommends technical standards for analog and digital communications.

CERN (Conseil Europeen pour la Recherche Nucleaire) European Laboratory for Particle Physics: birthplace of the World Wide Web.

CERT Computer Emergency Response Team (U.S. government): works with the Internet community on security awareness, hacker attacks, and so on.

Circuit Switching A communications network on which packets travel between hosts. The telephone system is an example of circuit switching.

Client The end user or his computer—or a program running on the computer—that requests a service, data stream, or other process from another computer or service. Depending on the context, the client can be a person or the program being run by a person who requests an audio stream, for example, from an Internet audio broadcaster.

Clipper Chip An encryption chip developed and sponsored by the U.S. government and decried by telephone companies and civil libertarians. The chip is intended to replace existing security measures and contains a back door that can be used by duly authorized government agencies via a court order or, for those with darker imaginations, by any hacker over the age of six.

Cyberspace A term coined by William Gibson in his novel *Neuromancer* to describe the world of computers and the society around them.

DARPA Defense Advanced Research Projects Agency: the U.S. government research and development agency that funded Arpanet.

Datagram A self-contained data package carrying so much onboard information that it can be routed from the origin to the destination computer without any previous exchanges between the two computers and the network. See also *Packet*.

DDN Defense Data Network: MILNET and several other Department of Defense networks.

DNS Domain Name System: the distributed naming and addressing scheme used on the Internet. For example, DNS enables us to assign aliases to a computer's numeric address: 206.190.33.162 becomes www.twolfpress.com.

Domain On the Internet, a part of a naming hierarchy. An Internet domain name consists of a sequence of names, such as microsoft.com or fun.net, that are separated by periods (dots).

Downloading The electronic transfer of information from one computer to another, generally from a larger computer to a smaller one, such as a PC.

DS1 Digital Signal 1: transmission standard at T-1 speeds, or 1.544 Mbps.

DS3 Digital Signal 3: transmission standard at T-3 speeds, or 44.736 Mbps. DS3 enables the combination of 28 DSls or a single DS3 facility, also known as a T-3 circuit.

DSU Data Service Unit: data transmission equipment used to interface to a digital circuit at a customer site. A DSU converts the customer's datastream, such as a T-1, for transmission through the CSU, which is often contained functionally within the DSU device. DSUs can convert data to or from a native port on a router to a leased line.

E1 European leased line connection: 2 Mbps.

E2 European leased line connection: 8 Mbps.

E3 European leased line connection: 34 Mbps.

E4 European leased line connection: 140 Mbps.

EBONE European backBONE: a European network backbone service.

EFF Electronic Frontier Foundation: established to address computer related social and legal issues.

E-Mail Electronic Mail: a means by which computer users can exchange messages and other information via a computer/communications network.

E-Mail Address A computer network address by which e-mail is sent to a specific user. For example, sending an e-mail to pseaman@twolfpress.com would cause your message to be routed to the e-mail server that services the domain `twolfpress.com`. That e-mail server would then deliver your e-mail to the user pseaman.

Encryption The reorganization, via crypto/cipher techniques, of a packet's data to prevent unauthorized access to its contents.

Ethernet A standard for LANs, initially developed by Xerox and later refined by Digital, Intel, and Xerox (DIX).

EUnet European Unix Network (the original name). EUnet is now a European ISP.

FDDI Fiber Distributed Data Interface: a high-speed networking standard that uses fiber-optic cable, although FDDI has subsequently been adapted to run over copper cabling.

Finger A program that displays information about a user or users logged on the local system or on a remote system. The information includes full name, last login time, idle time, terminal line, and so on. Finger predates the World Wide Web and, like Gopher and Veronica, is no longer widely used.

Firewall A system through which traffic between an internal and external network, usually the Internet, must pass. The firewall screens packets and permits only prespecified and tightly defined traffic to pass.

Flame An e-mail or group posting that often uses heated, inflammatory, and even bellicose language to criticize something or someone. The use of flames is often seen as the result of the insulating effect the Net has on people. The senders fear no face-to-face reprisal for their words, and as a result, feel free to express their feelings in a way they would never be willing to do in person.

Fragmentation The IP process in which a packet is broken into smaller pieces to fit the requirements of a given physical network. The converse is *reassembly*. Fragmentation can lead to some pieces arriving at the destination out of order. In streaming data, such as an audio stream, if the packet arrives too late, it is discarded. If a significant number of packets are discarded, the quality of the audio degrades.

Frame   A datalink layer packet that contains header and trailer information. Network layer packets are encapsulated to become frames.

Frame Relay   A packet-oriented protocol designed for interleaving data from multiple sources and packing it into the circuit whenever room is available. Frame relay is optimized for "bursty" rather than continuous types of network traffic.

FTP   File Transfer Protocol: the Internet protocol (and program) used to transfer files between computer systems. See also *Anonymous FTP*.

Gateway   The original Internet term for a *router*. For example, the phrase *What is your default gateway* refers to the default router that controls traffic going to and from your computer.

Gopher   The Internet Gopher is a distributed document delivery system by which a user can access various types of information on many different remote computers. Gopher predates the World Wide Web and, like Finger and Veronica, is no longer widely used.

Header   Precedes the actual data in a data packet and contains the origin and destination addresses as well as error-checking fields. A header also refers to the portion of an e-mail or Usenet news article that precedes the body of the message.

Hop   A term used in routing. A hop is one data link. A path from source to destination in a network is a series of hops. A hop is often used to measure the number of routers that a packet must traverse. For example, the following trace route shows the hops between the author's computer, and one of Microsoft's web servers

```
C:\users\default>tracert www.microsoft.com


Tracing route to www.microsoft.com [207.68.137.34]

over a maximum of 30 hops:


  1    170 ms    130 ms    120 ms   TWOLF1 [204.31.249.144]
```

```
 2    161 ms    160 ms    170 ms    dfw-tx-gw1.netcom.net [163.179.23.1]

 3    411 ms    320 ms    351 ms    h3-0.scl-ca-gw1.netcom.net
[163.179.208.7]

 4    270 ms    311 ms    230 ms    pb.mci.net [198.32.128.12]

 5    320 ms    321 ms    220 ms    core3-hssi3-0.SanFrancisco.mci.net
[204.70.1.201]

 6    240 ms    241 ms    330 ms    borderx1-fddi-1.Seattle.mci.net
[204.70.203.52]

 7    231 ms    240 ms    240 ms    borderx1-fddi-1.Seattle.mci.net
[204.70.203.52]

 8    240 ms    241 ms    240 ms    microsoft.Seattle.mci.net
[204.70.203.106]

 9    231 ms    230 ms    230 ms    msft1-f0.moswest.msn.net [207.68.145.46]

10    260 ms    241 ms    250 ms    www.microsoft.com [207.68.137.34]
```

Trace complete.

Host   A computer or device attached to a network to which a remote user or application can connect and do useful work. A router is not a host, but a web server or FTP is.

HTML   HyperText Markup Language: a language used on the World Wide Web to create web pages. HTML is the controlling syntax that defines links to other documents or objects, sets colors, controls fonts, and so on.

HTTP   HyperText Transport Protocol: the protocol for moving hypertext files across the Internet. HTTP requires a client program, such as a browser, on one end and an HTTP server on the other end.

Hypertext   Generally, any text that contains links to other documents. These links are words or phrases in the document that can be chosen by a reader and that cause another document to be retrieved and displayed.

IEEE   Institute of Electrical and Electronics Engineers.

Internet   An international collection of computers and networks interconnected by routers that enable the computers to function as a single, large virtual network that uses the IP protocol.

Internet Address   A 32-bit address assigned to hosts using TCP/IP. 207.68.137.34 is an Internet address that corresponds to www.microsoft.com. TCP/IP packets are routed on the basis of the destination Internet address. See also *IP*.

InterNIC   An organization formed to manage Internet Domain Names and addresses and provide various Internet Services. The InternNIC has evolved through a series of sponsorships and governmental involvement. Of late, some small challengers have been pushing for more top level domain names and greater efficiencies.

IP   Internet Protocol: a standard protocol that defines the IP datagram as a parcel of information that is transmitted across the Internet from origin IP address to destination IP address. The IP address is a set of four 1–3 digit numbers, represented as aaa.bbb.ccc.ddd. Each number is an 8- bit number from 0 to 255. Class A, or aaa, is the highest level; Class ranges B and C are typically used by second or third tier ISPs. See also *Internet Address.*

IRC   Internet Relay Chat: a real-time multiuser chat system in which people meet on channels to "talk" by typing messages privately, or in groups.

ISDN   Integrated Services Digital Network: a digital data line providing speeds up to 128 Kbps (128,000 bits per second). This data line is called a BRI, or Basic Rate Interface, and is composed of two B channels (the 64 Kbps digital lines) and a single D channel (16 Kbps, a low-speed packet data). Note: BRI's big brother is PRI, which is made up of 23 B channels (and a D channel), for a total of 1.54 Mbps of bandwidth, and is basically equivalent to a T-1.

ISP   Internet Service Provider: a company that resells Internet access to individuals or organizations at speeds ranging from 300 bps to OC-3.

Java   A programming language originally developed by Sun but now widely used on the WWW to spruce up web pages with graphics, animations, and so on.

Kermit   A file transfer and terminal emulation program used for communicating with character-based (non-WWW) host computers.

Kilobyte   1,024 bytes.

Knowbot   An independent, self-actuating program that seeks user-requested information. A knowbot sometimes replicates itself on other computers, and as it does its job, it sends updates (messages) to the user with the results of its efforts. When finished, the knowbot self-destructs. A knowbot is sometimes described as a "friendly" virus.

LAN   Local Area Network: a computer network designed to serve a local facility that is no larger than a few square kilometers. Multiple, geographically separated LANs can be interconnected to form a Wide Area Network, or WAN.

Leased Line   A leased phone line for 24-hour, 7-days-a-week, point-to-point use.

Listserv   Automated mailing list distribution system/server that enables users to easily add or delete themselves from distribution lists via keyword-embedded e-mail messages directed at the Listserv server.

LocalTalk   A LAN protocol developed by Apple Computer and designed to run on twisted pair with speeds up to 235 Kbps. All Macs contain a LocalTalk interface.

MAE-East, West   An interchange point for ISPs where they can peer together to exchange Internet traffic. Peering arrangements are made between respective ISPs. Metropolitan Fiber Systems (MFS) owns and operates the infrastructure used to interconnect the ISPs (`http://www.mfsdatanet.com/`). Current and planned locations include the following:

> MAE Chicago - Chicago, IL
> (`http://www.mfsdatanet.com/MAE/chicago.html`)
>
> MAE Dallas - Dallas, TX
> (`http://www.mfsdatanet.com/MAE/dallas.html`)
>
> MAE East - Washington, DC
> (`http://www.mfsdatanet.com/MAE/east.html`)
>
> MAE Frankfurt - Frankfurt, Germany
> (coming soon)

MAE Houston - Houston, TX
(`http://www.mfsdatanet.com/MAE/houston.html`)

MAE LA - Los Angeles, CA
(`http://www.mfsdatanet.com/MAE/la.html`)

MAE New York - New York, NY
(coming soon)

MAE Paris - Paris, France
(coming soon)

MAE West - San Jose, CA
(`http://www.mfsdatanet.com/MAE/west.html`)

MBONE   Multicast backBONE: Internet routers that support IP multicasting and enable the multicast of public and private audio and video programming.

Mbps   Megabits per second, not to be confused with MegaBytes per second.

MBps   MegaBytes per second, not to he confused with Megabits per second.

Megabyte   A million bytes, a thousand kilobytes.

MILNET   MILitary NETwork: originally part of the now defunct Arpanet. MILNET was partitioned off in 1984.

MIME   Multipurpose Internet Mail Extensions: a set of definitions to define program extensions that were not built-in to a web server or web client. The installation of website sound generally requires a web server's MIME-type table to be updated to support the new multimedia extension types (if the table isn't built in). In addition, end-user browsers also need to be configured to recognize the multimedia formats. Updating these configuration items is sometimes automatically handled by respective installation programs but often requires manual editing and updating.

Modem   MOdulator DEModulator: a device—sometimes built in, sometimes added on—that converts your computer's digital transmission to a format that can be carried over POTS (Plain Old Telephone) lines. The transmission is delivered via the phone system to another modem that is attached to another computer, which converts the now-analog signal back to digital format. After the data is converted to digital format, the other computer can understand and process it. In contrast, an ISDN line *is* a digital line, so a digital modem is really acting as a router or bridge, rather than as a modem.

Mosaic   The first WWW browser that was simultaneously available for Windows, Mac, and Unix with a uniform interface. Mosaic is the ancestor of market-leading current browsers, such as Netscape Navigator and Microsoft Explorer.

MPEG   Moving Picture Expert Group: set of international standards (`http://www.iso.ch/welcome.html`) that includes digital audio and video compression. Audio MPEG uses techniques that, in theory, can achieve compression rates of up to 26:1. In practice, however, it is often 12:1 or 6:1. Like most audio compression techniques, some data is sacrificed to achieve the desired results—that is, it is a lossy algorithm. This means that portions of the audio spectrum that the listener probably can't hear anyway are excised. In general, the level of audio compression is inversely proportional to the quality of the sound.

MPEG is primarily associated with video. On the Net, it is usually associated with both an audio and a video component. MPEG is also referred to as a *codec* (encoder/decoder). An MPEG encoder compresses both audio and video, and, conversely, the decoder decompresses both. MPEG encoders can also seperately encode video or audio.

The original MPEG Standard, MPEG-1 (ISO-11172, `http://www.iso.ch/isob/switch-engine-cate.pl?searchtype=refnumber&KEYWORDS=11172`), was introduced in 1991. Audio and video standards were established, with the video standard designed to provide up to VHS video quality at 1.2 Mbps, targeting CD-ROM game makers and other applications: 352-by-240, 30 frames/second.

MPEG-2 (ISO-13818, `http://www.iso.ch/isob/switch-engine-cate.pl?searchtype=refnumber&KEYWORDS=13818`) (circa 1994), was designed to be a higher-level standard, and was aimed at the cable and television broadcast networks and other digital media (720-by-480, 60 frames/second). In contrast to MPEG-1, data rates for MPEG-2 shoot up to as much as 2 Mbps—greater than T-1 speeds!

MPEG-4 (ISO-14496) is a draft specification scheduled for completion in 1997 or 1998. It is aimed at the *low* end, including applications such as seemingly forever imminent videophones, multimedia e-mail, games, remote sensing, mobile multimedia communications, and so on. The new algorithms are proposed to max out at 64 Kbps, or one ISDN B channel, and will likely include fractal and other advanced techniques, with video up to 176-by-144, 10 frames/second.

For the latest news, information, and developments in MPEG technology, check out `http://www.mpeg.org`.

Multicasting   A process of delivering one stream to a network, in which the network itself multiplies the stream to clients that request it. Multicast-enabled routers do the work of replicating the stream; end-user client software applications transmit the user's request to receive a copy of the stream from the router. On receipt of the request, the router transmits the stream to the client. See also *Broadcast, MBONE.*

Network   Two or more computers connected so that they can share resources.

Network Address   See *Internet Address; IP.*

Newsgroups   Public message exchange forums, delineated by subject or topic, in which people interested in specific subject areas can exchange e-mail messages. These e-mail messages are like any other e-mail, except that each is addressed to the group and can be read by and replied to by anyone visiting the group. The following examples include a variety of newsgroups: `dfw.jobs` is a listing of e-mail messages about job opportunities in Dallas, `rec.music.makers.guitar.jazz` and `alt.music.enya` are devoted to music lovers who enjoy jazz and the works of Enya. There are thousands of newsgroups, with subjects in almost every conceivable area.

NFS   Network File System: a distributed file system on which computers can access each other's system.

NIC   Network Information Center. A Network's command and control center. Originally only one NIC existed to serve Arpanet. Today, many NICs exist, operated by local, regional, and national networks.

NOC Network Operations Center: any center tasked with the operational aspects of a production network. These tasks include monitoring and control, troubleshooting, user assistance, and so on.

Node A single computer connected to a network.

NSA National Security Agency: created by President Truman in 1952. NSA is charged with intercepting, collecting, and analyzing foreign communications of all types; establishing communications security for American diplomatic, military, and other governmental bodies; and establishing computer security standards for use throughout the American government and guarding against unauthorized access. Many rumors exist about the NSA. People believe that the NSA has the capability to break popular cryptosystems like DES; people also believe that the NSA has placed trap doors in DES; finally, some people believe that the NSA mirrors the entire Internet on terabytes worth of hard disk space. These rumors have neither been proved nor disproved.

NSF National Science Foundation: it sponsors NSFNET.

NSFNET National Science Foundation NETwork.

OC-1 Optical Carrier level 1: it has a Sonet (Synchronous Optical NETwork) optical transmission rate of 51.48 Mbps.

OC-3 OC-3 Optical Carrier level 3: it has a Sonet optical transmission rate of 155.52 Mbps.

Octet An octet is eight (8) bits. In networking, the term *octet* is often used rather than *byte* because some computer architectures do not use 8-bit bytes.

ODBC Open DataBase Connectivity: generic SQL programming interface for database connectivity with access to Apple, PC, minicomputer, and mainframe systems.

Packet A self-enclosed parcel of information that contains origin and destination header information for transmission across a network. See also *IP*.

Ping Packet INternet Groper: a program used to test whether a target Internet device can be reached by sending an ICMP echo request. Failure to receive a reply can indicate several things, including a network problem between origin and destination or an offline destination. In the following example, the author's computer requested that its Domain Name Server resolve www.netscape.com. The name server returned the corresponding Internet address for Netscape's web server (205.218.156.44). The Ping program then sent four data packets to the Netscape server, which then replied to each with response times ranging from 220ms to 251ms.

```
C:\ping www.netscape.com


Pinging www3.netscape.com [205.218.156.44] with 32 bytes of data:


Reply from 205.218.156.44: bytes=32 time=251ms TTL=247

Reply from 205.218.156.44: bytes=32 time=220ms TTL=247

Reply from 205.218.156.44: bytes=32 time=221ms TTL=247

Reply from 205.218.156.44: bytes=32 time=220ms TTL=247
```

POP   Point Of Presence: a physical location where an ISP maintains tele-communications equipment, leased lines, servers, and routers.

POP   Post Office Protocol: designed for users to retrieve mail from a server.

Port   16-bit unsigned integer used by IP to distinguish among several possible simultaneous connections to a host. For example, a WWW port can be 8080, whereas an FTP or other private port can be 759752.

PPP   Point-to-Point Protocol: primarily used by users with modem dial-up connections to ISPs. PPP succeeded SLIP.

PRI   See *ISDN*.

Private Key   Your private key is used to decrypt a message encrypted with your public key. Both keys are generated on your computer by various means. You keep the private key encrypted in a password-protected file on your computer.

Protocol   An agreed-upon standard by which computers on the same or different networks transmit information.

Public Key (cryptography) Uses separate keys for encryption and decryption. One key is private, and the other is public. In contrast, Private Key Encryption, such as DES, uses the same key for encryption and decryption. This creates a problem because you have to share the key with others, making the system more vulnerable. RSA is the best-known public key cryptosystem. See also *Private Key*.

RBOC Regional Bell Operating Company.

Replication A (usually) automated process that copies data from one location to another. Mirroring is an example of replication.

Router A specialized computer designed to route network or Internet traffic to the next router or attached computer.

RSA The abbreviation for a public-key cryptosystem. See also *Public Key/ Private Key*.

Server A network device providing services—such as file servers, name servers, web servers, audio servers, and so on— for multiple users.

SLIP Serial Line IP: an Internet protocol primarily used by users with modem dial-up connections to ISPs. SLIP was succeeded by PPP.

SMTP Simple (Internet) Mail Transfer Protocol: used to route e-mail between servers.

SNMP Simple Network Management Protocol: a network management protocol for TCP/IP-based networks.

Spam Term used to describe unsolicited e-mail or newsgroup postings, often in the form of commercial announcements. The act of sending a spam is called spamming.

Sonet Synchronous Optical NETwork: transmission rates, signals, and interfaces for fiber-optic signals. The level runs at 51.840 Mbps and can go as high as the multigigabit range.

SQL Structured Query Language: a standard language for defining and accessing relational databases.

Sysop   SYStems OPerator: the person responsible for the physical operations of a computer system or network.

T-1   A leased line carrying data at speeds up to 1.544 Mbps. A T-1 is often called a DS1, for the transmission standard.

T-3   A leased line carrying data at speeds up to 45 Mbps (44.736, actually), providing the bandwidth of 28 T-1s. A T-3 is often called a DS3, for the transmission standard.

TCP   Transmission Control Protocol: uses IP for delivery.

TCP/IP   Transmission Control Protocol/Internet Protocol: a combined set of protocols that facilitates the transfer of data between computers. TCP monitors and validates data transfer. IP receives data from TCP, breaks it into packets, and then transmits, or forwards, it on.

Telnet   A simple character-based terminal emulation program that is no longer widely used by end users but is still used by system administrators for quick administration of remote devices, such as routers.

Traceroute   A command that displays the relay sites used by your packets as they transit between your machine and the destination. The command also displays transit times in milliseconds. See also *Hop.*

Trumpet Winsock   Widely distributed third party Microsoft Windows 3.1 SLIP/PPP shareware software.

Twisted Pair   A cabling system in which pairs of wires are twisted together at a precise angle to cancel out em (electromagnetic) interference.

UDP   User Datagram: uses IP for delivery, like TCP. However, UDP does not require an acknowledgment from the destination computer. RealAudio uses an enhanced, proprietary, error-correcting UDP by default, but it optionally uses TCP at the request of the client.

Unix   A computer operating system.

URL   Uniform Resource Locator: a WWW address, such as `http://www.realaudio.com`.

Usenet   See *Newsgroups*.

Veronica   Very Easy Rodent-Oriented Net-wide Index to Computerized Archives: a database of the menu items on thousands of Gopher servers. Veronica predates the World Wide Web and, like Gopher and Finger, is no longer widely used.

Virus   A program that replicates itself on computer systems by incorporating itself into other programs.

WWW   World Wide Web: See *Internet; Browser*.

APPENDIX B

GLOSSARY OF AUDIO TERMS

1's Complement   A binary number system in which negative numbers are represented by inverting the equivalent positive number. For example, –10011 = 01100.

2's Complement   A binary number system in which negative numbers are represented by inverting the equivalent positive number and adding 1. For example, –10011 = 01101).

Active Circuit   Any device in which an external power source is used as a source of energy to boost or modify an input signal.

A/D Converter (ADC)   Analog-to-Digital Converter: a device for converting an analog audio signal into digital form. The input is an analog audio signal, such as that available from a preamp or mixer output. The output is a stream of binary numbers.

AIFF   Audio Interchange File Format: the Macintosh standard audio file format widely used on the Internet. AIFF supports mono, stereo, three-channel, quadraphonic, and four- and six-channel surround sound. AIFF also supports MIDI. Arbitrary word lengths from 1 to 32 bits, and arbitrary sample rates are supported. Each sample is a linear 2's-complement number.

AIFF-C or AIFC   AIFF with compression. See also *AIFF*.

Aliasing   False measurement of an audio signal's frequency during analog-to-digital conversion. Aliasing is caused by not sampling a signal fast enough. Aliasing takes the form of "whooshing" sounds and other noises that are not present in the original analog signal.

Amplifier   An active circuit used to boost an audio signal to a higher voltage or power level.

Anti-Aliasing Filter   A low-pass filter used during analog-to-digital conversion. It prevents aliasing by blocking frequencies in an analog audio signal that are higher than half the sampling rate of the A/D converter.

AU (.au)   The Unix sound format, which is fairly common on the Internet. AU is also called Sun audio, NeXT audio, MU-law, and u-law.

Audio   The electrical or digital encoding of sound.

Balanced   Having two input or output lines for an audio signal. One line is the send path, and the other is the return path. Neither of the signals flows through the ground.

Band-Pass Filter   A filter that passes only those frequencies between an upper and lower limit and rejects all others.

Bandwidth   The range of frequencies contained in a signal. Audio, for example, ranges from 20 Hz to 20 KHz, and thus has a nominal bandwidth of about 20 KHz. A signal consisting only of frequencies in the range of 2 KHz to 5 KHz would have a bandwidth of 3 KHz.

Bass Trap   A structure that is composed of acoustic insulation and sound-diffusing materials; it is designed to absorb low frequencies.

Boom   An adjustable horizontal or diagonal bar used on a microphone stand for holding a microphone.

Bouncing   Mixing two or more source tracks to create a new track.

Buffer   An amplifier (usually low gain) used to interface one circuit to another.

Cable   Two or more insulated wires bundled together to carry audio signals. Cables usually have one or more hot wires and a sheath to provide shielding.

Capacitance   The capability of a circuit to store electrical charge.

Cardioid   A mathematical curve resembling a Valentine heart. A cardioid microphone has a polar pattern that is a cardioid.

Compression   1. A mathematical technique used to encode and store audio or other data in a more efficient format to save space. 2. The reduction of the dynamic range of an audio signal.

Compressor   A type of signal processor used to reduce the dynamic range of an audio signal. Gain is reduced at high signal input levels to produce a more uniform output level.

Condenser Microphone   A microphone in which the sound-sensitive element is a charged capacitor (condenser).

Control Console   A device for combining a large number of audio inputs in various ways to create two or more outputs. Most control consoles have preamps, equalization, and other features. Also known as a mixer, control board, or mixer board.

Cutoff Frequency   For a filter, the frequency in which gain begins to drop off rapidly.

DAT   Digital Audio Tape recorder: a two-track digital recorder using a tape cartridge and a rotating recording/playback head.

DB SPL   Decibels of Sound Pressure Level: a unit of measure of the loudness of sound.

DBm   A decibel system in which 0 DBm = 1.0 milliwatts.

DBu   A decibel system in which 0 DBv = 0.775 volts.

DBv   A decibel system equivalent to DBu. See also *DBu*.

DBV   A decibel system in which 0 DBV = 1.0 volts.

Decade   A 10 times increase or decrease in frequency. There are 2 decades between 100 and 10000 Hz.

Decibel (DB)   A logarithmic unit of sound loudness, audio power, or audio voltage. It is also used to express the ratio of two values.

De-Esser   A frequency-sensitive compressor used to reduce excessive hissing—such as "ess," "cee," and similar sounds—associated with sibilance.

Destructive Editing   Sound (audio) editing in which the original audio is not preserved.

Differential Amplifier   An amplifier with balanced inputs. It is sensitive to the difference in voltage level between the two input lines, not their absolute voltages. Differential amplifiers are useful for reducing certain types of noise.

Direct-to-Disk Recorder   A digital audio recorder using a computer hard disk drive as the primary storage medium.

Directionality   A microphone's capability to reject unwanted sounds coming from off-axis directions.

Distortion   Corruption of an audio signal; nonlinearity. Distortion is usually undesirable, but it can be used as a special effect.

Dry   Refers to unprocessed audio.

Dynamic Microphone   A microphone that works by moving a conductor through a magnetic field. In effect, this microphone is a sound-powered generator.

Dynamic Range   The relative difference between the loudest and faintest sound (or audio) from a source. Dynamic range is usually measured in decibels.

Dynamic Ribbon Microphone   See *Ribbon Microphone*.

Effects Unit (Effects Box)   A device for adding simulated reverberation, echoes, and other special effects to an audio signal.

Electret Condenser Microphone   A special type of condenser microphone that uses an electret, which is a permanently charged capacitor.

EMI   ElectroMagnetic Interference: stray electrical or magnetic fields that cause noise in an audio circuit.

Equalization (EQ)   Adjusting the frequency content of an audio signal. Some frequencies can be boosted, some attenuated, and others unaffected to achieve the desired effect.

Equalizer   A device used for equalization. Analog equalizers consist of a set of adjustable filters that split the audio into different frequency bands. The outputs of these filters are then mixed back together to produce an equalized output. Digital equalizers perform the same function, but use a digital signal processor chip instead of analog filters.

Error Detection and Correction   A mathematical process in which minor to moderately severe errors in audio or other digital data can be found and fixed. Error detection and correction techniques are used on audio CDs and CD-ROMs to prevent data loss due to scratches, dirt, and minor defects.

Expander   A signal processor used to increase the dynamic range of an audio signal.

Fader   An audio gain control; a volume control.

Feedback   A condition in which some part of an amplifier's output is applied to its input. Feedback is positive if it reinforces the input and negative if it counteracts it.

Filter   1. An audio circuit used to either boost or attenuate only selected audio frequencies. 2. A mechanical structure having a similar effect.

Formant Frequencies   The resonant frequencies of the larynx. A large part of the energy of the voice is concentrated at these frequencies. They give each person's voice its unique qualities, despite changes in pitch.

Frames   A block of data in an audio format file. A frame can contain one sample from each audio channel, or it can contain a sequence of samples from a single channel.

Frequency   The number of times a signal repeats in a given period of time. All audio signals are composed of a series of simple sine waves of a single frequency.

Frequency Response   The range of frequencies that a piece of equipment is sensitive to or can respond to. For example, a microphone or an amplifier can have a frequency response of 20–20,000 Hz.

Gigahertz (Ghz)   One billion hertz.

Gooseneck   A flexible metallic tube used to support a microphone.

Ground Loop   A condition in which current flows in the shield of an audio cable due to voltage difference between the two ends of the cable. Ground loops are a common problem in many audio systems, and they often result in severe hum and other noises.

Headphone Amplifier   A mono or stereo amplifier with multiple outputs, each with its own volume control. This amplifier is used to drive a number of headphones.

Headroom   The amount of margin an amplifier has to produce high-level peaks.

Hertz (Hz)   The basic unit of frequency. One hertz is equal to one cycle per second.

High-Pass Filter   A filter that passes high frequencies and rejects low frequencies.

Hum-Bucking Coil   An extra coil inside a dynamic microphone—particularly one of moving-coil design—that is used to detect stray magnetic fields. This coil is used to cancel (buck) hum when it is wired out of phase with the main voice coil.

Hypercardioid   Similar to cardioid or supercardioid, but more extreme. A hypercardioid microphone is sensitive to sounds from one axis only. Other sounds are strongly rejected.

Impedance   The apparent resistance to current flow. At DC, it is equivalent to resistance. At higher frequencies, it takes inductance and capacitance into account. Impedance is measured in ohms.

Inductance   An effect caused by a changing magnetic field. A voltage is generated (induced) in a conductor by moving it through a magnetic field or by changing the strength of the field.

Instrument Microphone   A microphone designed for the broad frequency range and large peaks produced by musical instruments.

Kilohertz (KHz)   One thousand hertz.

Limiter   A device used to prevent overload of an audio circuit. A limiter prevents a signal from going above a preset limit.

Line Level   A signal level of roughly 0 DBv.

Linear   Literally, on a line. This term is sometimes used as a synonym for analog. It also refers to a circuit, encoding scheme, or other system in which the output is directly proportional to the input. In this sense, an amplifier with a fixed gain (10, for example) is linear. Its output is always X times the input. An amplifier in which the output is the logarithm or square of the input is not linear.

Linear Encoding   An audio encoding method used in AIFF and other formats in which samples are represented by their actual values. See also *Logarithmic Encoding*.

Logarithmic Encoding   An audio encoding method used in WAVE and other audio file formats, in which samples are represented as their logarithms rather than actual values. PCM (Pulse Code Modulation) is one example of logarithmic encoding.

Lossless   Adjective applied to an audio compression or format conversion process in which no information is lost. The process can be reversed with perfect recovery of the original audio.

Lossy   Adjective applied to an audio compression or format conversion process in which some information is lost. The process can be reversed, but the recovered audio is degraded. Lossy compression algorithms are often used because they offer high compression ratios with only slight degradation.

Low-Pass Filter   A filter that passes low frequencies and rejects high frequencies.

Megahertz (Mhz)   One million hertz.

Mic Stand   An adjustable, upright fixture for holding a microphone.

Microphone   Any device for converting sound into an audio signal.

MIDI   Musical Instrument Digital Interface: a serial interface designed to connect electronic musical instruments with each other and to computers. A MIDI bus carries commands, not audio. First proposed in the early 1980s, MIDI has since grown into an industry standard.

MIDI Format   A file format widely used on the Internet to distribute instrumental music. A major strength of these files is their very compact size.

MIDI Sequencer A device that generates MIDI control codes that are used to control MIDI-compatible synthesizers, samplers, and other devices. A sequencer can involve dedicated hardware, or it can be implemented in software on a computer.

MIDI Time Codes (MTC) Special commands on a MIDI bus for synchronizing MIDI-compatible musical instruments. These codes are the MIDI equivalent of SPMTE time signals.

Mixer A device for combining two or more audio signals; a control console.

MOD An audio format that stores samples and playlists rather than digitized audio. MOD is the most common sampled-audio format. It is used for music, although nonmusical samples can also be stored. Originally developed for the Amiga computer, MOD spread to other computers. Once relatively popular, it is now declining.

Monitor Speakers (Monitors) Speakers used in a studio or other location to play back a recording or to listen to a live mix. Monitor speakers generally have a flatter frequency response and are more rugged than consumer-grade speakers.

Mono Monophonic: pertaining to a single audio channel.

Moving-Coil (Dynamic) Microphone A dynamic microphone that uses a coil of wire mounted on a thin, flexible diaphragm. Both coil and diaphragm are suspended in a magnetic field. Sound strikes the diaphragm, causing both it and the coil to move. A small voltage is induced in the coil that is proportional to the sound.

MPEG A multimedia format—defined by the Motion Picture Experts Group—that is often associated with video but also supports sound. MPEG-1 is designed for movie-quality audio. MPEG-2 is for TV-quality audio. MPEG uses a lossy compression method that achieves high compression with only a slight loss of sound quality. MPEG files are thus somewhat smaller than many other equivalent audio files.

Multitrack Recorder Any recorder capable of recording and playing back more than two channels.

Multitrack Recording Unit   Complete (or nearly so) mixing and recording consoles in a single box. Also called portable studios, they support four to eight audio channels, each with a preamp, equalizer, and mixer input. The recording section contains either a multitrack tape or disk recording unit.

Neodymium   A metallic chemical element whose compounds and alloys are used to make the strongest known permanent magnets. Such magnets are often used in high-quality dynamic microphones and headphones.

Noise   Any unwanted sound or audio, particularly that of a random nature.

Noise Floor   The background noise level in an audio signal.

Noise Gate   A device that passes high-level signals unaltered, but attenuates low-level signals. It is used to eliminate or reduce noise during pauses in music or speech.

Nondestructive Editing   Sound (audio) editing in which the original audio is preserved.

Notch Filter   A filter than passes all frequencies, except those between an upper and lower limit.

Nyquist Rate   Twice the highest frequency contained in a signal. It is the minimum rate at which an A/D converter must operate to prevent aliasing.

Nyquist Theorem   A mathematical proof that a signal can be completely reconstructed from discrete samples, provided that the samples are taken at a rate at least twice the highest frequency contained in the audio signal.

Octave   A doubling or halving of frequency.

Omnidirectional   Sensitive to sound coming in from all directions. The term is usually used to refer to microphones.

Pass Band   For a filter, the frequency range that is unaffected by the filter, or even boosted by it.

Passive Circuit   Any device in which all energy comes from the input signal. Such a device can only attenuate the signal.

Period   The reciprocal of frequency; the time required for a signal to repeat itself.

Phantom Power Supply   An external power source used to operate a condenser microphone. Many mic preamps and mixers have built-in phantom power supplies.

Phase   For two signals of the same frequency, phase is a measure of the time shift between the signals.

Phase Angle   A periodic signal requires 360 degrees to repeat itself. A phase angle between 0 and 360 degrees is used to locate any spot on that periodic signal.

Phone Jack/Plug   A two- or three-conductor connector. The two-conductor plug has a round barrel with a tip and a sleeve contact. The three-conductor version adds a ring contact between the tip and sleeve. A barrel diameter of 1/4 inch is most common in pro-audio equipment. Often, 1/8 inch or smaller versions are used on consumer audio gear. Two-conductor versions are used for an unbalanced mono signal. Three-conductor versions are used either for balanced mono or unbalanced stereo connections.

Pitch Shifting   Increasing or decreasing the frequencies in an audio signal without changing the time scale. Pitch shifting can be used to make a sound deeper or higher.

Polar Pattern   A circular graph showing the sensitivity of a microphone to sounds coming from all directions.

Pop Screen   One or more layers of mesh cloth stretched across a metal hoop. Mounted in front of a microphone, a pop screen reduces breath and mouth noises.

Power Amp   An amplifier designed to drive heavy loads, such as speakers.

Power and Light Module   A power module with small lamps for lighting the front of a rack.

Power Module   A rack-mounted surge suppressor and noise filter used to protect audio equipment from surges and noises on the 120 VAC power line.

Preamp (Preamplifier)   A high-gain amplifier used to boost a low-level signal (such as that from a microphone or electric guitar) to line level.

Quantization Error   Imperfections in the analog-to-digital conversion process caused by finite word lengths. These imperfections are equivalent to introducing noise.

Rack   An equipment rack or case with standard 19-inch mounting bays.

Rare-Earth Magnets   See *Neodymium*.

Raw Audio   Digital audio, taken as-is from an A/D converter. Digital audio is sometimes stored in this form without reformatting.

RCA Jack/Plug   A two-conductor concentric connector used on unbalanced audio circuits. The inner conductor carries the signal, and the outer conductor is the shield.

Recorder   Any of a variety of devices used to store audio in digital or analog form.

Resonances   Natural frequencies of a room or other space. The room's acoustics tend to strongly reinforce these frequencies, resulting in a "booming" effect.

Reverberation (Reverb)   A series of echoes produced as a sound reflects off multiple surfaces; the simulation of natural reverberation by an electronic device.

Reverberation Time   The time required for sound levels to die down to 60 DB below their initial value. Used in acoustics to measure how "lively" a studio, concert hall, or other room is.

RFI   Radio Frequency Interference: stray radio waves that cause noise in an audio circuit.

Ribbon Microphone   A dynamic microphone using a thin corrugated metal ribbon suspended in a magnetic field. When sound strikes the ribbon, it vibrates, generating a small voltage that is proportional to the sound pressure.

Sampler   An electronic musical instrument capable of storing and playing many short digitized audio samples. Under control of a MIDI bus or built-in keyboard, a synthesizer then generates music audio based on these samples. Pitch, length, frequency content, and so on can be adjusted to generate musical notes and various effects.

Sampling Rate   The rate at which audio is sampled during conversion to digital form. The sampling rate must be at least twice the highest frequency present in the audio, or aliasing will result.

Self-Describing Format   Any audio file format that has a header that defines the type of audio stored. Header information includes sample rate, word length, number of tracks, and other information.

Sensitivity   The capability of a microphone to pick up faint sounds, or the microphone's voltage or power output level for a given sound pressure level. Sensitivity is also the capability of any circuit to detect and process a low-level signal.

Shield   A layer of fine wire or foil in an audio cable used to prevent the cable from picking up noise from outside sources. It is also called a sheath or ground sheath.

Shotgun Microphone   A long, highly unidirectional microphone. This type of microphone is often used for recording sound for movies and other situations involving a noisy, relatively uncontrolled environment.

Signal Processor   Any of a variety of devices used to modify an audio signal. A signal processor is used for reducing or increasing dynamic range, reducing noise, or performing special effects such as distortion, echoes and reverb.

Signal-to-Noise Ratio (SNR)   A measurement of how strong an audio signal is compared to the noise level. For a piece of audio equipment, this ratio is a measurement of how much noise is added by the equipment.

Single-Ended   Having a single input or output line for an audio signal. The return path for the signal is through the ground. A single-ended line is said to be unbalanced.

SMPTE   Society of Motion Picture and Television Engineers: a time-code standard defined by SMPTE that is used for synchronizing recorders, musical instruments, and other audio and MIDI devices.

SND (SND Resource)   A Mac-specific sound (audio) format used by the Macintosh operation system and such applications as Hypercard. SND is rarely used on the Internet. AIFF is the preferred Mac format.

Sound   1. Acoustic energy.   2. A collective term encompassing both acoustic energy and audio.

Sound Pressure   Fluctuations in air pressure caused by sound.

S/PDIF   A serial data interface for transferring digital audio data.

Static Sound (Audio) Format   Any nonstreaming audio format. A file using this format that must be downloaded before it can be played.

Stereo   Stereophonic: pertaining to a pair of separate, but closely related audio channels used to add a dimension of space to audio.

Stop Band   For a filter, the frequency range that is rejected or at least attenuated.

Subsonic   Inaudible sound below 20 Hz.

Supercardioid   Similar to cardioid, but more extreme. A supercardioid microphone is more directional than a cardioid microphone.

Synthesizer   An electronic musical instrument that can combine multiple tones in complex ways to create musical notes. The first synthesizers were analog, but most modern units are digital. Most synthesizers are controlled via a MIDI interface.

Thermal Noise   Random noise created in an audio circuit by heat.

Threshold of Hearing   A sound-pressure level corresponding to the faintest sound detectable by a person with normal hearing. This threshold has been standardized at 0.0002 dynes per square centimeter, or 0 DB SPL.

Threshold of Pain   The lowest sound-pressure level that begins to cause pain. The pain occurs at about 130 DB SPL.

Tube   A vacuum tube. The British call them valves.

Tube Microphone   Any microphone with a built-in vacuum tube amplifier.

Twisted-Pair Cable   Two insulated wires, tightly wrapped around each other, and protected with a plastic covering. A shield is optional. Such cables are usually used for carrying balanced signals.

Ultrasonic   Inaudible sound above 20 KHz.

Unbalanced   See *Single-Ended.*

Undersampling   A problem in which a signal is not sampled fast enough during A/D conversion. The result is aliasing.

Unidirectional   Sensitive to sound coming in from one direction and tending to reject sounds from all other directions. This term is usually used to refer to microphones.

Valve   A vacuum tube (chiefly British).

VOC   A proprietary audio format created by Creative Labs for use with its SoundBlaster audio cards.

Vocal Microphone   A microphone designed primarily for recording the human voice, although it can be used for other purposes. Vocal microphones usually have built-in wind screens to reduce pops and other breath noises.

VU   Volume Units. A VU meter on a mixer or recorder indicates the strength of an audio input. 0 VU is the ideal level. 0 VU usually corresponds to 4 DBm (1.226 volts into a 600 ohm load).

WAVE (.WAV)   Waveform Audio File Format is the Windows-native audio format. It is the most common audio format on the Internet. WAVE was developed by IBM and Microsoft as part of the RIFF (Resource Information File Format) specification for various files used with Windows.

Wavelength   The distance required for a tone or other signal to repeat itself once. Wavelength is equal to the velocity of the signal divided by the frequency.

Wet   Refers to processed audio as opposed to dry (unprocessed) audio.

Wind Screen   A foam cup, or similar device that fits over a microphone to reduce wind and breath noise. Wind screens can also be built into the microphone.

XLR   A three-pin connector commonly used on microphones and balanced audio circuits. Two pins are dedicated to the audio signal, and one is for the shield.

APPENDIX C

WEBSITE AUDIO URLs

URL/SITE

Description. *Note: Site description is within the context of how the site is relevant to website sound and related topics. The actual scope of these sites is greater than what is detailed in the following descriptions.*

`http://java.sun.com`

Sun Microsystems' JavaSoft website. Resource for Java programmers.

`http://www.adaptec.com`

Mass storage (hard disk) controller products, networking products, and so on. Resource for high-speed data and networking.

`http://www.adobe.com/`

Resource for high-quality graphics creation and other products.

http://www.adsl.com/

ADSL Forum's (industry group) website. Resource for ADSL technology information.

http://www.alliance.net/lav/sound.html

Example of TrueSpeech site.

http://www.alphaWorks.ibm.com/

IBM Internet Multimedia effort: Bamba.

http://www.apcc.com/

American Power Conversion (APC). Produces a highly successful line of power-protection products.

http://www.ascap.com/

American Society of Composers, Authors, and Publishers (ASCAP).

http://www.ascend.com/

Popular ISDN router manufacturer.

http://www.asiansources.com./tsmicro.com/

FanCard. Resource for protecting computer equipment from the dangers of overheating due to fan failure.

http://www.AudioNet.com

The largest broadcast network on the Internet.

http://www.audionet.com/radio/talk/klif/

Example of a talk radio station being broadcast on the Internet.

http://www.bestpower.com/

Best Power manufactures a wide range of UPS products, including the highly regarded premium line of Fortress UPSs.

http://www.bmi.com/

Organization representing songwriters, composers, and music publishers.

`http://www.boardwatch.com`

Magazine and Internet site that publishes a detailed directory of Internet service providers.

`http://www.broadcast.harris.com`

Supplier of an enormous line of radio and television equipment in more than 150 countries. Harris sells everything from connectors to television broadcast vans and trucks.

`http://www.cisco.com`

Internet router manufacturer.

`http://www.conpub.com.au/Conmag/index.htm`

Connections is the online version of an Australian magazine of the same name. Billed as "Australia's Entertainment and Technology Monthly," it contains information on audio and other equipment and techniques used in Australian studios, concerts, films and so on.

`http://www.sweetwater.com/Home.html`

Home page for Sweetwater Sound Inc., an audio and music retailer. Between the ads for various products, you can find information on new products, catalogs from vendors, and reports on current events in the music and audio industry.

`http://www.keyboardmag.com/homepage.htm`

Keyboard Central, the online version of the monthly magazine *Keyboard*, contains reference information, manufacturer's contacts, product information, and downloads.

`http://www.musictrades.com/`

Online version of *The Music Trades*, a trade magazine for the music and recording industry.

`http://www.dform.com/inquiry/spataudio.html`

The Ultimate Spatial Audio Index. If you're interested in 3D audio or the audio aspect of virtual reality, this is a page to see.

Audio Manufacturers' Home Pages

The following web pages are operated or sponsored by leading manufacturers of audio equipment and software. The manufacturers are entirely responsible for the content and accuracy of their pages. NOTE: Pages may contain more types of equipment than what is mentioned in this listing.

`http://www.audixusa.com/`

Audix Corporation. Microphones and monitors.

`http://www.creaf.com/zonemenu.html`

Creative Labs. Makers of Sound Blaster sound cards and related products.

`http://www.dbxpro.com/`

dbx Professional Products. Mic preamps, compressors, limiters, noise gates, synthesizers, noise reduction, EQ, and so on.

`http://www.dolby.com/`

Dolby Laboratories, Inc. Noise reductions technology, multichannel audio technology, and so on.

`http://www.digidesign.com/Newdigiweb/`
`digihome.html`

Digidesign. Complete line of digital audio capture and editing software and hardware.

`http://yamaha.com:8000/index.html-ssi`	Yamaha's information station. Acoustic and electronic instruments; various pro-audio gear including mixers, effects processors, recorders, and so on.
`http://www.neumannusa.com/`	Neumann USA. Studio microphones.
`http://www.rolandus.com/`	Roland Corporation U.S. Musical instruments, keyboards, direct-to-disk recorders, voice processors, and so on.
`http://www.sennheiserusa.com/sennh.htm`	Sennheiser USA. Microphones, headphones, wireless, audiology, and so on.
`http://www.shure.com/`	Shure Brothers. Microphones, phonograph cartridges, preamps, mixers, and wireless.

`http://cons3.sel.sony.com/`
`http://cons3.sel.sony.com/`
`SEL/cgi-bin/online/index`
	(Home Page)
	(Product List) Sony Electronics. A broad line of audio, video, and computer products.

`http://www.teac.com/`	TEAC America, Inc. TASCAM pro-audio products, consumer audio, and so on.
`http://www.macromedia.com/`	Macromedia. Sound editing and multimedia software.
`http://www.peavey.com/`	Peavey Electronics. A full line of pro-audio products.

http://www.ensoniq.com/

Ensoniq. Musical instruments, multimedia sound cards, and so on.

http://www.sfoundry.com/

Sonic Foundry. Makers of Sound Forge software.

http://www.cnet.com/Content/Radio/

c|net radio site.

http://www.dspg.com/

DSP Group, Inc. TrueSpeech technology information and licensing information site.

http://www.gandalf.ca/

Internet router manufacturer.

http://www.gentner.com/

Radio/talk show equipment supplier.

http://www.iso.ch/welcome.html

MPEG (Moving Picture Expert Group). Industry group site for more information on MPEG standards.

http://www.isochrone.com/

Internet streaming audio software manufacturer.

http://www.javasoft.com/

Sun Microsystems's JavaSoft website. Resource for Java programmers.

http://www.macromedia.com/

Macromedia (Shockwave). Software manufacturer of Internet multimedia tools, including audio and video products.

`http://www.macromedia.com/shockwave/`
`epicenter/shockedsites/waterdragon/`
`swa.html`
	WaterDragons. Example of Shockwave site.

`http://www.microsoft.com/games/hellbender/` 	An example of an Internet-enabled game site.
`http://www.microsoft.com/netshow/`	Microsoft NetShow. Internet multicasting audio/video product.
`http://www.mids.org`	Matrix Information and Directory Services publishes legal and technical analysis of web topics, including a subscription-based Internet weather map in MPEG format.
`http://www.minuteman-ups.com/` 	Para Systems, Inc. Makes the MinuteMan line of Uninterruptable Power Supplies (UPSs).
`http://www.mot.com/MIMS/ISG/Products/` `isdn/bitsurfr_family.html`	Motorola's BitSURFR Pro ISDN modem.
`http://www.mpeg.org`	Industry support group site for more information on MPEG standards and news.
`http://www.realaudio.com` 	Progressive Networks (RealAudio). Manufacturer of leading Internet streaming audio software.
`http://www.seagate.com`	Manufacturer of high-capacity data storage products, such as large hard drives and related technologies.

`http://www.sgi.com/`

Silicon Graphics. Manufacturer of high-performance digital workstations and servers and a wide range of Internet-related products and services.

`http://www.sfoundry.com/`

Sonic Foundry. Makers of Sound Forge software.

`http://www.sony.com/Music/`

An example of a record publisher website.

`http://www.spco.com/`

Software Publishing Corporation. Software manufacturer of ASAP WebShow slide show/audio product. An example of an audio software development kit product, using the RealAudio SDK.

`http://www.streamworks.com/`

Xing Streamworks. Manufacturer of MPEG-based audio/video streaming product.

`http://www.thebone.com/`

Example of blues club site in Dallas that broadcasts a weekly live blues jam and archives past performances.

`http://www.thedj.com`

TheDJ, an example music site.

`http://www.thelist.iworld.com`

Database for obtaining information on the Internet's service providers by region, graphic map, area code, and so on. To use the map, you simply point and click anywhere on the map to get a listing.

`http://www.timecast.com`	RealAudio-maintained site that attempts to create a listing of all Internet broadcasts that use RealAudio software.
`http://www.twolfpress.com`	Site used in this book for various examples. Site is owned and operated by the authors.
`http://www.vdo.net/` 	VDONet. Manufacturer of Internet video streaming product with audio capabilities.
`http://www.virtualnoise.com/tsindex.htm`	TrueSpeech site.
`http://www.vocaltech.com` 	Maker of the Internet Phone and Internet Wave Audio, IWAVE.
`http://www.voxware.com`	Manufacturer of an Internet telephone application and a voice-grade audio encoder and player.
`http://www.WebSiteSound.com`	Publisher-maintained website for the latest information on *Website Sound*.
`http://www.zephyr.com/` 	Manufactures products for sending high-quality audio over the dial-up telephone network. Telos Zephyr, for example, can transmit near-CD quality audio over a single ISDN line.

APPENDIX D

JAVA AND NET SOUND

Using Java, SDKs, the various versions of C++, and Microsoft's ActiveX, programmers can create exciting, dynamic enhancements for any website, bringing them beyond the pale of ordinary HTML and into a more vibrant and interactive stage of evolution.

The much heralded Java programming language is certainly making waves on the Net; however, it isn't without problems and limitations, including a growing trend at some corporations to use firewalls to filter out Java. The desire to keep Java as platform-independent as possible has resulted in some weaknesses in its armor, especially in the area of website sound, as discussed in this appendix. Overall, the supporters and developers of Java are working to improve these areas, so it will take time to see how these issues are addressed.

Java and Website Sound

Many excellent books are available on Java programming; therefore, this section will not be treated as a tutorial, but rather as an overview of the current possibilities and a small taste of what it takes to add an audio component to your Java application(s).

In its current incarnation, Java provides limited support for audio. In fact, it only supports eight bit, µlaw, eight KHz, one channel .AU files. If you have existing audio files that you want to incorporate into your Java application, you'll need to convert them with a tool such as CoolEdit or Goldwave, as described in Chapter 6, "File/Format Conversions."

Because .AU files are best suited to voice-only audio, your Java application is limited to low-fidelity sound effects and speech clips. .AU is a nonstreaming format, so the file sizes need to be kept very small. The Java application needs to be designed to automatically download the files to the browser, to be played only after they have been completely downloaded and requested by the user.

Examples might include adding sound effects that correspond to user interaction with the web page. This could be as simple as a "click" or other sound effect that does any of the following: plays when the user clicks on an option; alarms when invalid selections are chosen; or even accompanies an animated .GIF.

The java.applet.AudioClip has three controls: play, loop, and stop. The basic functionality can be broken down to something like the following code:

```
AudioClip SoundClip;
SoundClip = applet.getAudioClip(getCodeBase(), "mysound.au");
SoundClip.play();   //Play it
SoundClip.loop();   //Play it in a loop
SoundClip.stop();   //Stop the sound loop.
```

Naturally, you'll want to include all the usual error trapping, button definition, or other application functionality you want in any other Java application. Note that you can play several clips simultaneously, and they can be used to create interesting effects—pushing the technique at least a little beyond the voice-only limitations of the .AU format.

With the severe limitations on the types of audio Java can currently support, its viability for significant audio applications is thin at best. When this is added to the extremely primitive controls available to manipulate the user interface, it's clear that this is a work-in-progress. Much more functionality and flexibility needs to be added for the situation to change.

Fortunately, organizations such as Sun Microsystems' JavaSoft (http:// www.javasoft.com/ or http://java.sun.com), Silicon Graphics (http:// www.sgi.com/), and Adobe (http://www.adobe.com/) are working hard to update application programming interfaces (APIs) that include more sophisticated audio and multimedia controls and support.

Developers can integrate C++ or other compiled programs with Java to create exciting multimedia programs; however, they'll need to create a version for each platform they want to support and require the users to download and install the applications on their computers. As the Internet population is increasingly diluted with less sophisticated users, the prospect of delivering these kinds of applications to a large percentage of Internet users competent to download and install software is slim.

SDKs: Custom Applications

Software manufacturers such as Progressive Networks (http://www.realaudio.com) have released Software Development Kits that provide developers with the tools to create customized interfaces to their software, supporting Windows, Shockwave, ActiveX, and Java.

SDKs can be used to create customized client front-ends for delivery of audio content, games, presentations, training materials, educational programs, and more using live or archived content.

An example of using an SDK to create a custom plug-in is Software Publishing Corporation's (http://www.spco.com/) WebShow, which presents a slide-show type interface that is integrated with RealAudio. Another example is TheDJ (http://www.thedj.com), which creates a customized jukebox-like interface for its listeners.

Similarly, with Macromedia Director, you can create custom interfaces for your listeners. An example of a custom interface is WaterDragons, which can be found at http://www.macromedia.com/shockwave/epicenter/shockedsites/waterdragon/swa.html. Where is all of this going? As discussed in Chapter 12,

"What Makes Good Net Sound?," custom interfaces point the way to increasingly virtual reality-like interfaces. Although many of these applications are visually compelling, they are for the most part fairly simple.

The expanding feature set of Java and other initiatives is gradually improving the level of sophistication and ease of use we can expect in future Java applications and plug-ins. As high-quality animation is combined with streaming audio, we inch closer to truly interactive landscapes.

INDEX